AF723778

David Balaam is a retired businessman who took up photography in 2012, and is now an enthusiastic amateur photographer.

Although he photographs many different *'genres'*, church photography is his passion. He has visited over one hundred churches and cathedrals in the UK and across Europe, and brings here some of his self-gained knowledge for others to experience.

This is not an in-depth technical publication, but more of a '*how to*' book for the keen and eager amateur photographer looking to further their photographic experience.

Throughout this book, it is assumed the reader has some knowledge of post-processing in either Lightroom and Photoshop, or similar software applications.

www.debphotosonline.com

CONTENT

Published by: davidbalaam-books.co.uk

ISBN 978-0-9935864-7-7

www.debphotosonline.co.uk

To

Friend and mentor, Ron Smith ARPS, DPAGB

1935 - 2024

Thank you for your encouragement and wisdom.

To

My friend Vic Piper.

The knowledge base for all things architectural.

Typical layout of an early church, facing East

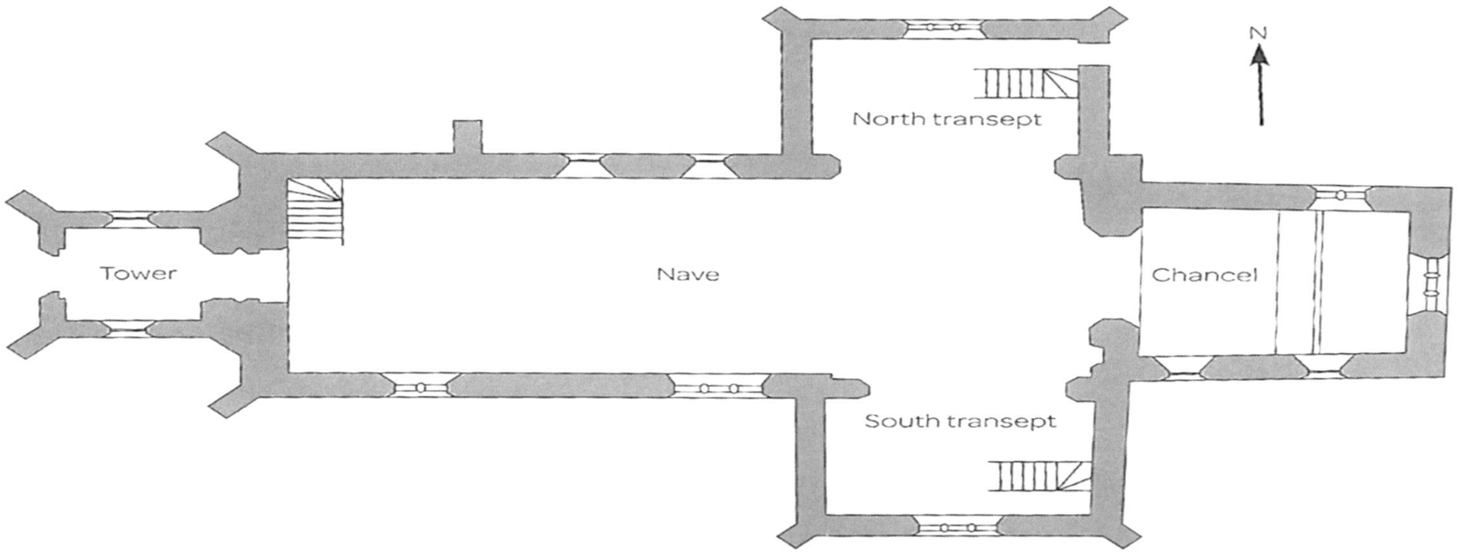

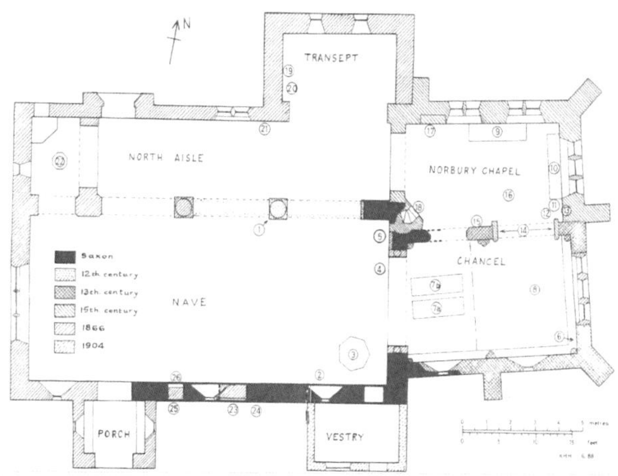

A more detailed layout identifying the time-line of alterations.

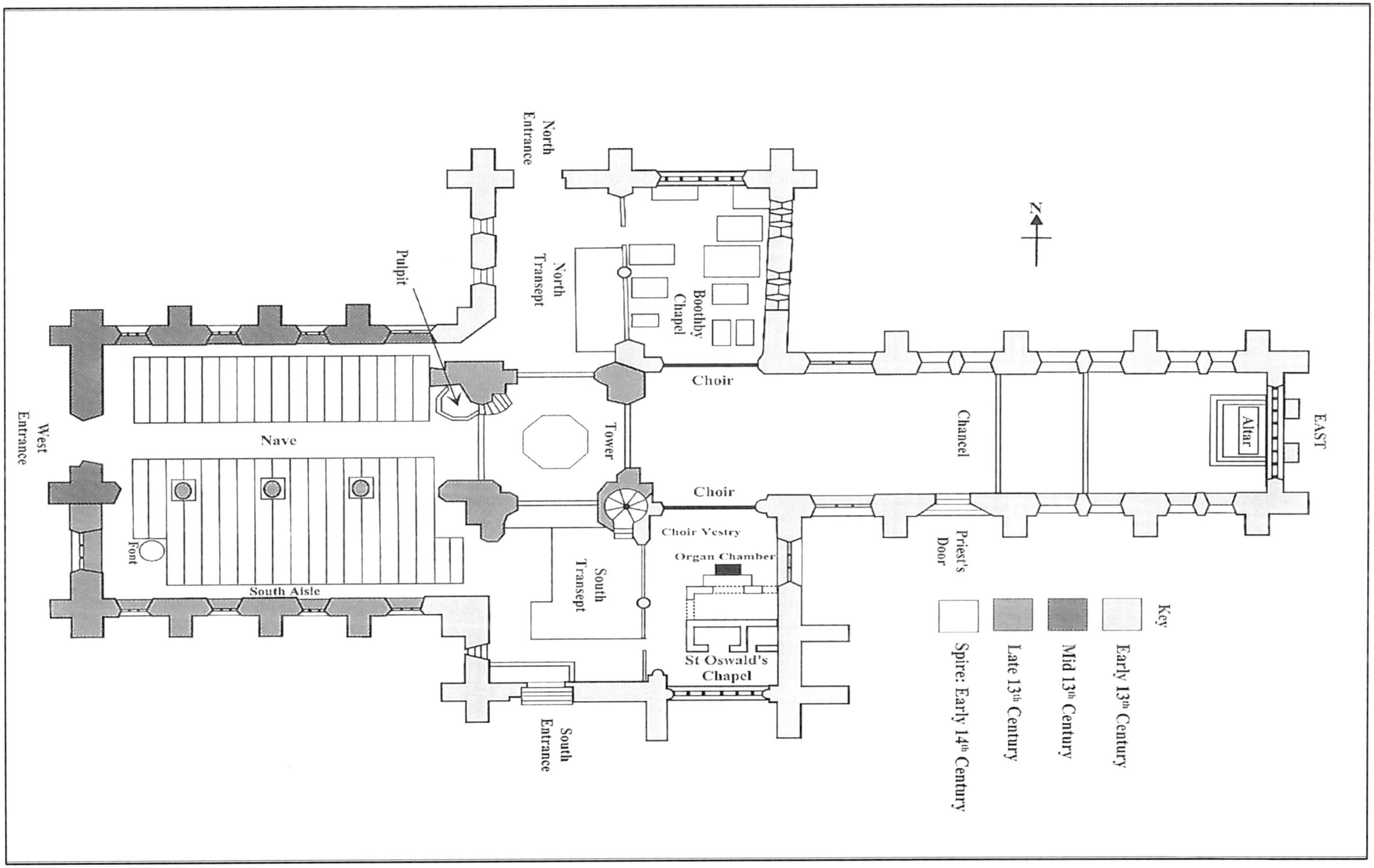

A larger 13c church including chapels in the North and South Transept's. Usually the Lady Chapel or dedicated to the Lord of the Manor

Tips for the Enthusiastic Amateur by David Balaam

Although I have been interested in photography for many years, like many people I have met, I did not take up the hobby seriously ur I retired in 2012. Digital photography is ideal for someone like me; I have never used 'film' or been in a darkroom. Being able now take images, and then deleting them, was a 'god-send.'

I am self-taught, but joined firstly the local u3a camera group, where I met Ron Smith, and then I joined a local camera club, meeti once a week. I found these clubs most interesting and ideal for learning new techniques and gaining experience in club competitior although this is not mandatory, and should not put anyone off wanting to join a club.

Ron was already an experienced photographer, specialising in cathedral and church work, but not exclusively. The image on the ne page is a prime example of his work, and, in my opinion, one of his best.

Inevitably, I got the 'bug' to photograph churches and cathedrals where I found them; in the UK or Europe. My preference, howev was to find some of the smaller, village churches; anything from the 11th century to the 18th century. Stepping into a Saxon or Norm church is stepping into another world. The walls, ceilings and artefacts can tell you a story, if you look closely.

Many of the following examples are from a group of churches belonging to the **Church Conservation Trust (CCT).** The have sever hundred churches in England and most are accessible all the year round. Their website is https://www.visitchurches.org.uk/vis church-listing.

Another group of custodians are **The Friends of Friendless Churches** who have many ancient churches in England and Wales. The website is; *https://friendsoffriendlesschurches.org.uk*

So, why have I written this book, offering my advice to you? Simply, because I have learnt the hard way photographing interiors, ar I have always found a little help goes a long way. This is ***not*** a highly technical book. I want to show you how to produce a *'good'* imag and eventuality, an even better one.

TIP ONE: Travel light. If you are in a church or cathedral for a few hours, carrying a rucksack is not comfortable. I take; a lightweig sturdy tri-pod (essential), Camera with no more than two lenses, spare batteries, a Speedlite, and a spare SD card.

TIP TWO: Walk around the church first getting to know it. Look for the unusual; wall art, sculptures, stained glass, pews, pulpits ar fonts. There is a lot more than photographing the *'nave'* and *'alter,'* no matter how good they look.

TIP THREE: Do *not* use a flash. Many of the older churches will have little or no lighting (some even do not have electricity), but tha is fine. We rely on natural light and long exposures to get the results we need. However, there is a technique using a Speedlight, or torch, described on page thirty-four, to target specific areas of interest.

TIP FOUR: I work with a Canon 6D Mk1 DSLR using either a prime 24mm f2.8 lens, or a medium telescopic 24-85mm f3.5mm len These lenses allow me to stop down to f22 or even f32 to get the amount of light needed on a prolonged exposure; anything betwee 10 – 30 seconds.

I recommend using a DLSR or Mirrorless digital camera that is mounted on a tri-pod. Having said that, I do carry a Fuji X-T3 mirrorless with a 18mm – 55mm lens as well, if, for any reason I am unable to use the Canon. The Fuji is also exceptionally good when using high ISO's handheld, at 30th sec.

I have made sections, starting with the first thing you will usually see on entering a church – *The Nave.* I mentioned earlier that some churches will be either dark, fully lit with artificial light (annoying spotlights), or will have sensor lighting. This can also be annoying; you set up a shot, the camera senses the right metering and you are happy with the 'pre-view.' The lights go out. You run up the nave waving your hands to turn the lights on again and hope you have enough time to take the shot.

TIP FIVE: I use 'manual' setting (not 'auto'). ISO 100. F24. I always set the camera to take '*bracketed*' images, allowing -1/4 and +1/4. This way, as we will see later, allows for correcting the aperture, especially in very dim settings.

TIP SIX: You can photograph a church or cathedral in any whether, but more importantly, do *not* visit on a *very sunny day* or too *early* in the morning (times of year may vary). Most churches, although there are exceptions, were built with the altar facing East, in line with the rising of the sun. Again, most churches will have, sometimes, a beautiful stain-glass window on the East wall which when caught by the sun, looks good, but is a pain to photograph. You would not normally shoot into the sun, so do not do it in a church. You will get burn-out which cannot be corrected in Photoshop. You can wait until the sun moves slowly around, following other stain-glass windows, or you can concentrate on many of the other interesting artefacts around you. (many examples to come).

I will also show you how you *can* cheat the daylight when you have a blown-out stain-glass window.

TIP SEVEN: My '*modus operandi*' is much the same whenever I start to photograph a church. After a quick wander around, I set-up at the back of the nave facing the altar and take my first wide-angle image. This can be portrait or landscape depending on the width of the church. I move halfway down the nave for a second shot, usually taking in just the front of the chancel; the pulpit (if visible) the rood screen (if one), choir and altar. The third image is standing on the edge of the chancel taking in the altar and stain-glass window. You should now have your first nine images.

From here on it's up to you. There may be interesting objects around the chancel; bishop's chair, flower arrangements, candelabras, icons etc. The following pages will, I hope, give you further ideas of what to look for, and how to shoot them. The way you photograph your church, or anything come to that, is how *you* want it to look. I like dark, moody images of old churches, with soft ambient light, but that may not be for you – that's fine.

Other Tips will include *cheating the light*, and *adjusting the horizontals* – especially important with any building photography.

And before we continue, don't forget to take some photos of the church you are standing in, and to remember its name (I have lost count of the nameless churches I have records of).

<u>Architecture periods to look out for are</u>;

Early Medieval (Anglo Saxon/Norman) 500-1150, Medieval/Gothic 1150-1485, Renaissance/Tudor/Jacobean 1485-1660, Baroque/Stuart 1660-1730, Palladian/Georgian/Regency 1720-1840, Victorian 1837-1901.

Some of these periods will overlap. What was new in London would take time for that style to be adopted later by provincial and rural architects and builders. For example, the baroque style continued in rural areas right up to about the 1780's.

ERIC DE MARE

In addition to the advice and Tips I will be offering, I wanted to take some time out to introduce you to a famous early photographer c architecture, Eric de Mare.

Eric de Mare was born in 1910 in Essex, England, and was a pioneer in architectural photography, and published many books on th subject, (as well as other interesting subjects such as canals and bridges).

I am not sure if his title, *Architectural Photography*, published 1975, is out of print, but secondhand copies can be found on-line.

His knowledge of combining Art with photography is fascinating and equally relevant today, if not more so. He also talks c '*Composing*' in terms of *Contrast, Repetition, Balance* and *Climax*; which are all essential elements, especially on our subject c interior photography.

Other observations, which he records intelligently, are the *Three Kinds of Architectural Photography*; he observes, rightly, that mos building photography is taken as a '*Record*' of the building and used 'as is' without any consensus desire to change its appearance.

The second he calls the *'Illustration'*; here the image can be manipulated to make a 'personal comment' through enhancing the imag in the 'darkroom'. (we now use modern applications such as Photoshop or Lightroom).

Thirdly, he calls this '*The Picture*'; A collection of images in or around a building showing the detail of an object, or a collection c pottery, dusty candles or carved pillars and walls with ancient drawings.

His books also include a large number of Monochrome images highlighting many different aspects of Architecture photography, som of which I cover in this publication, including, *Perspectives, Aspect Ratio, Depth of Field, Textures* and *Detail*.

I hope you will find time to investigate this master photographer and his works in more detail.

Eric de Mare 1910 – 2002

https://en.wikipedia.org/wiki/Eric_de_Maré

Disused Steelworks - Sheffield (c)

by

Ron Smith ARPS DPAGB

1935 - 2024

Photographed in almost total darkness.

A fine example of interior photography using natural light.

Reproduced by kind permission of the photographer.

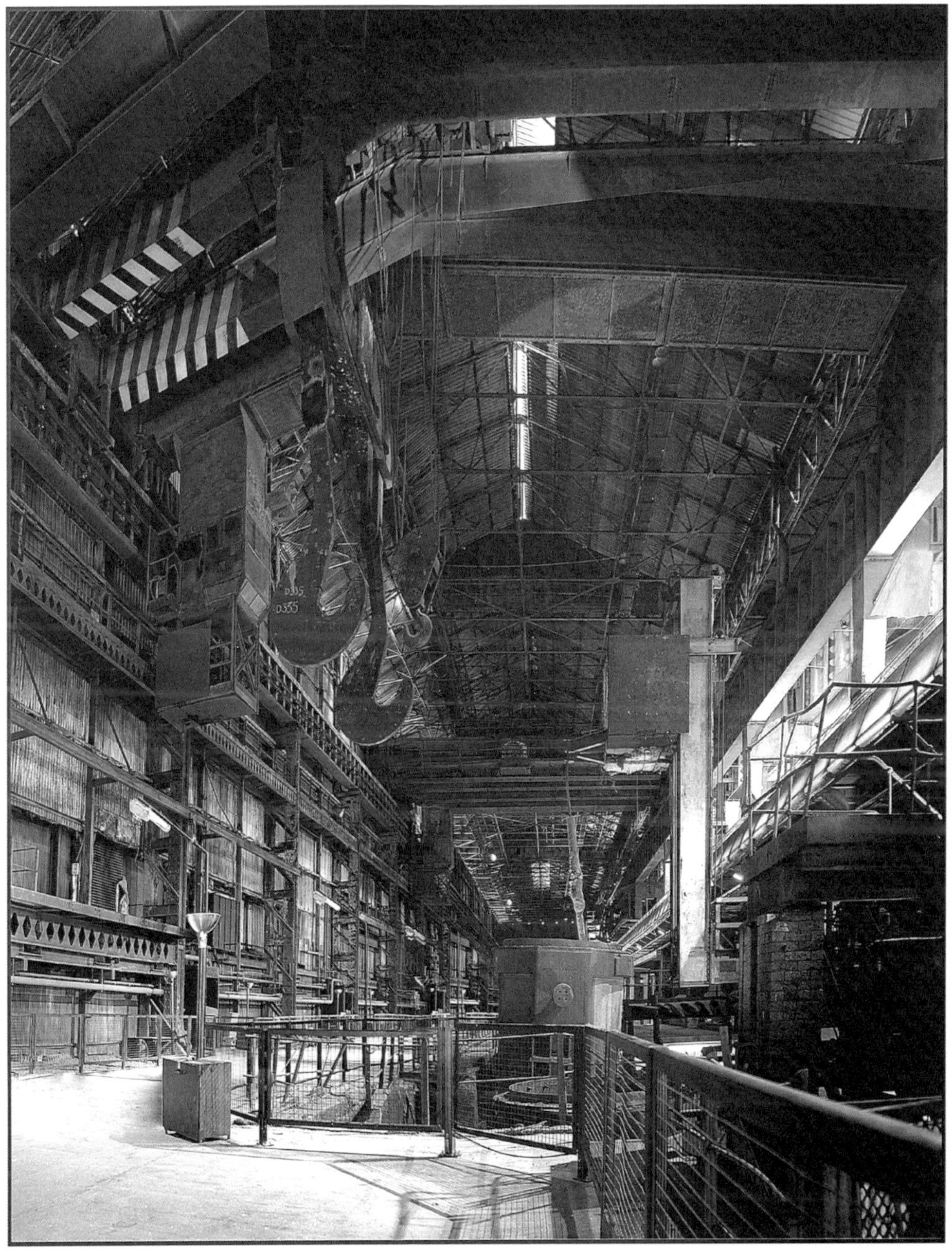

THE NAVE

A wide angle lens, 28mm to 50mm will be able to take the width of most churches in landscape mode.

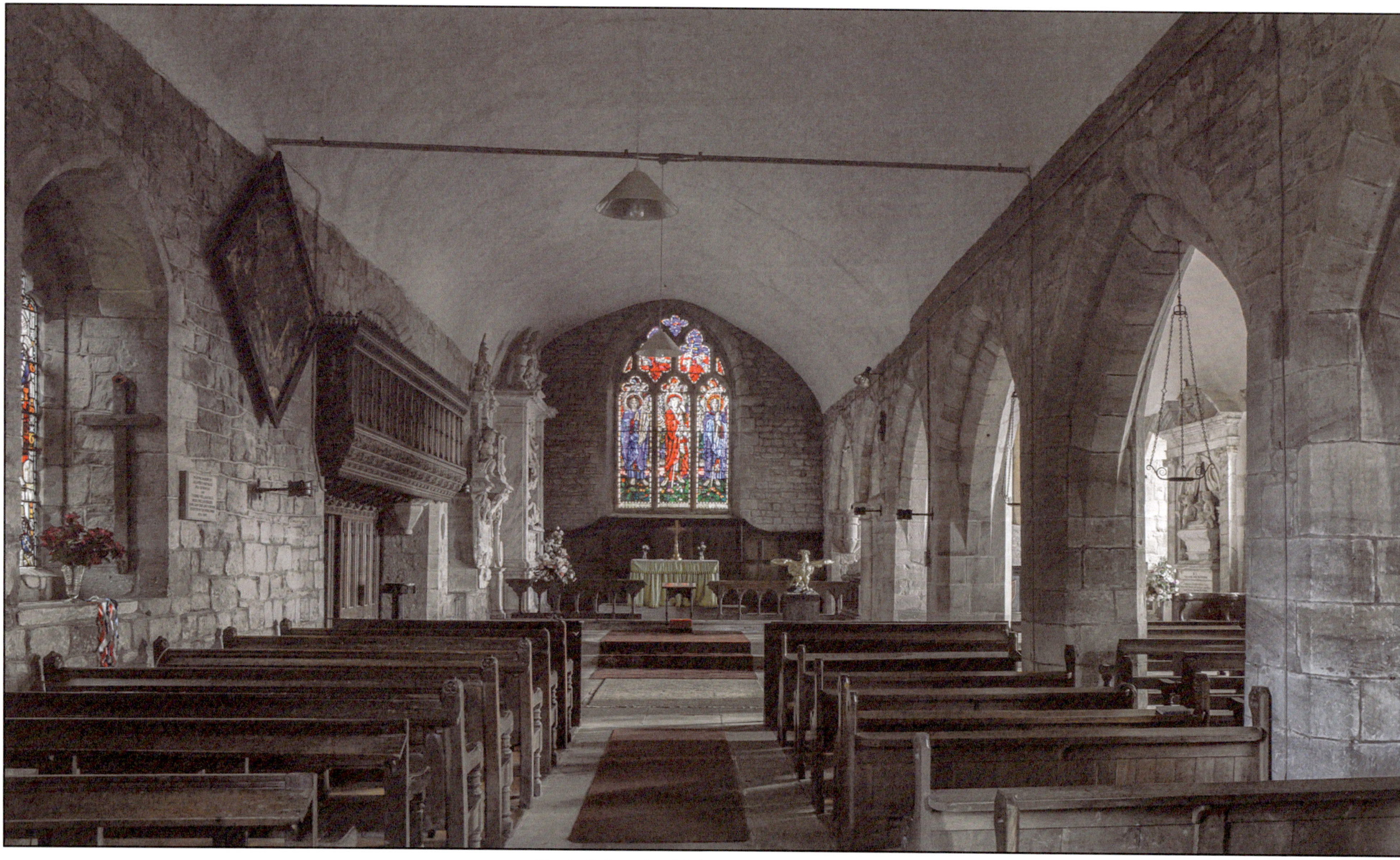

St Cuthbert's, Holme Lacy, Hereford

2sec 24mm f18 ISO100

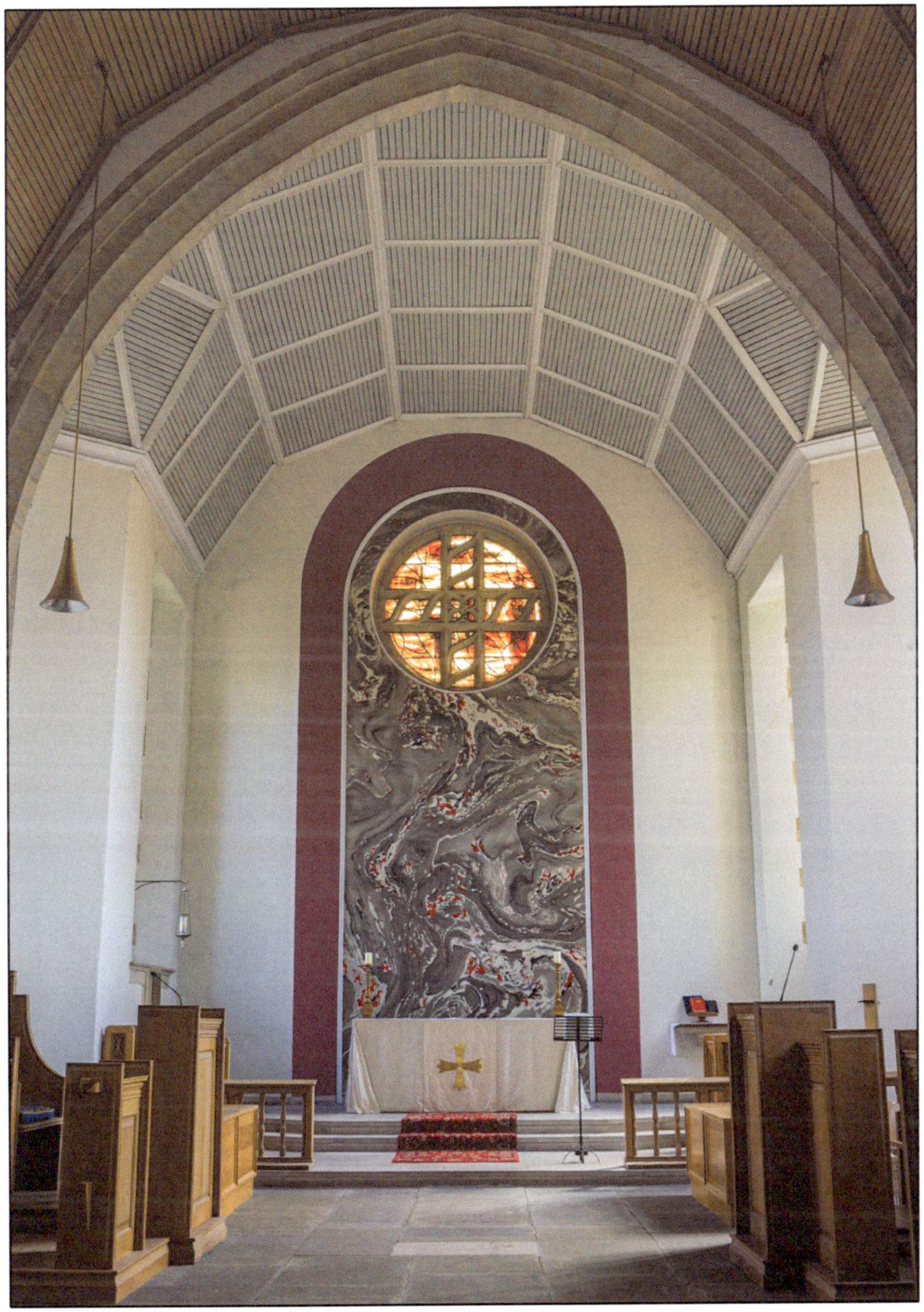

1/2sec F13 ISO100 Canon 6D

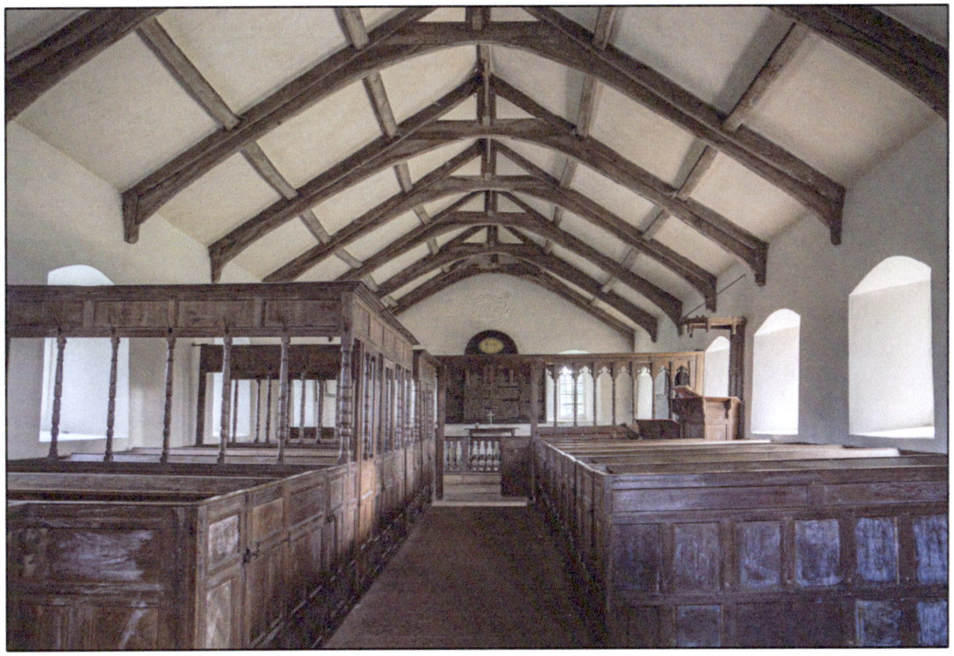

0.7sec f 6.7 24 mm ISO100 Canon 6D

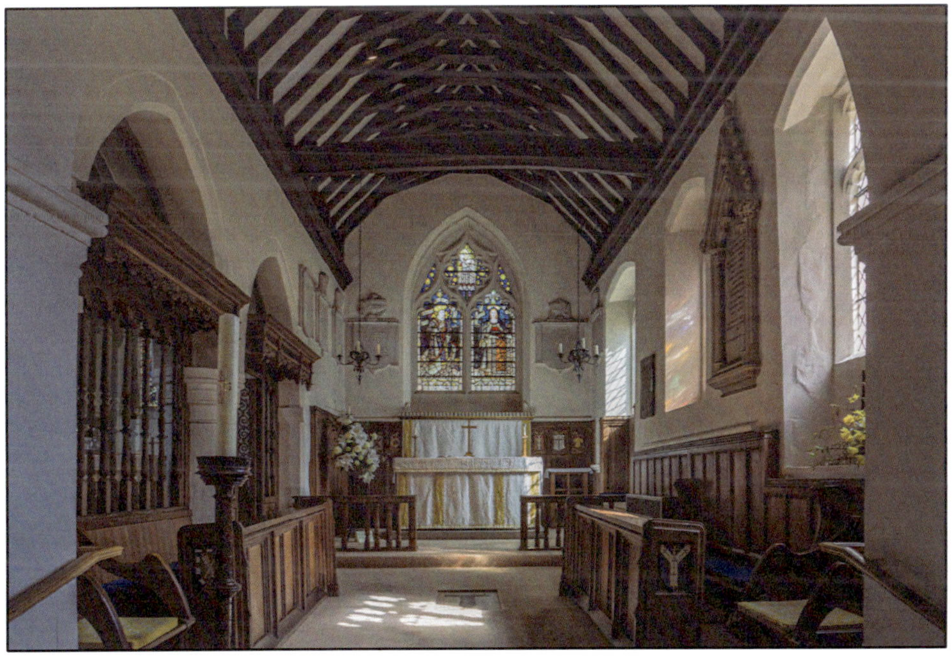

1/13sec f 7.1 24 mm ISO100 Canon 6D

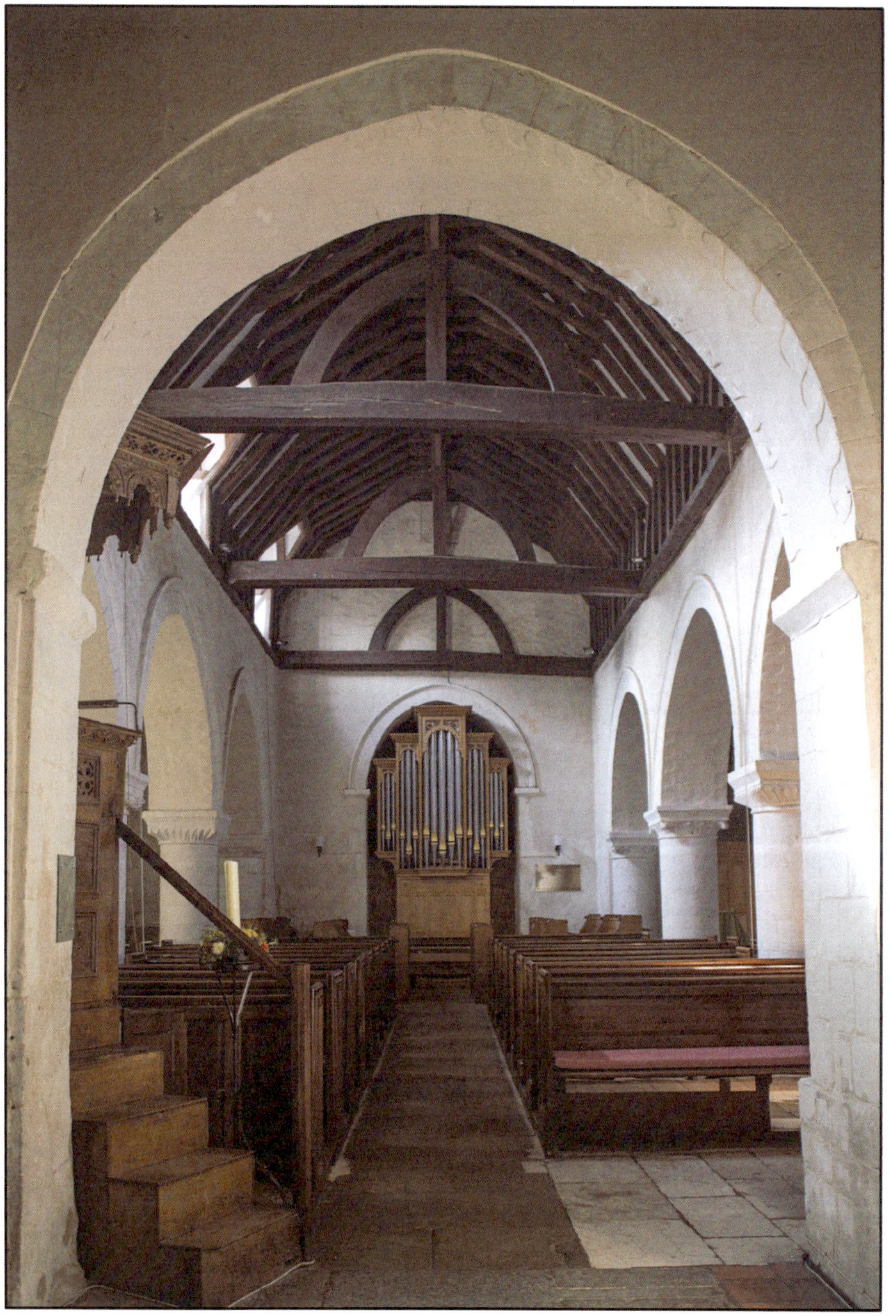

1/6sec f 2.8 24 mm ISO100 Canon 6D

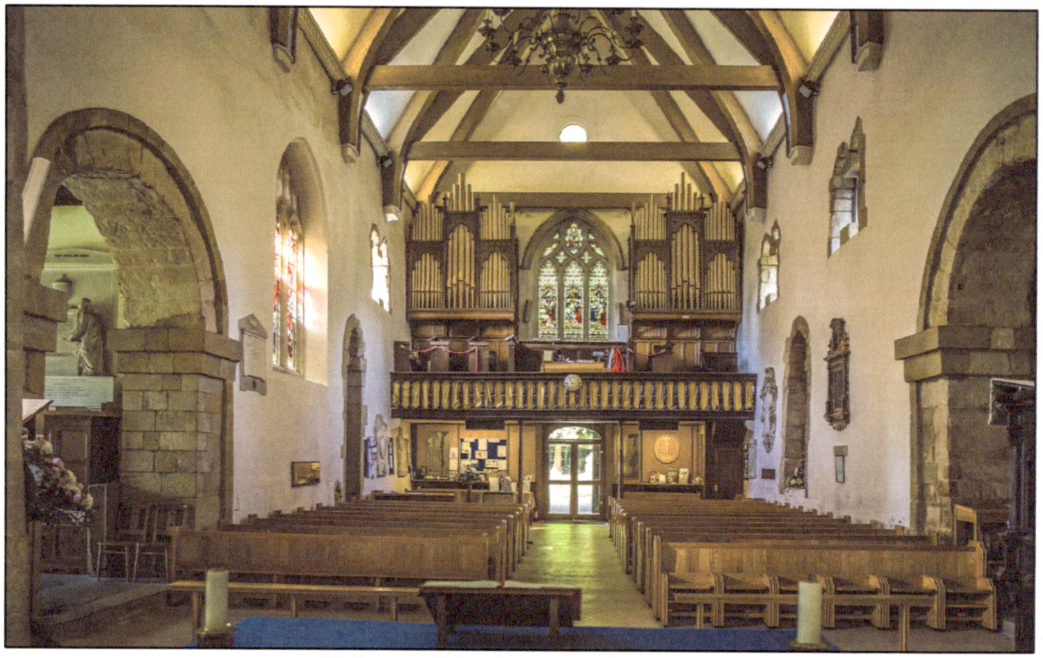

1/10sec f3.5 24 mm ISO100 Canon 6D

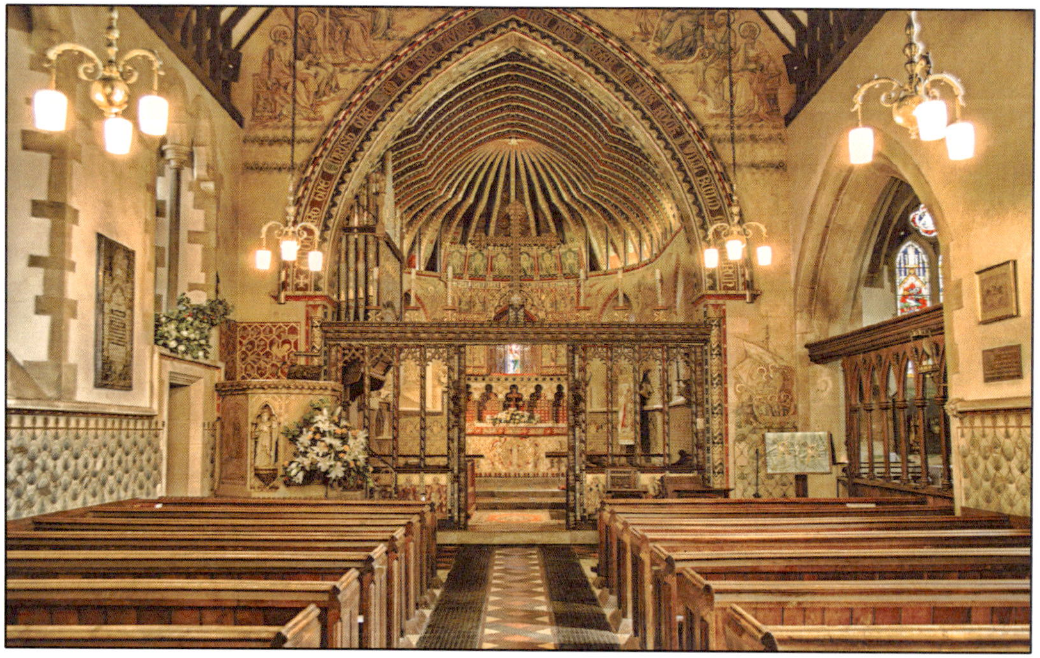

1.5sec f4.5 32mm ISO100 Canon 6D

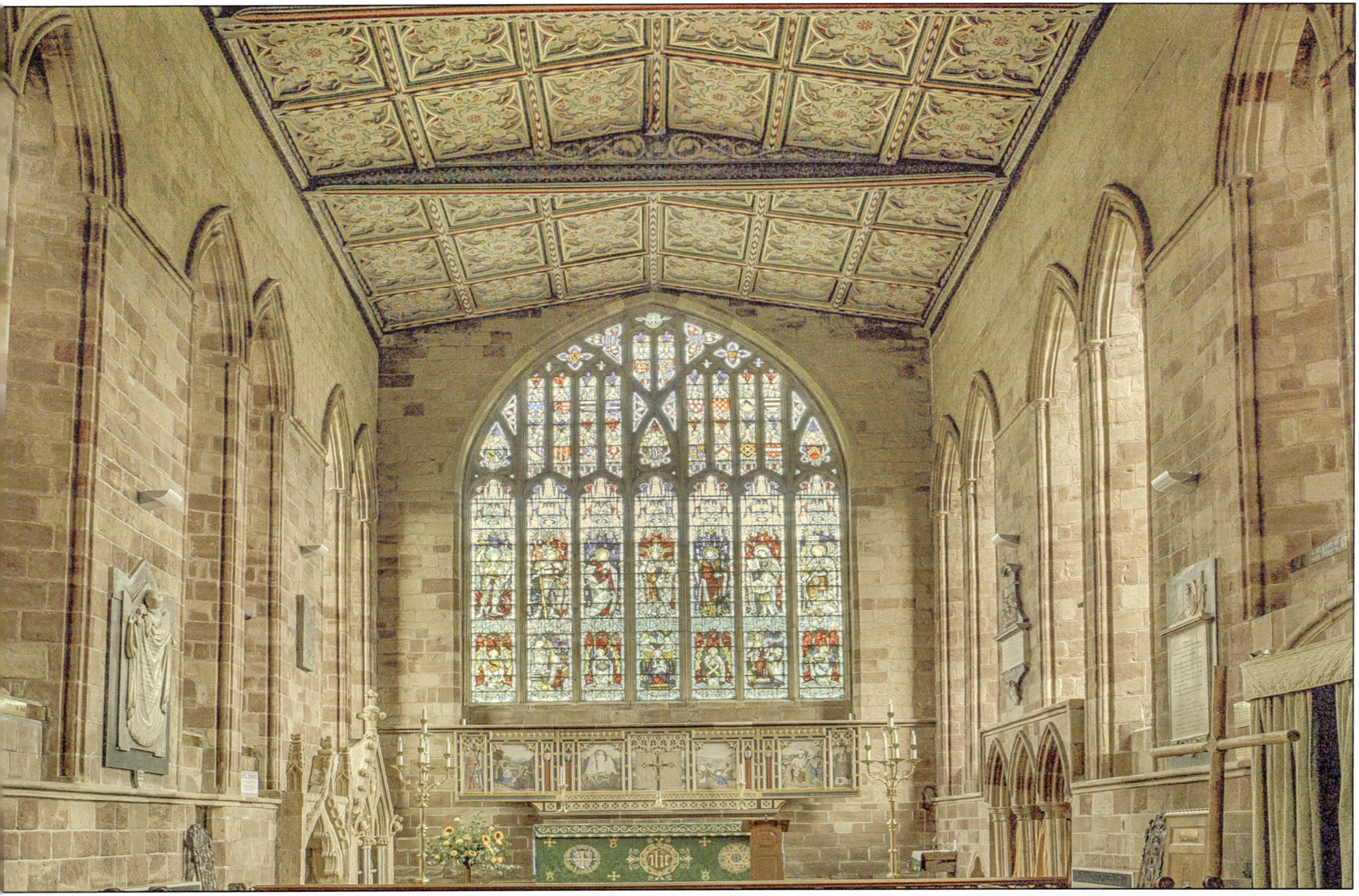

St Oswald's, Ashbourne, Derbyshire

0.6sec f13 24 mm -1.3 EV ISO100 Canon 6D

With additional processing in Nik software (to my liking)

EXAMPLES OF BRACKETING

This will allow you to select the correct exposure for further processing, or for combining as HDR. (See page 36)

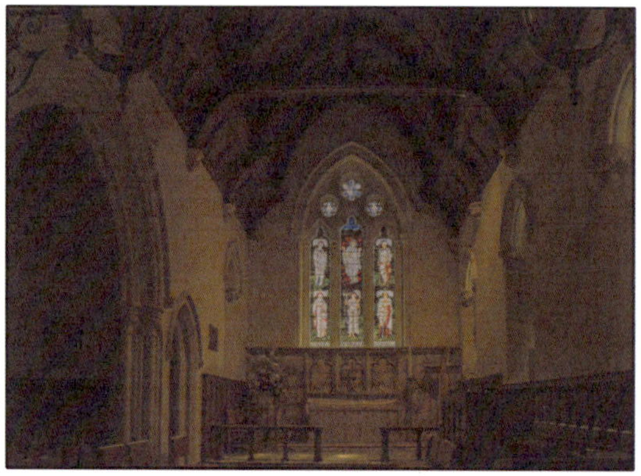

0.3 sec f 8 24 mm -1.2 EV ISO100 Canon 6D

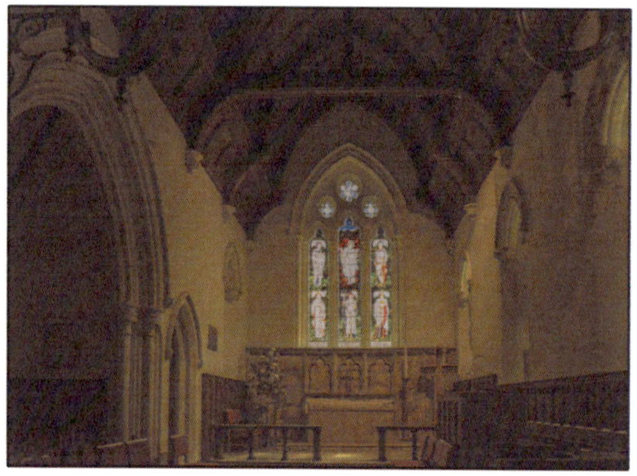

0.5 sec f 8 24 mm 0 EV ISO100 Canon 6D

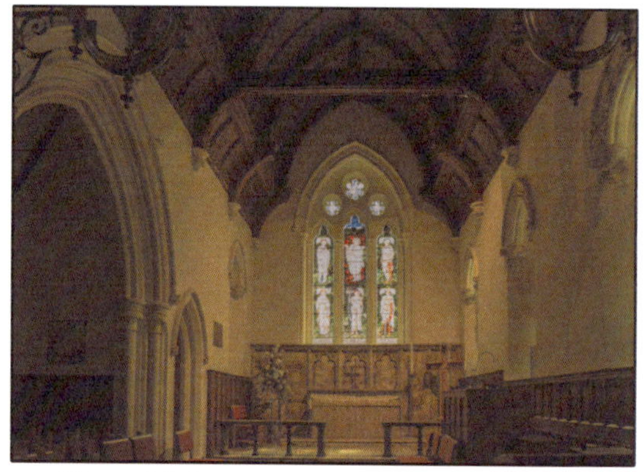

07 sec f 8 24 mm +1.2 EV ISO100 Canon 6D

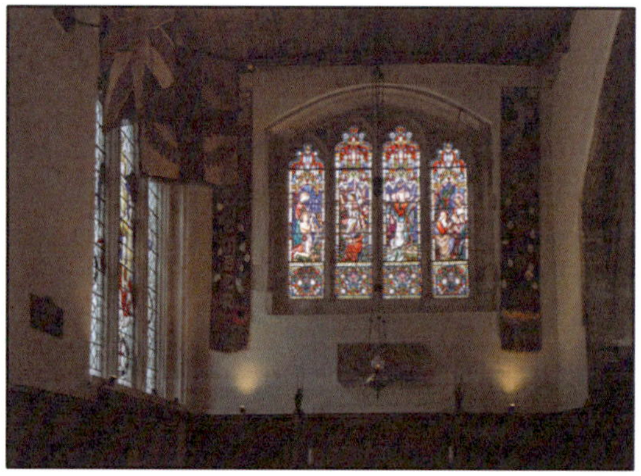

3 sec f22 28mm ISO100 Canon 6D

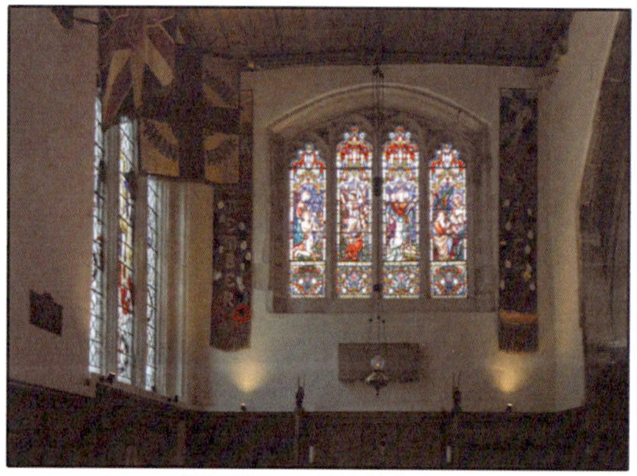

4 sec f22 28mm ISO100 Canon 6D

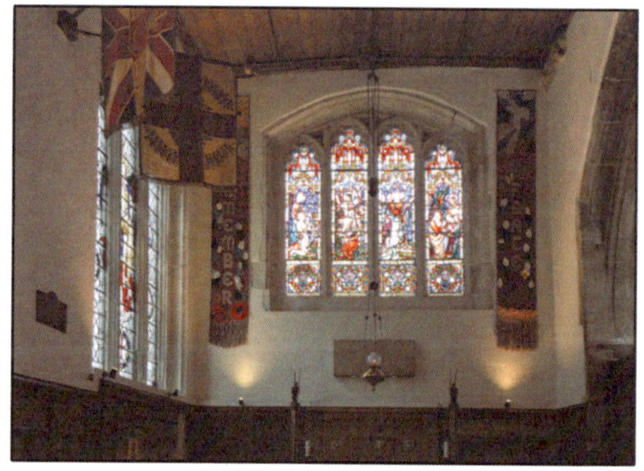

6sec f22 28mm ISO100 Canon 6D

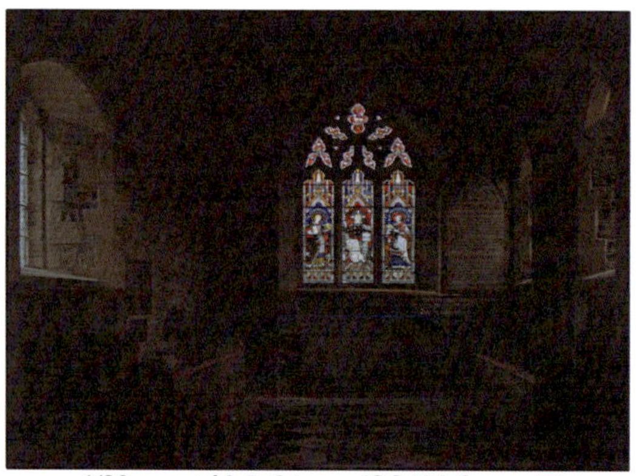

1/20 sec at f 3.5 24 mm ISO100 Canon 6D

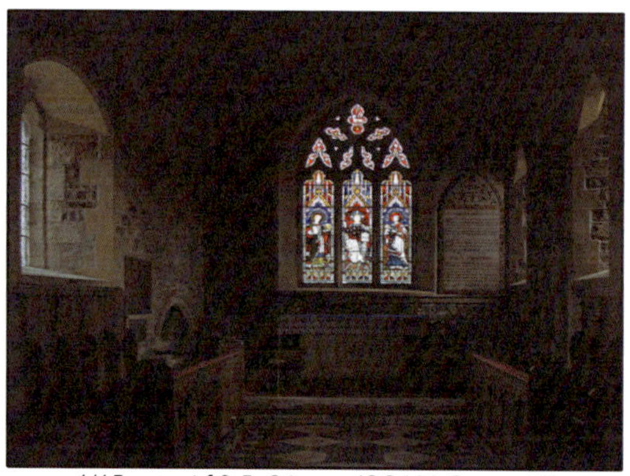

1/15 sec at f 3.5 24 mm ISO100 Canon 6D

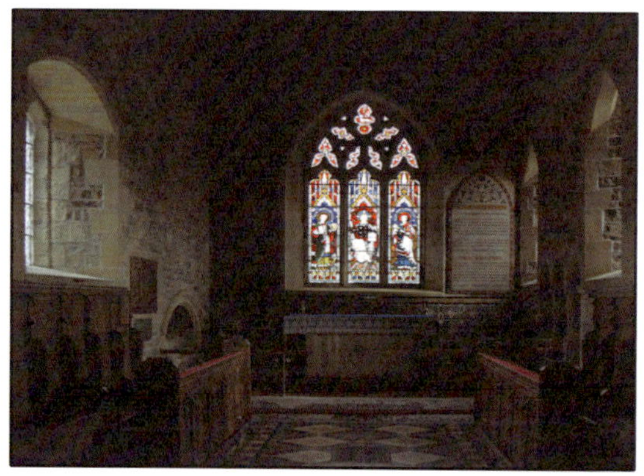

1/10 sec at f 3.5 24 mm ISO100 Canon 6D

PORTRAIT v LANDSCAPE

The orientation is how you prefer it to be.

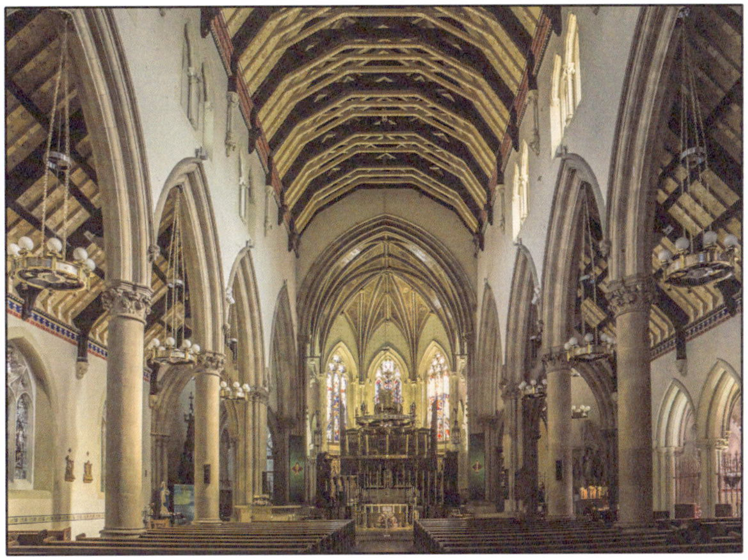

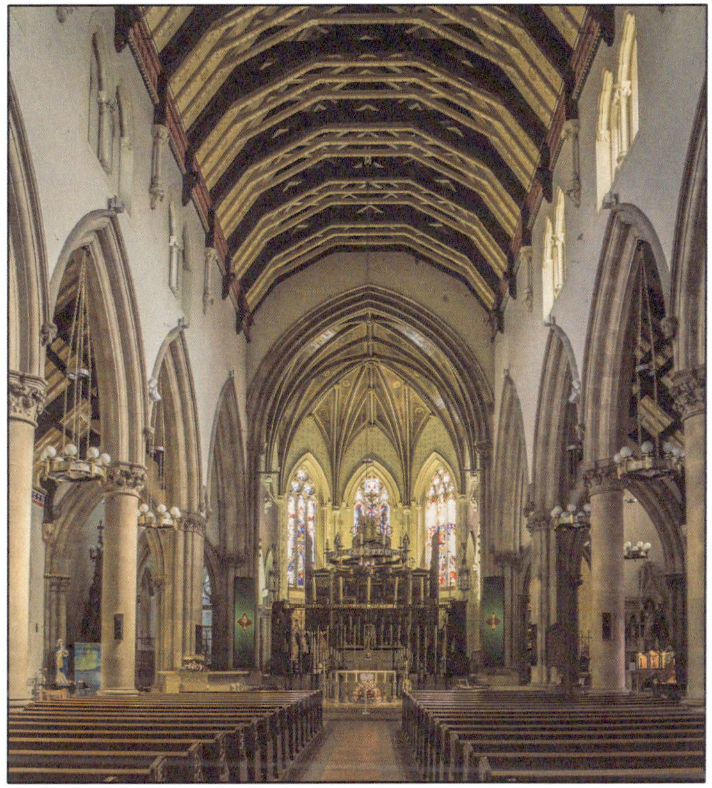

Portrait mode will usually include more of the ceiling and introduce prominent *'leading lines'*.

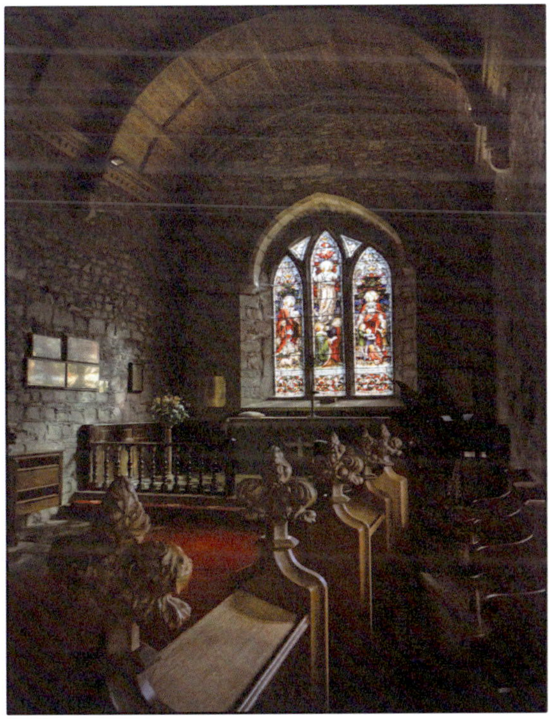

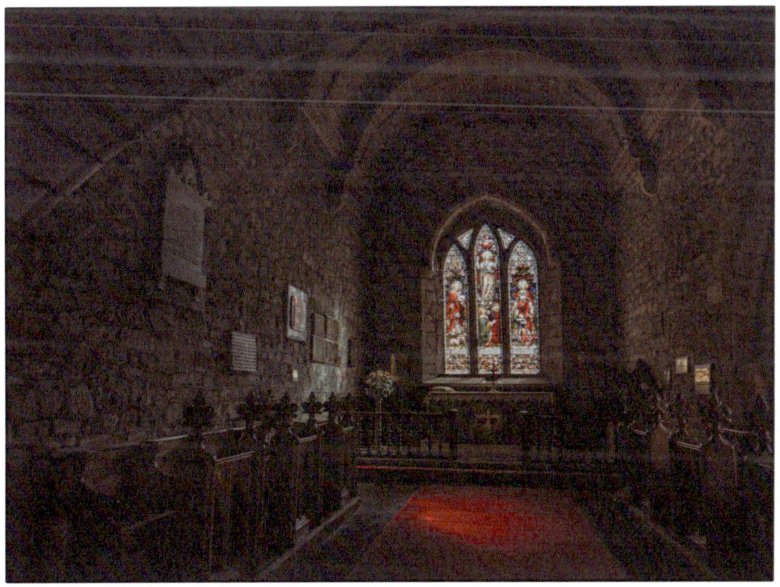

CEILINGS

Look Up! Ceilings will range from 10th century wooden beams held in places by modern supports (and wood-worm), or elaborate designs with painted panels and crests. Photographing them can be tricky. I have laid on the floor more than once to get the right perspective. Experiment with taking two or three images and stitching them in Lightroom.

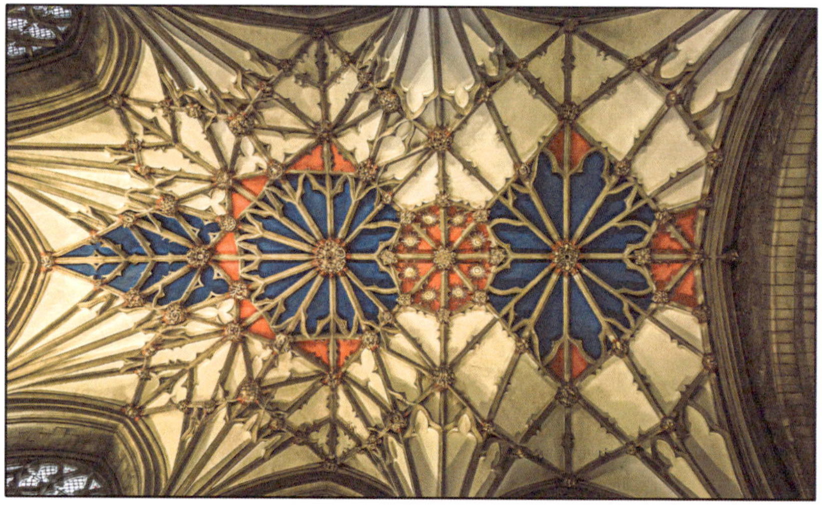

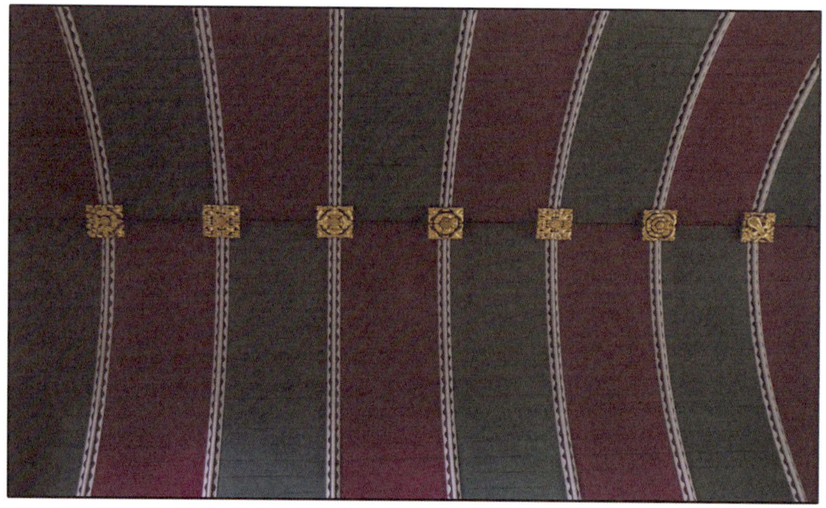

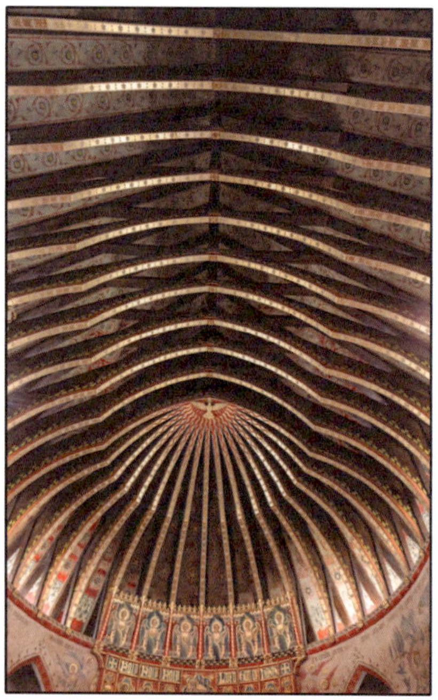

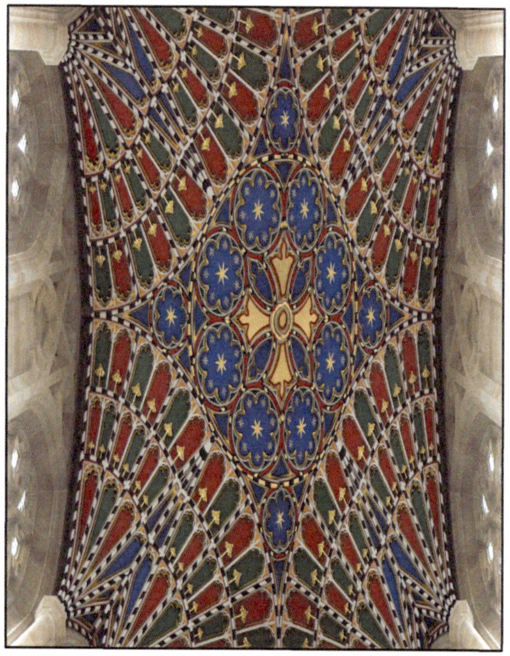

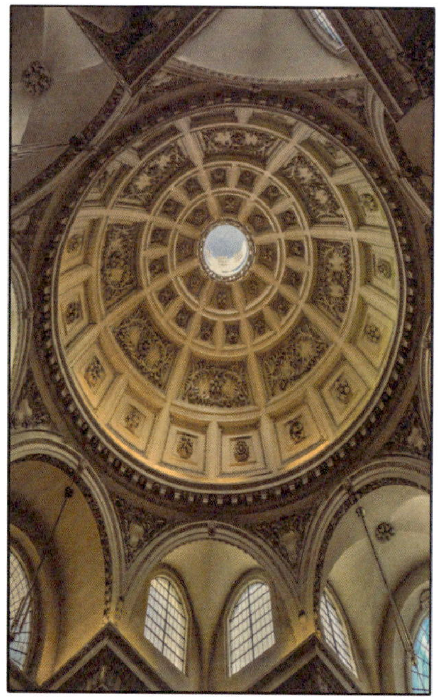

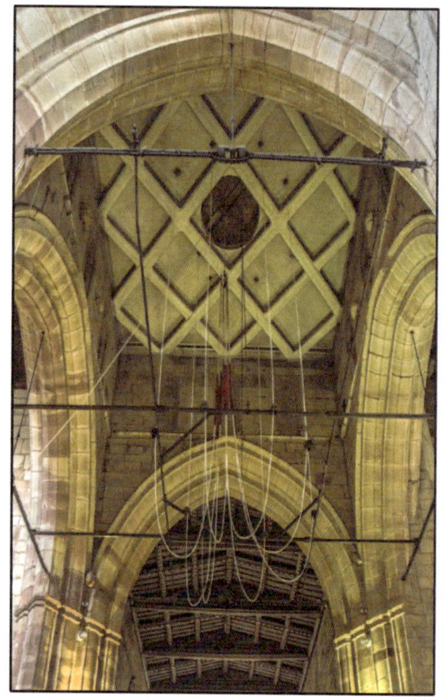

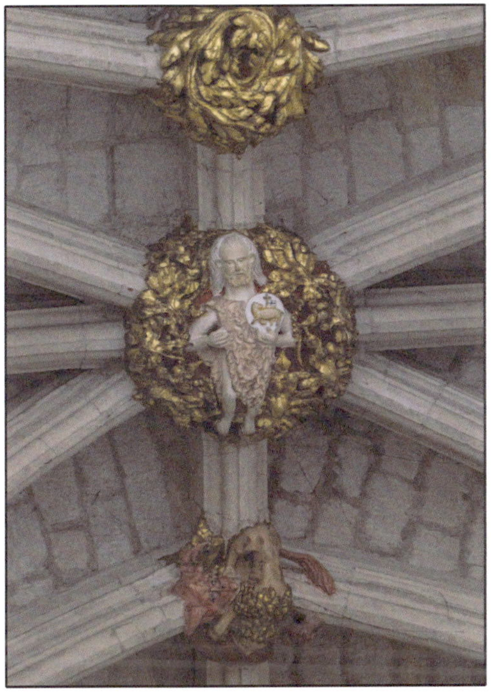
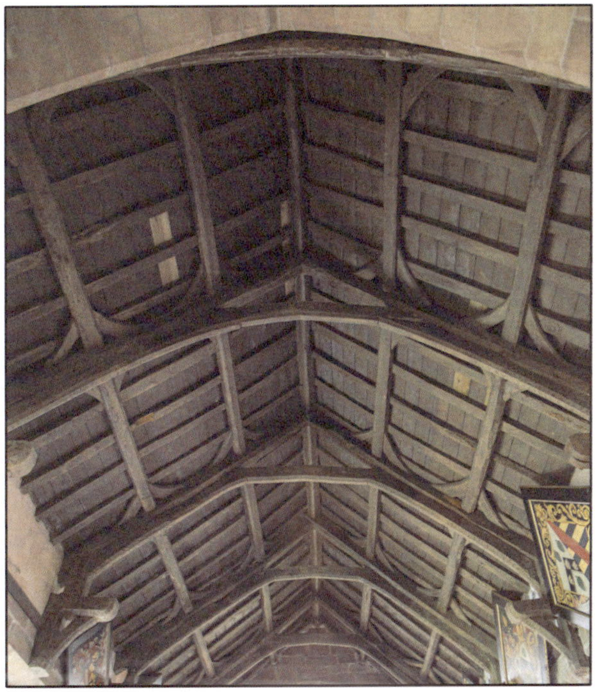
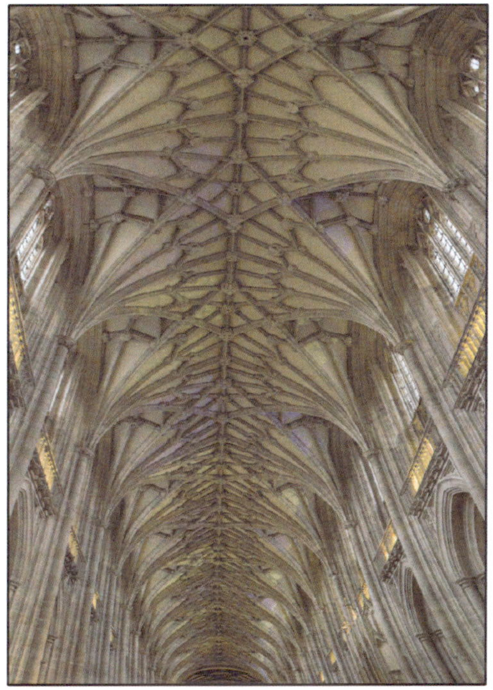
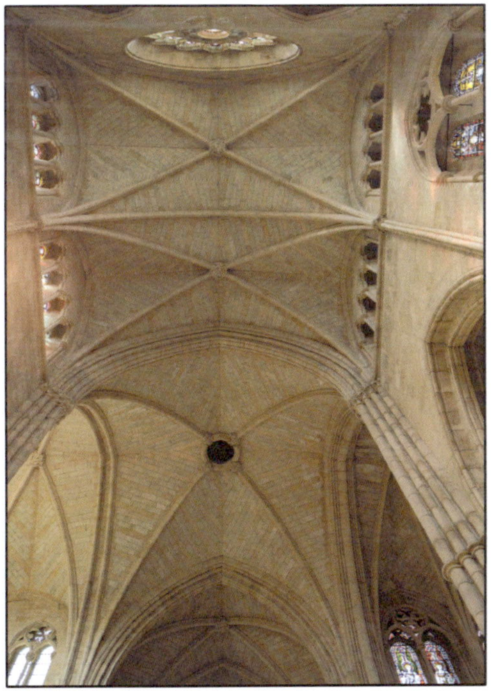
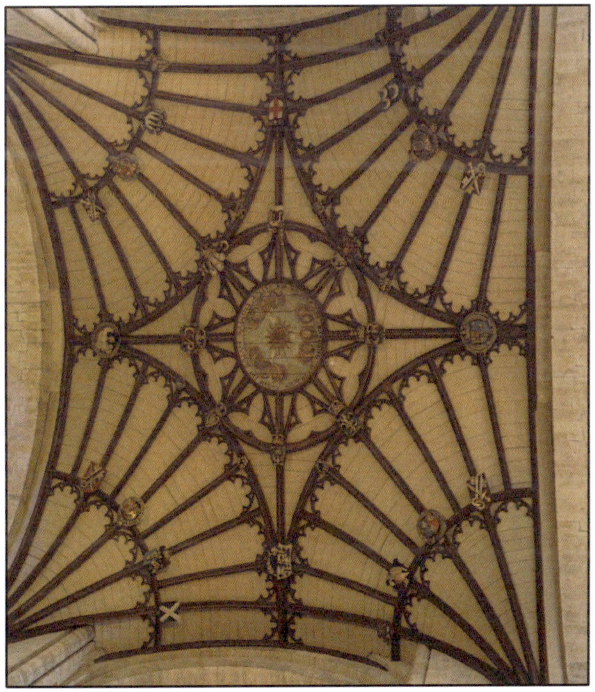
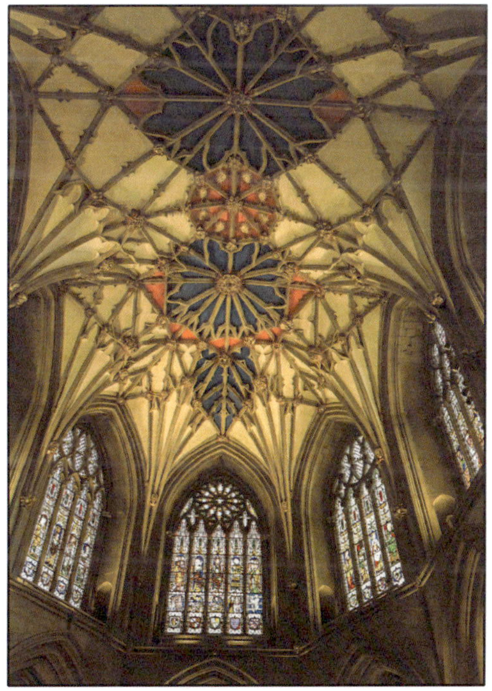

PULPITS

No two Pulpits are alike - they can be simple structures with a lectern light, or elaborate carved wood, stone or marble in many shapes and sizes. High pulpits have a grand staircase and some are topped with an ornate canopy or sounding board. Look out for the intricate craftsmanship in the wood or stone carving. These are works of art.

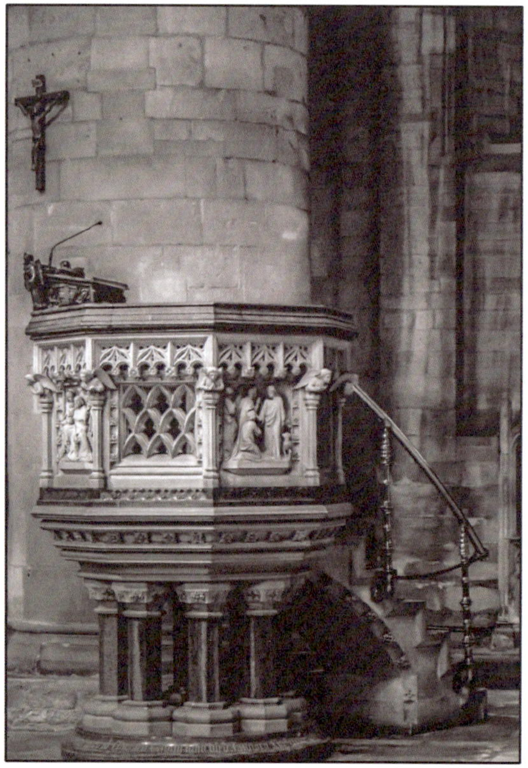

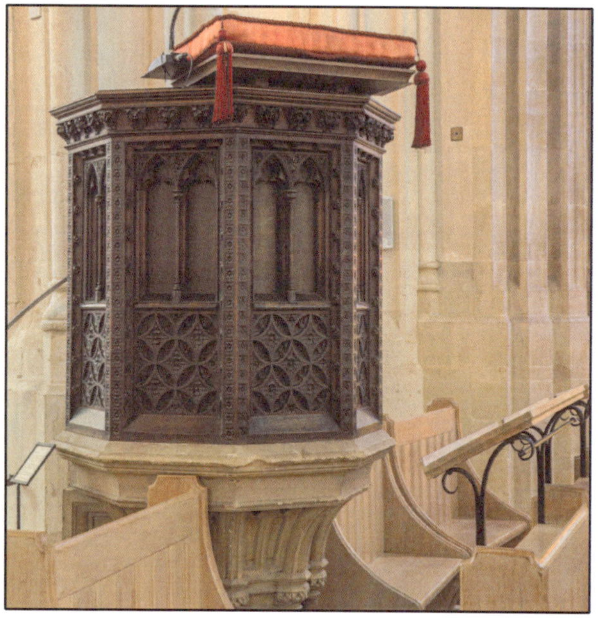

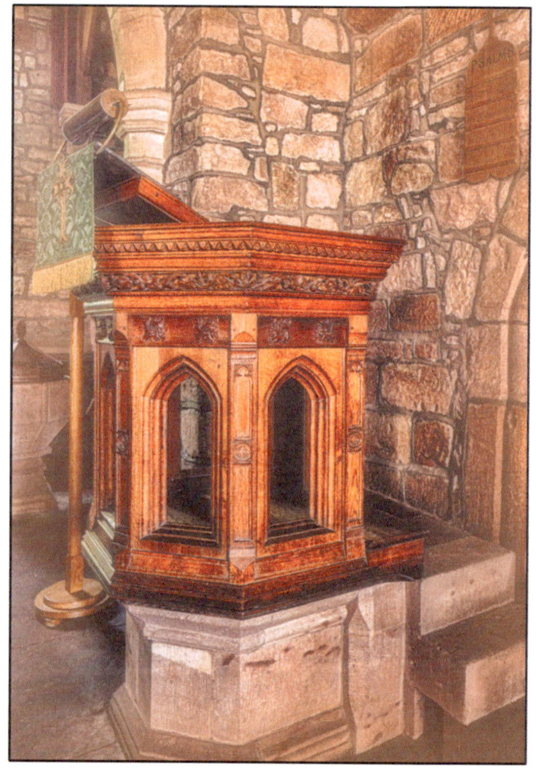

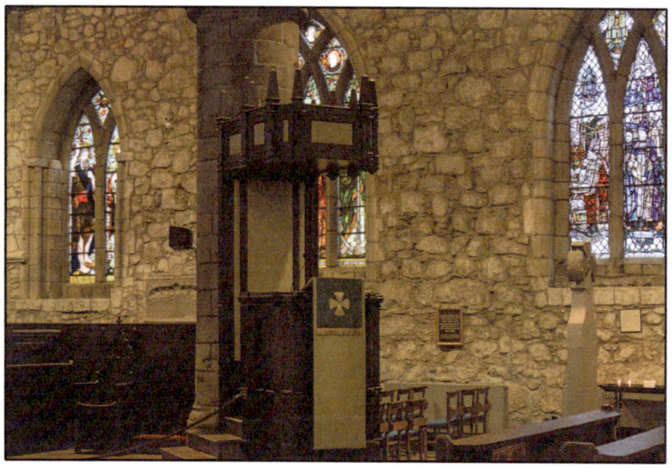

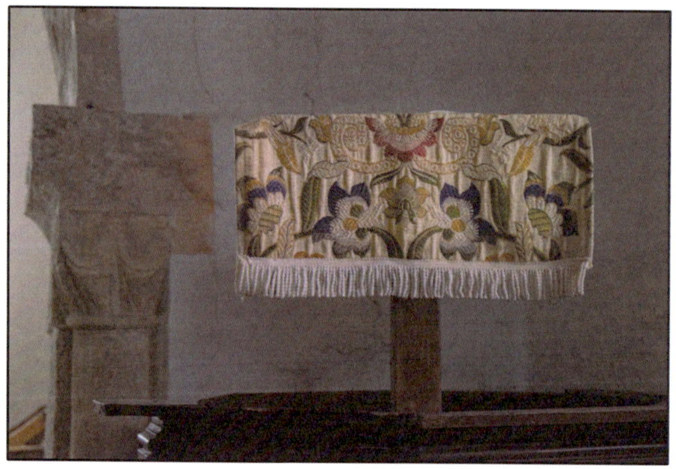

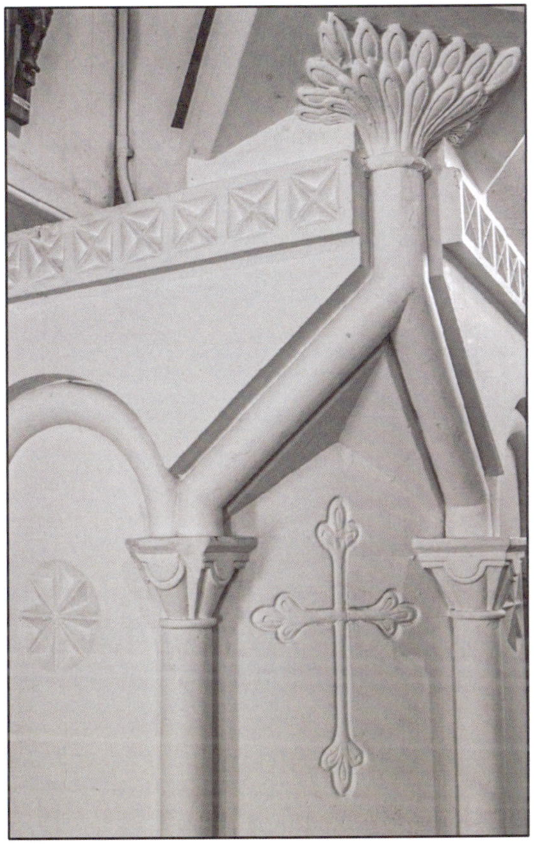

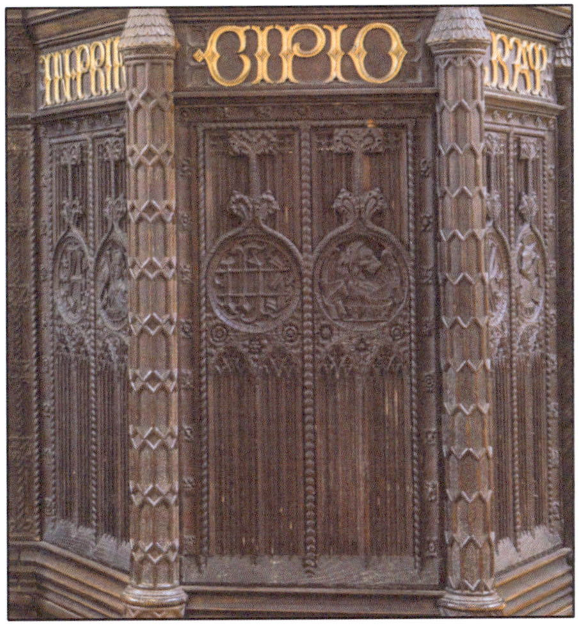
CIPIO

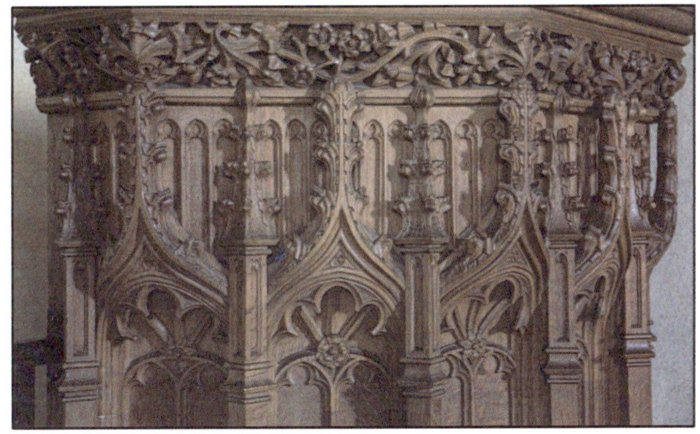

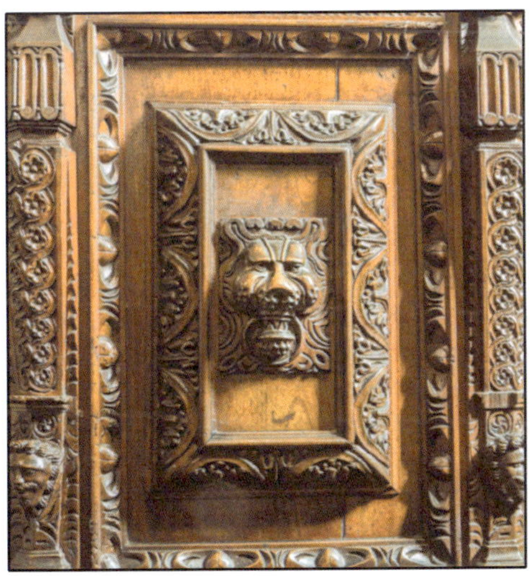

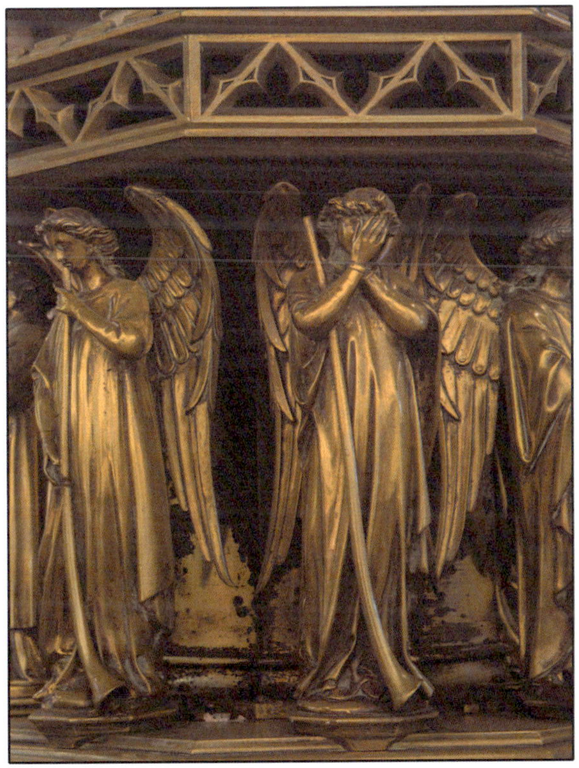

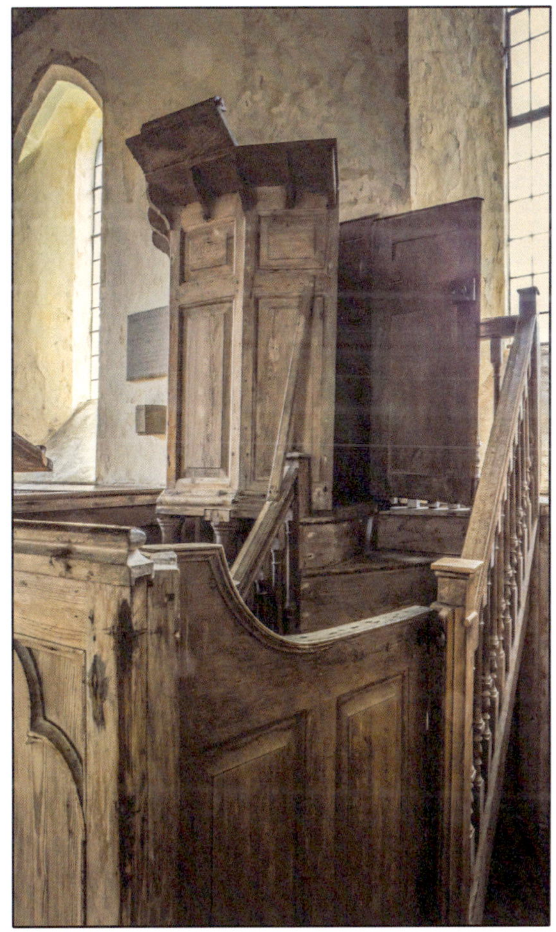

SCULPTURES

Most churches, and especially cathedrals, will have a dedication to a local benefactor or lord of the manor. Many smaller village churches started out as private chapels and will be filled with coat-of-arms, flags, statues, and wall plaques. Most of these are made of white marble or stone, so be careful with your white balance. I keep mine on auto. Also, many of these benefit, like the pulpits, from being photographed close-up to show off the detail in the workmanship.

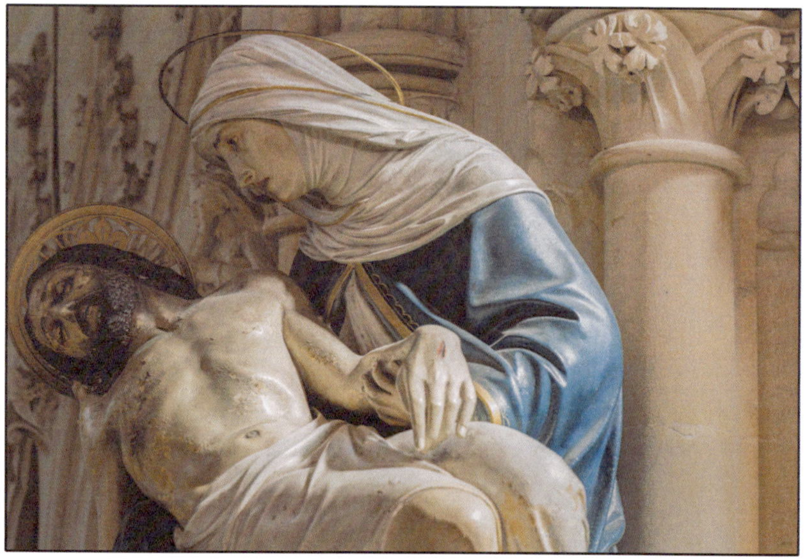

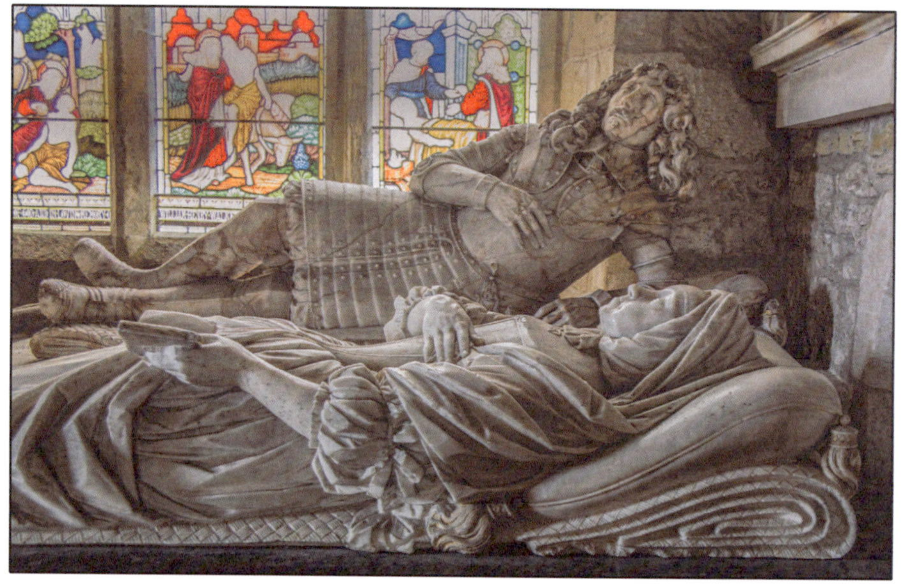

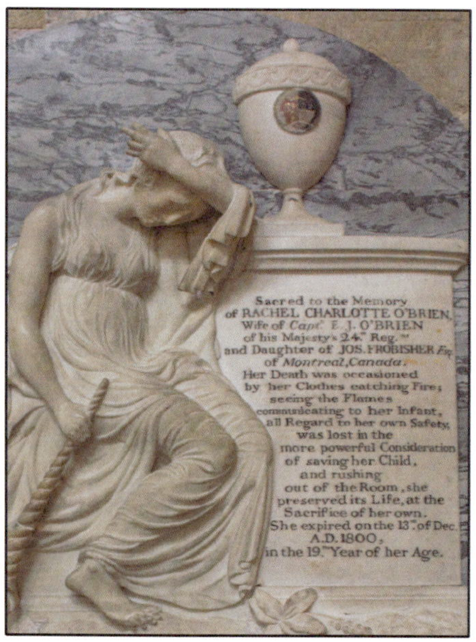

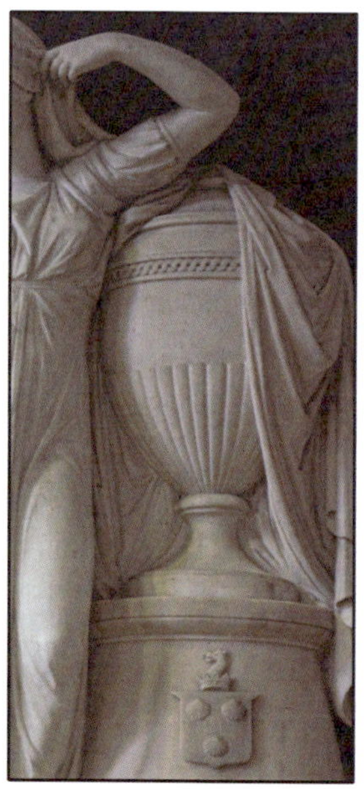

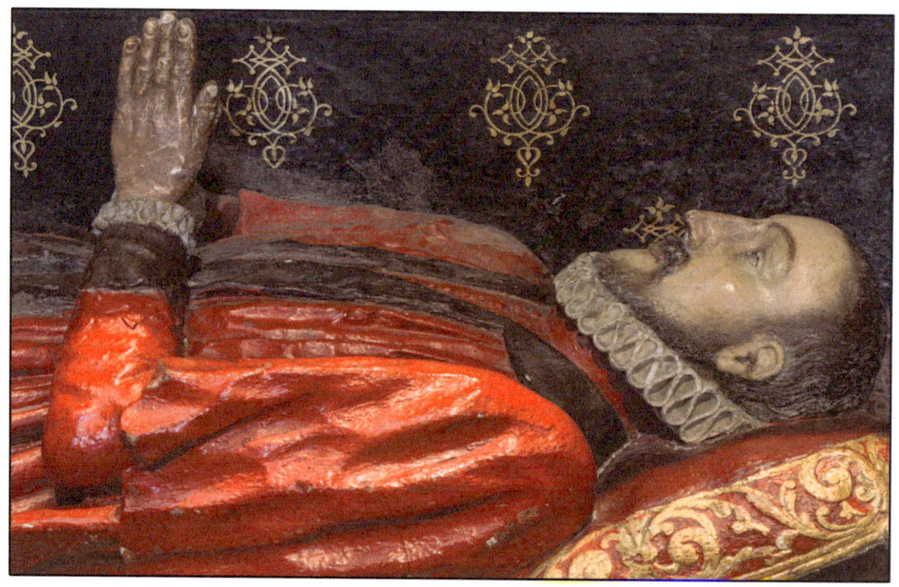

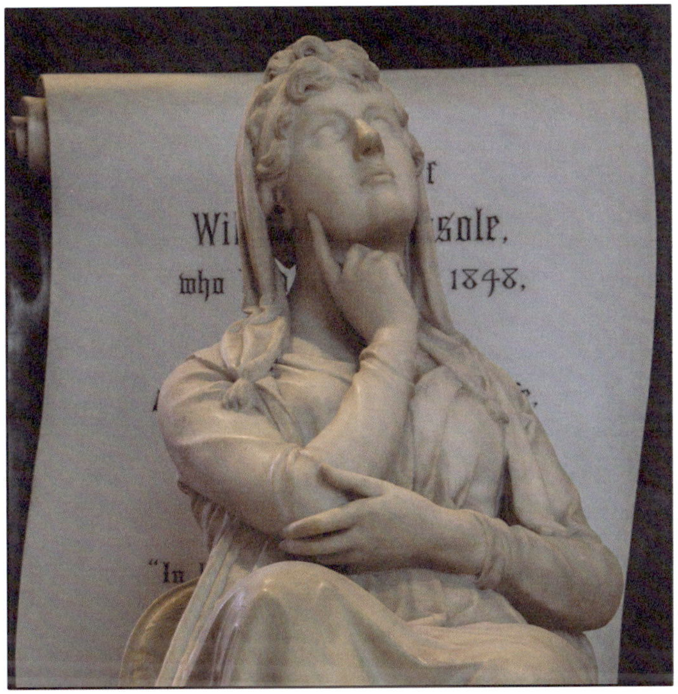

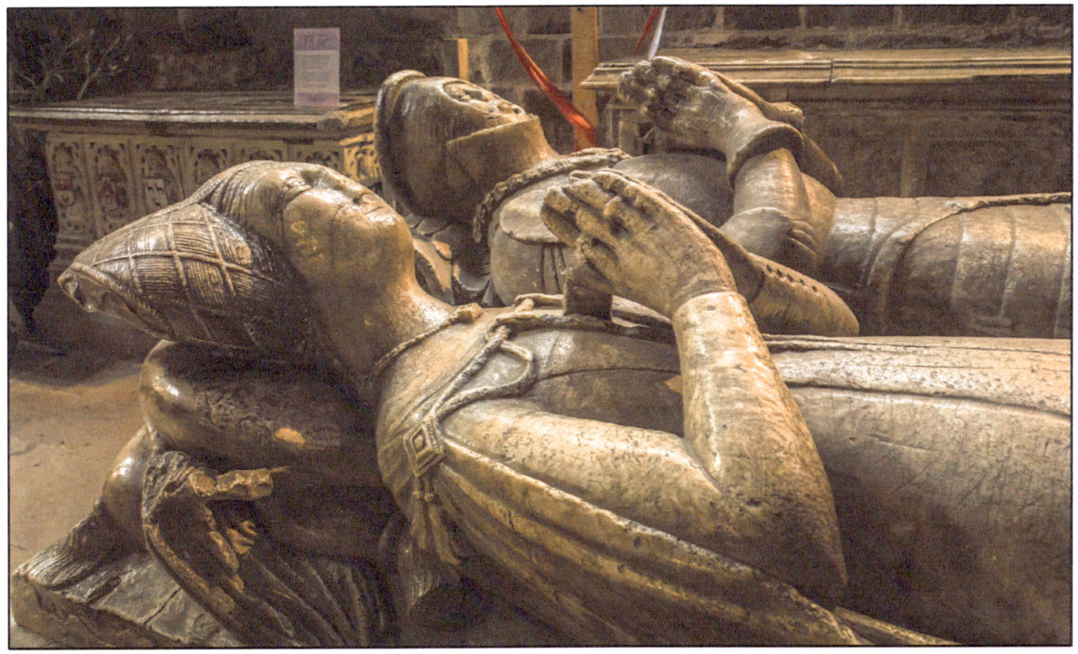

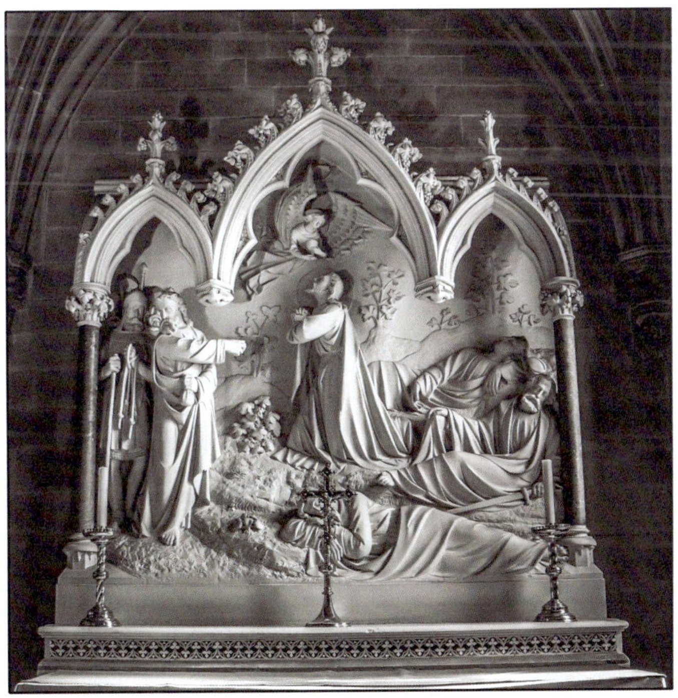

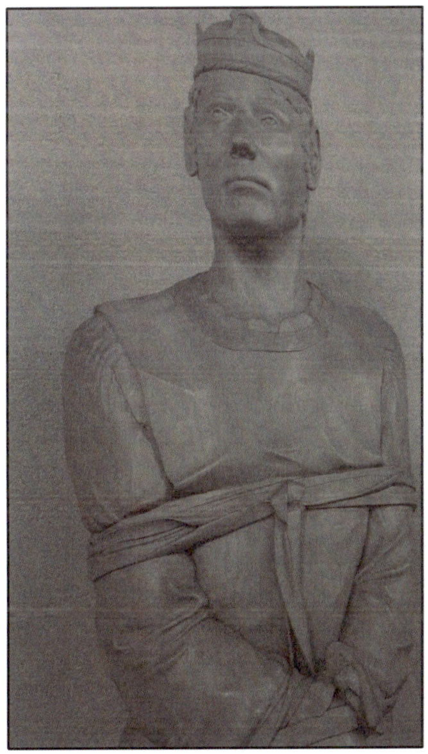

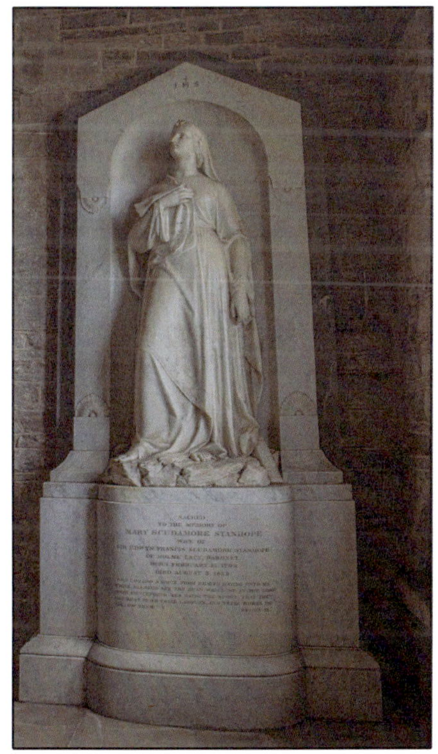

MISCELLANEOUS

Keep an eye out for something different. Old churches are full of interesting artefacts - *be creative*.

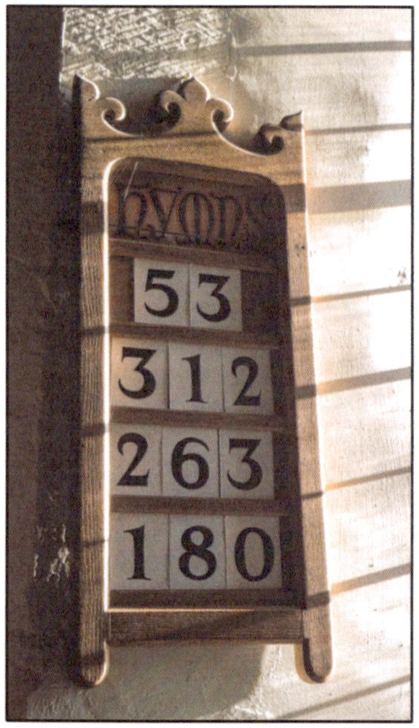

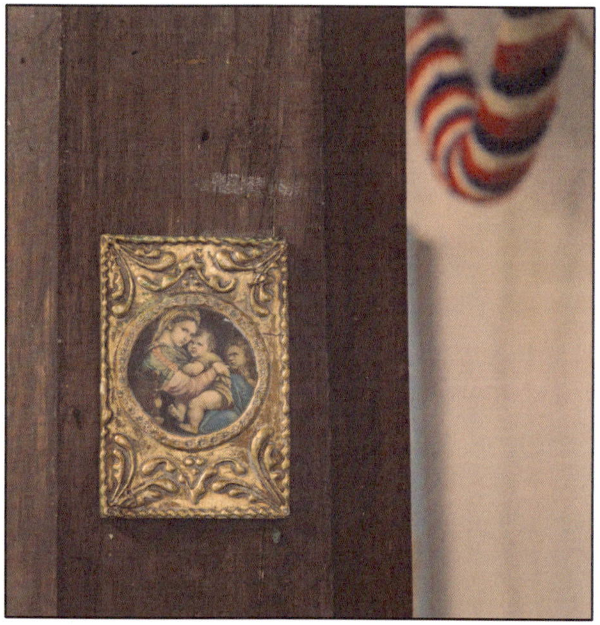

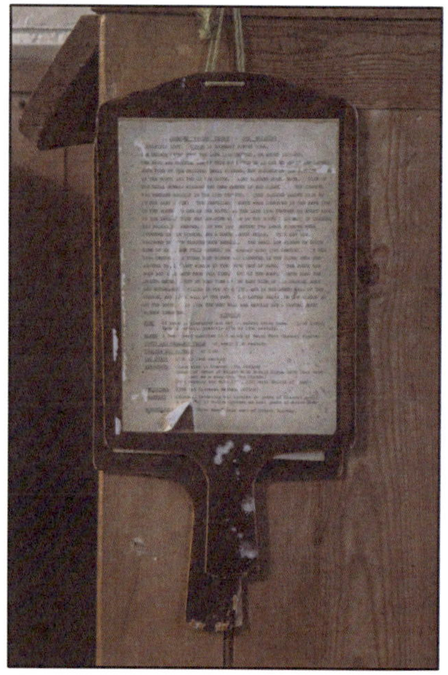

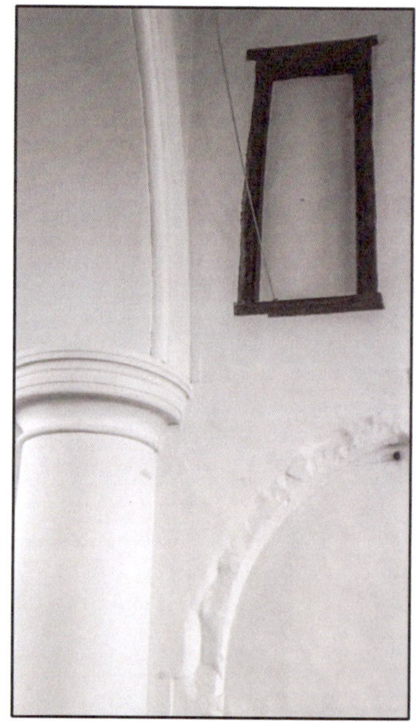

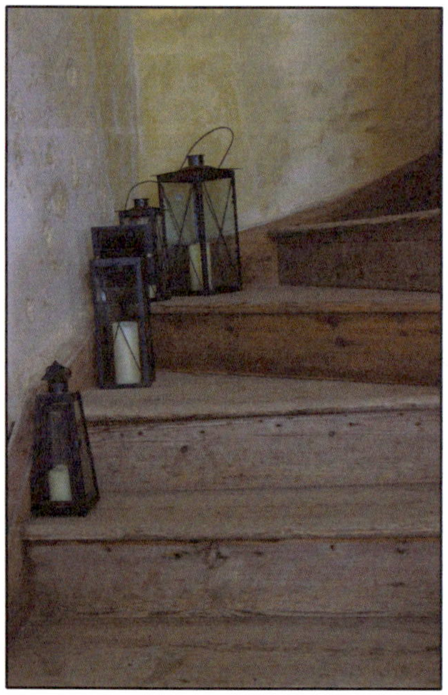

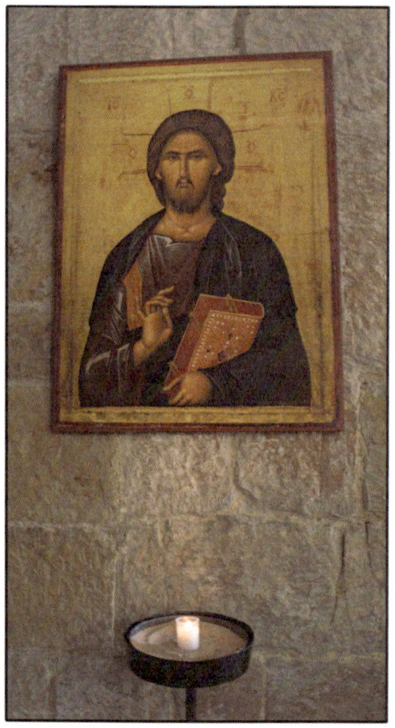

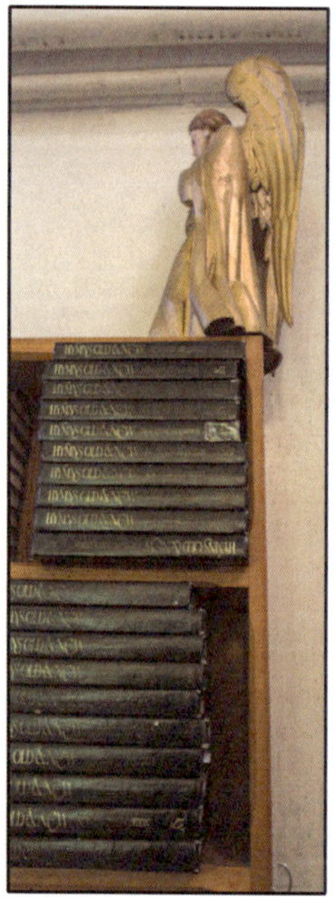

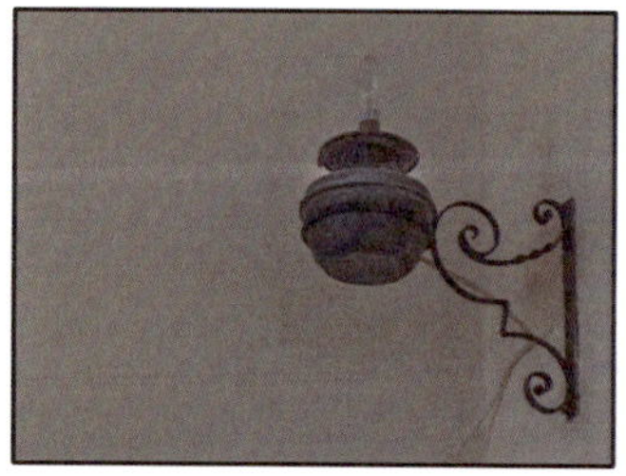

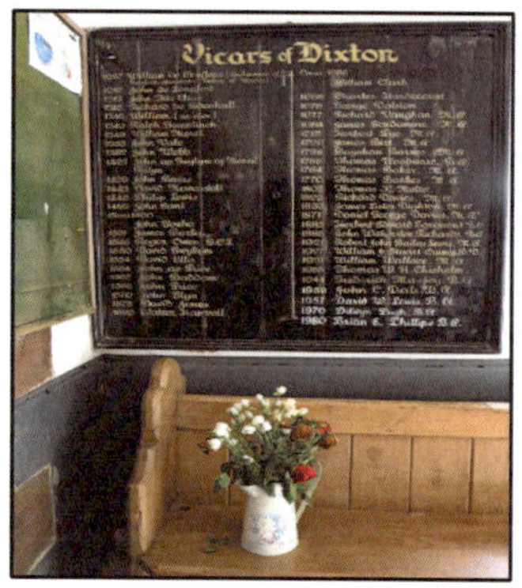

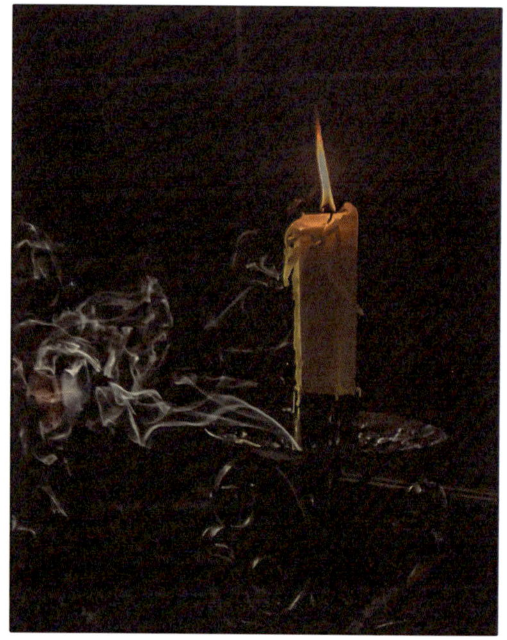

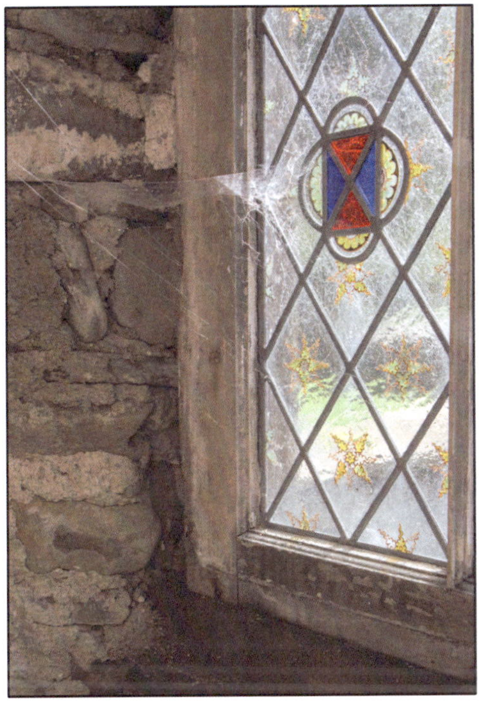
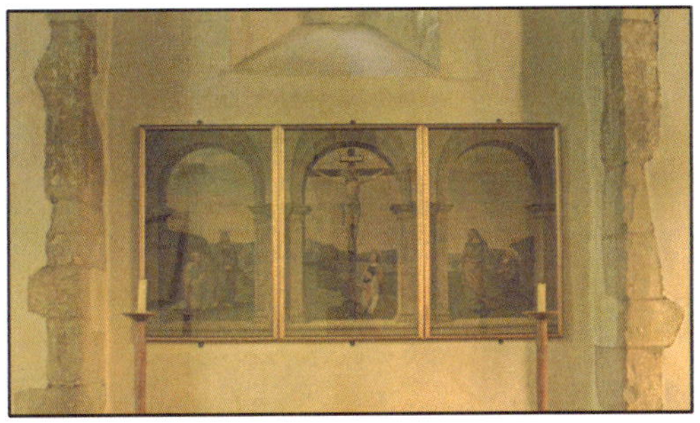
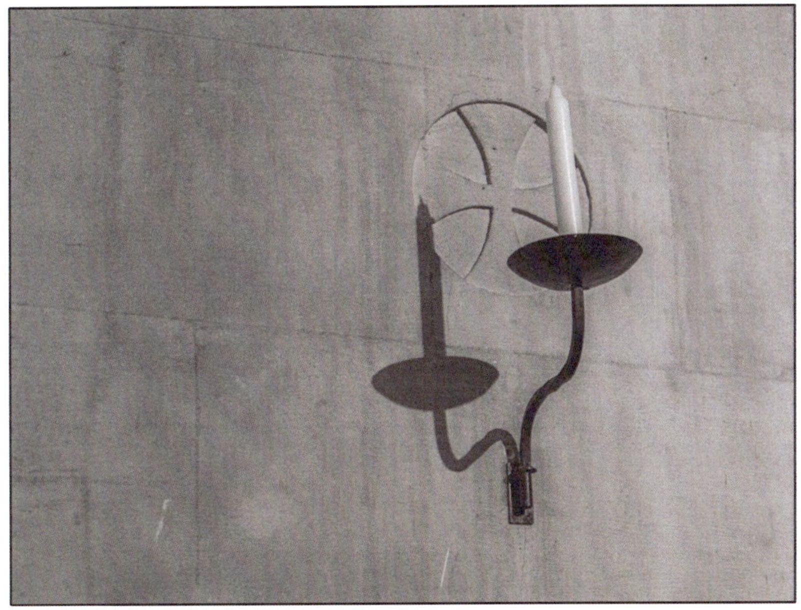
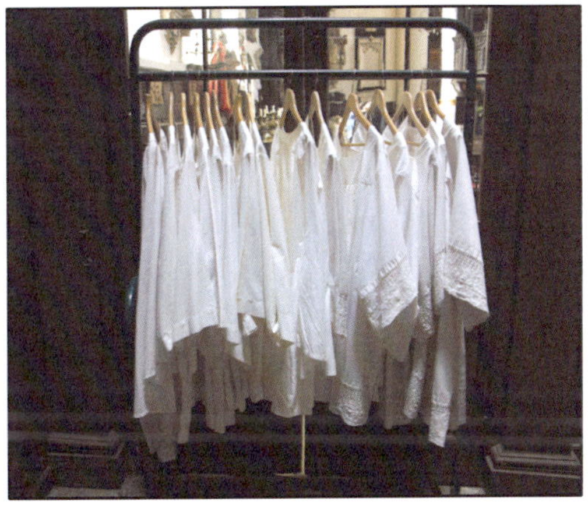
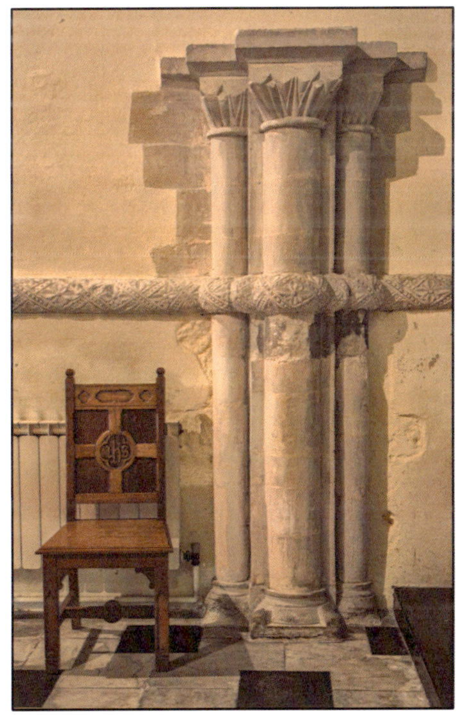
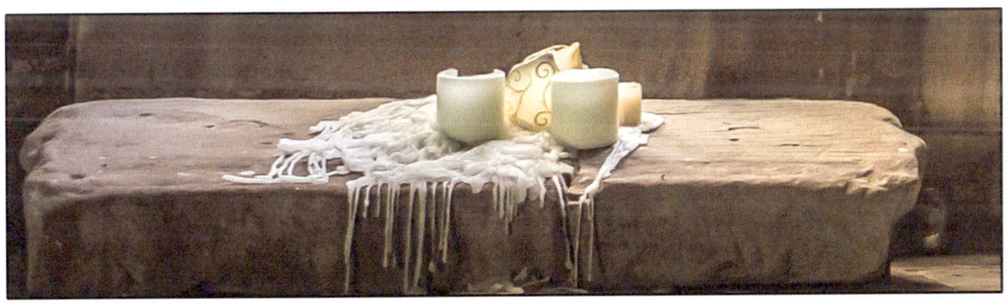
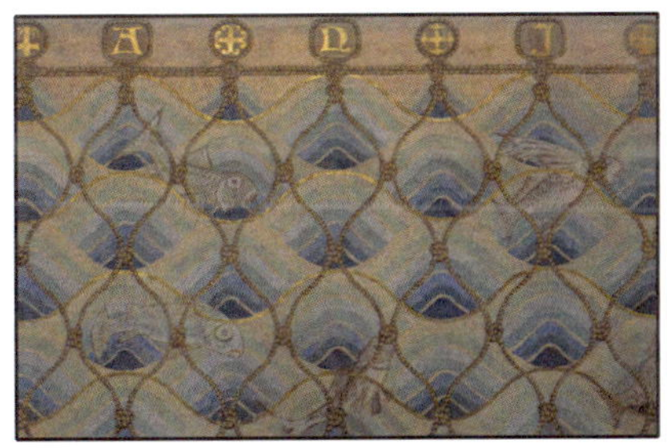
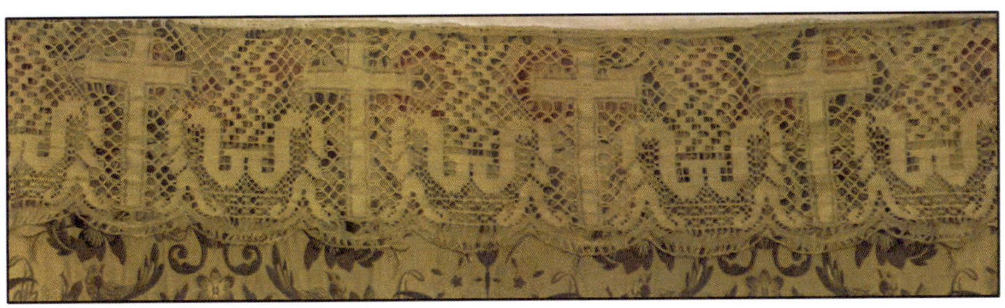
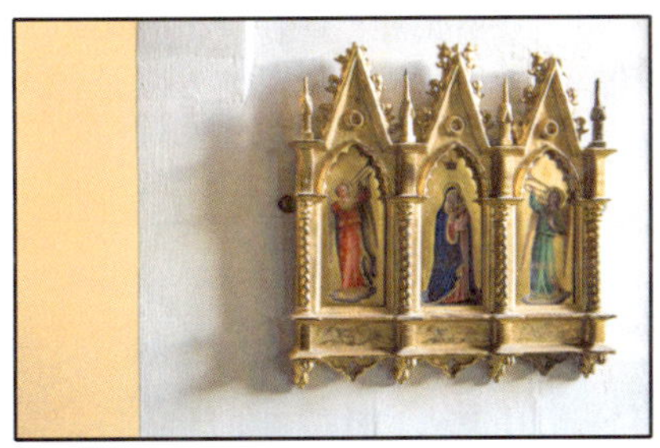

HORIZONTALS and VER12TICALS

Lens distortion is very noticeable when photographing architecture, and is a result of the lens bending the mage to fit the frame. An 18mm – 35mm lens will show less distortion, but still may occur. Fear not, most Adobe software including Elements, Photoshop and Lightroom can adjust your image automatically. These examples were adjusted in Lightroom using *Transform*. Check the *'constrain crop'* then click on Auto. *Photoshop has a straightening tool and Elements has a correct distortion tool*

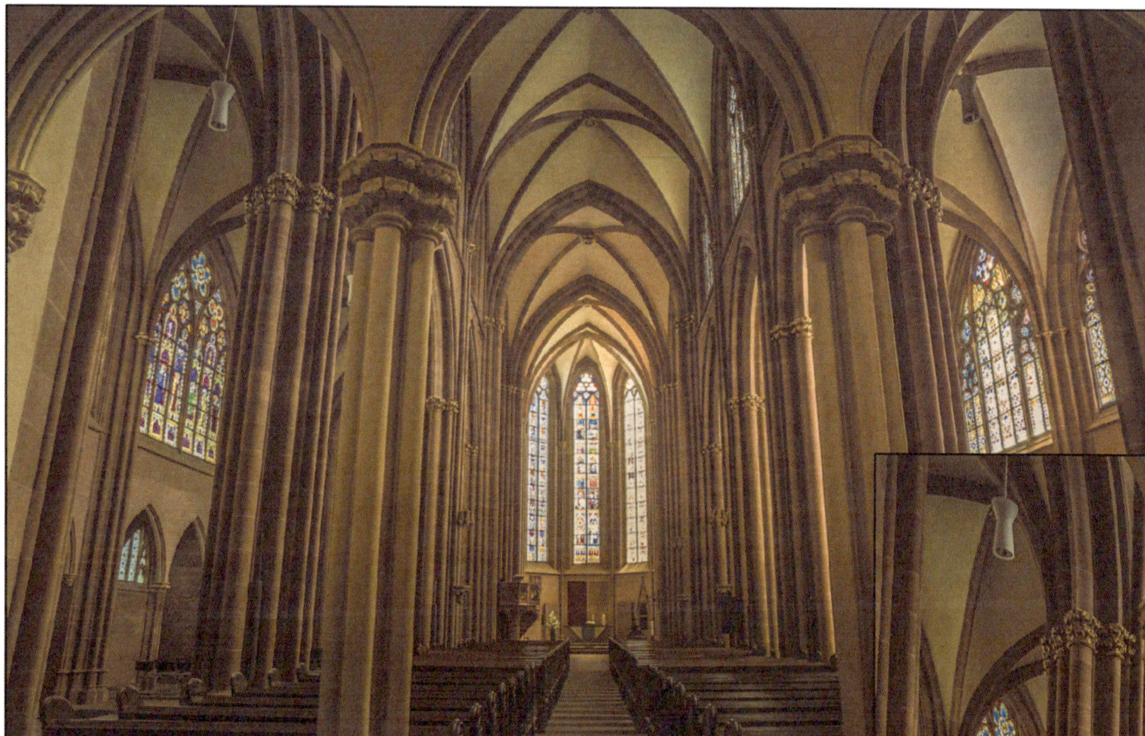

Before correction

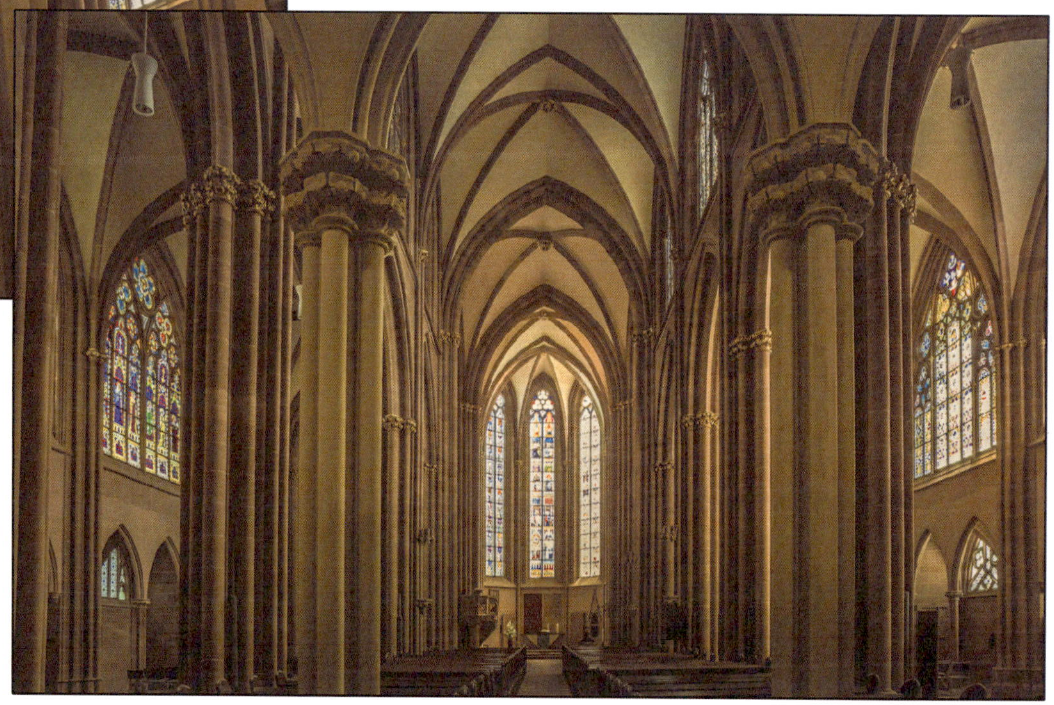

After correction using the *Transform* feature in Lightroom

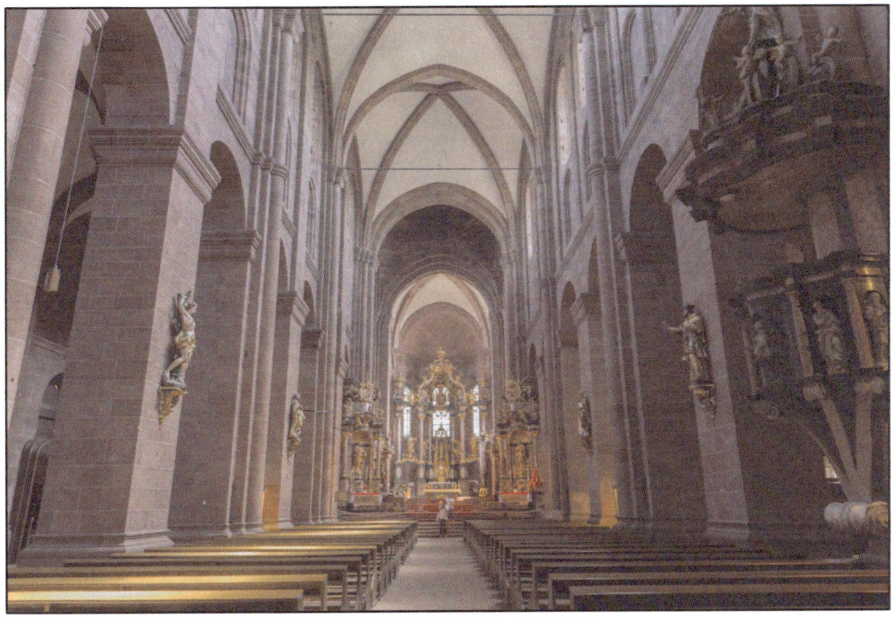

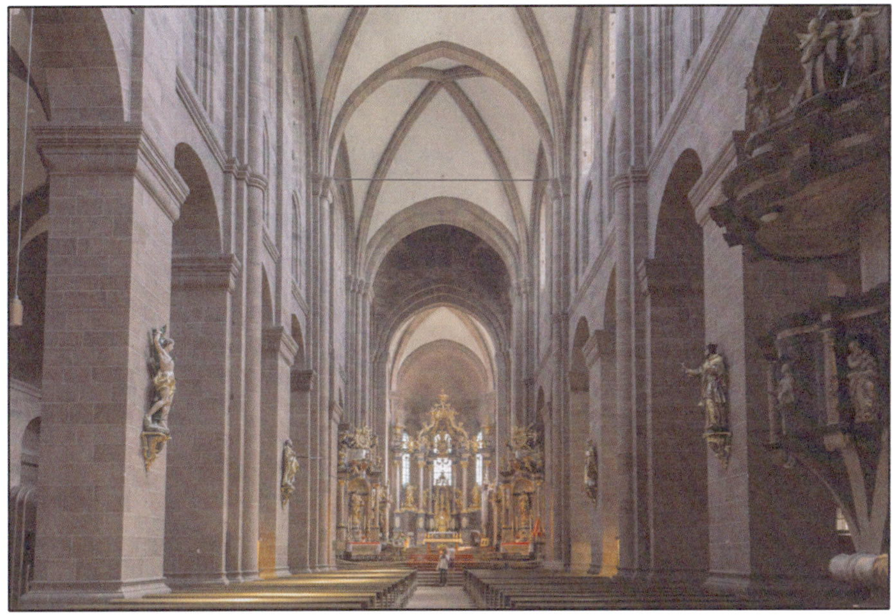

If you know your image will need to be adjusted for verticals in post-processing, it is advisable to *'step-back'* a few paces, as some cropping will occur when editing, which you will not be able to correct, or, worst still, never be able to revisit that particular place again

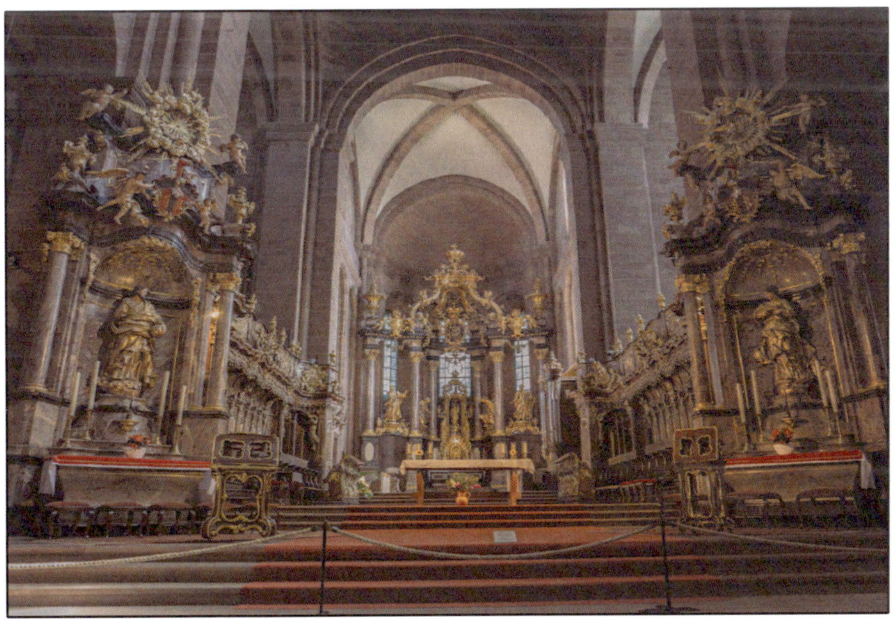

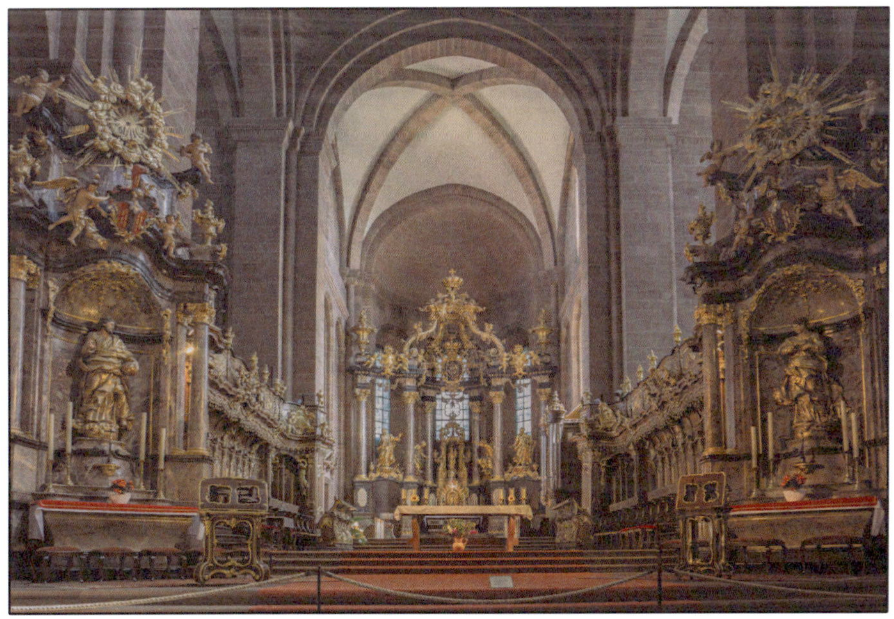

SHADOWS and LIGHT

How you prefer your finished image to be is entirely up to you as the photographer. We all have our *'style.'* Having said that, you will have been told there are only two elements to photography: *light and composition.* This applies to most genre of photography, but none so more than interiors. Take a look again at Ron Smith's image at the front of this book. Although not a church, this disused building was eighty per cent devoid of natural light. The exposure was over three minutes, yet Ron captured perfectly all the elements of the vast interior to produce this award winning image. The following pages are some of my favourite *'atmospheric'* images.

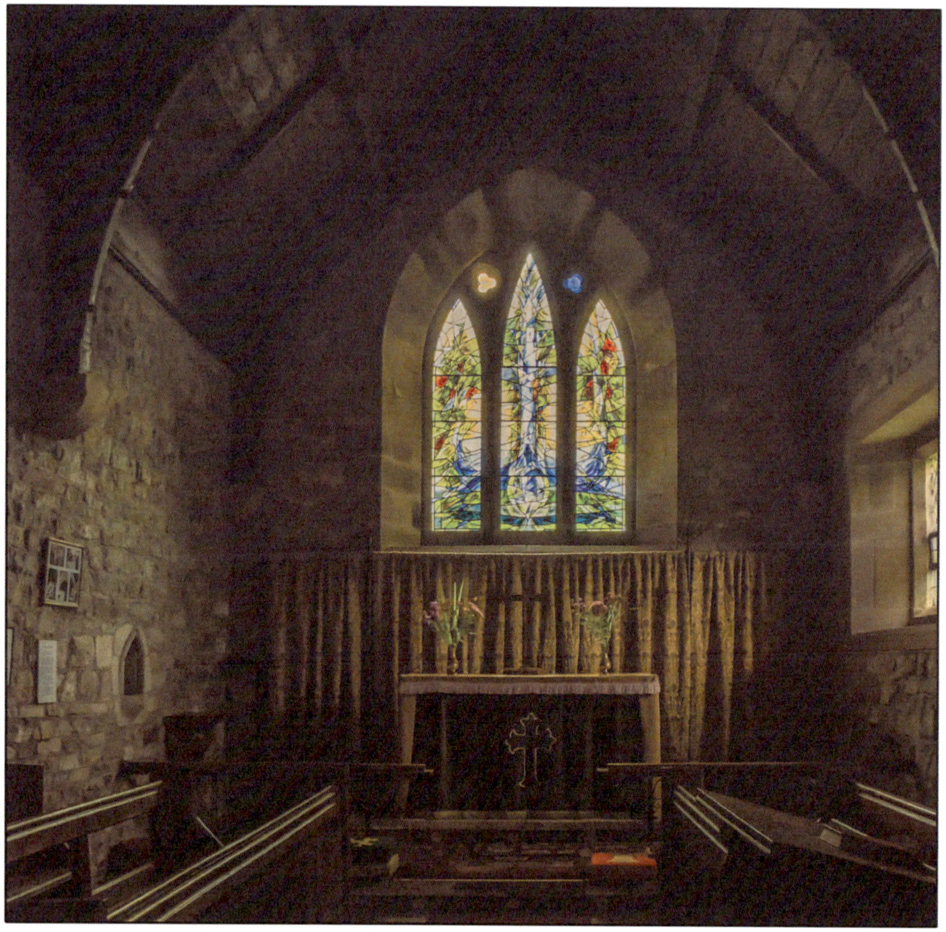

0.3sec f 22 24 mm ISO100 Canon 6D

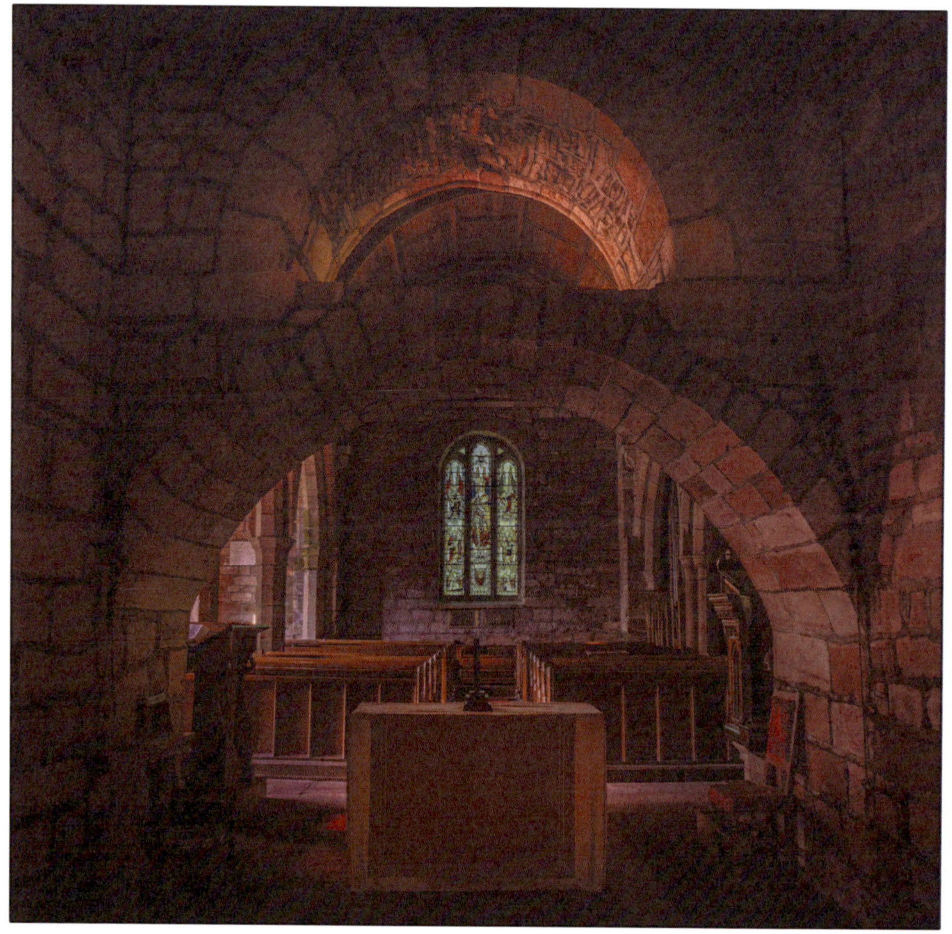

1.4sec f 22 24 mm ISO160 Canon 6D

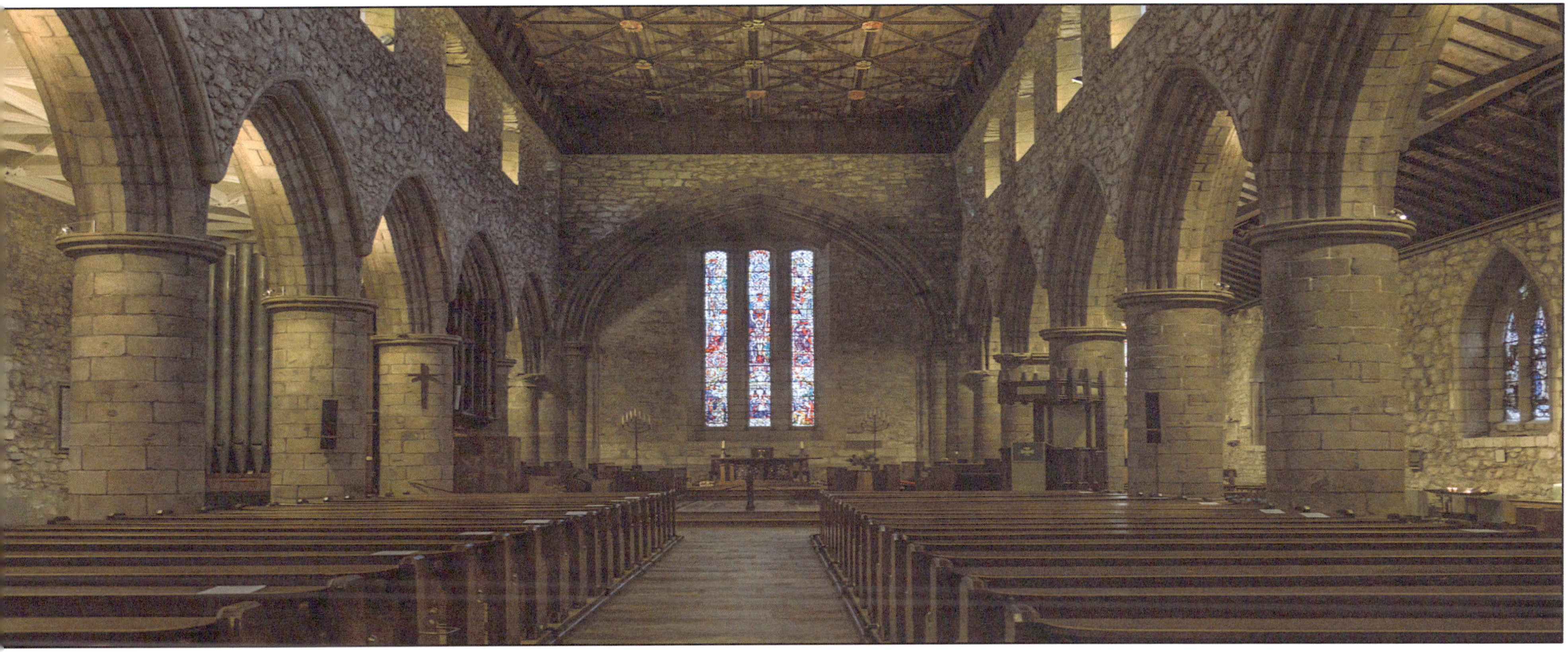

1/60sec f3.6 20mm ISO100 Fuji X-T1

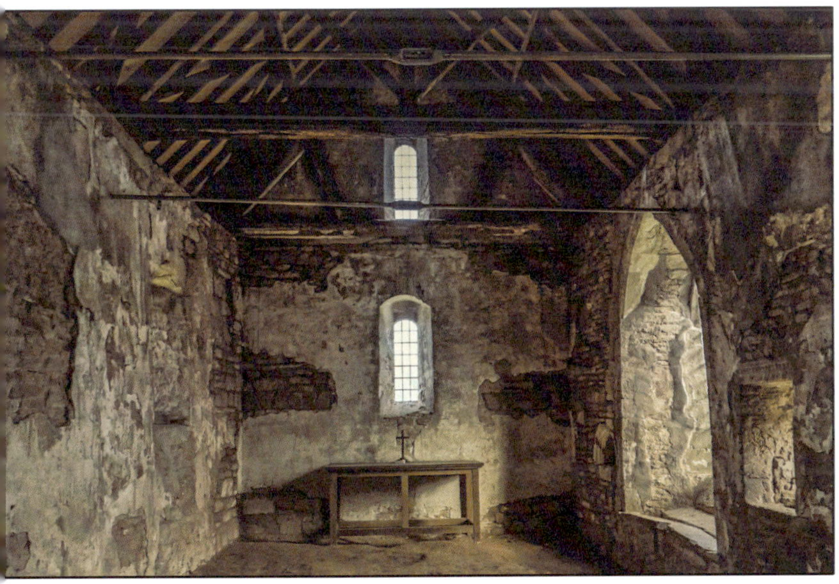

1/60sec f7.1 18.5mm ISO1000 Fuji X-T1

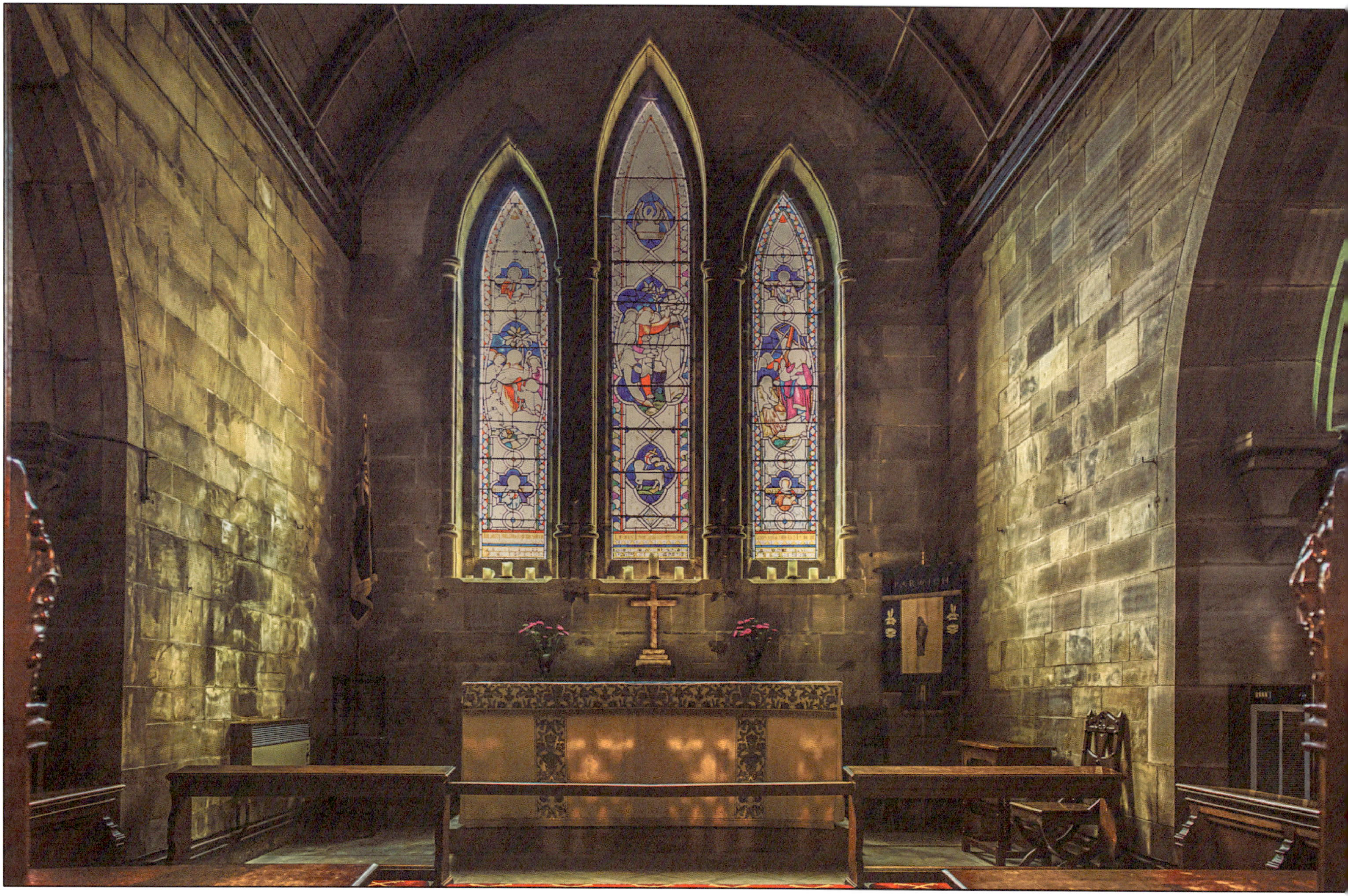

5sec f7.1 24mm ISO100 Canon 6D

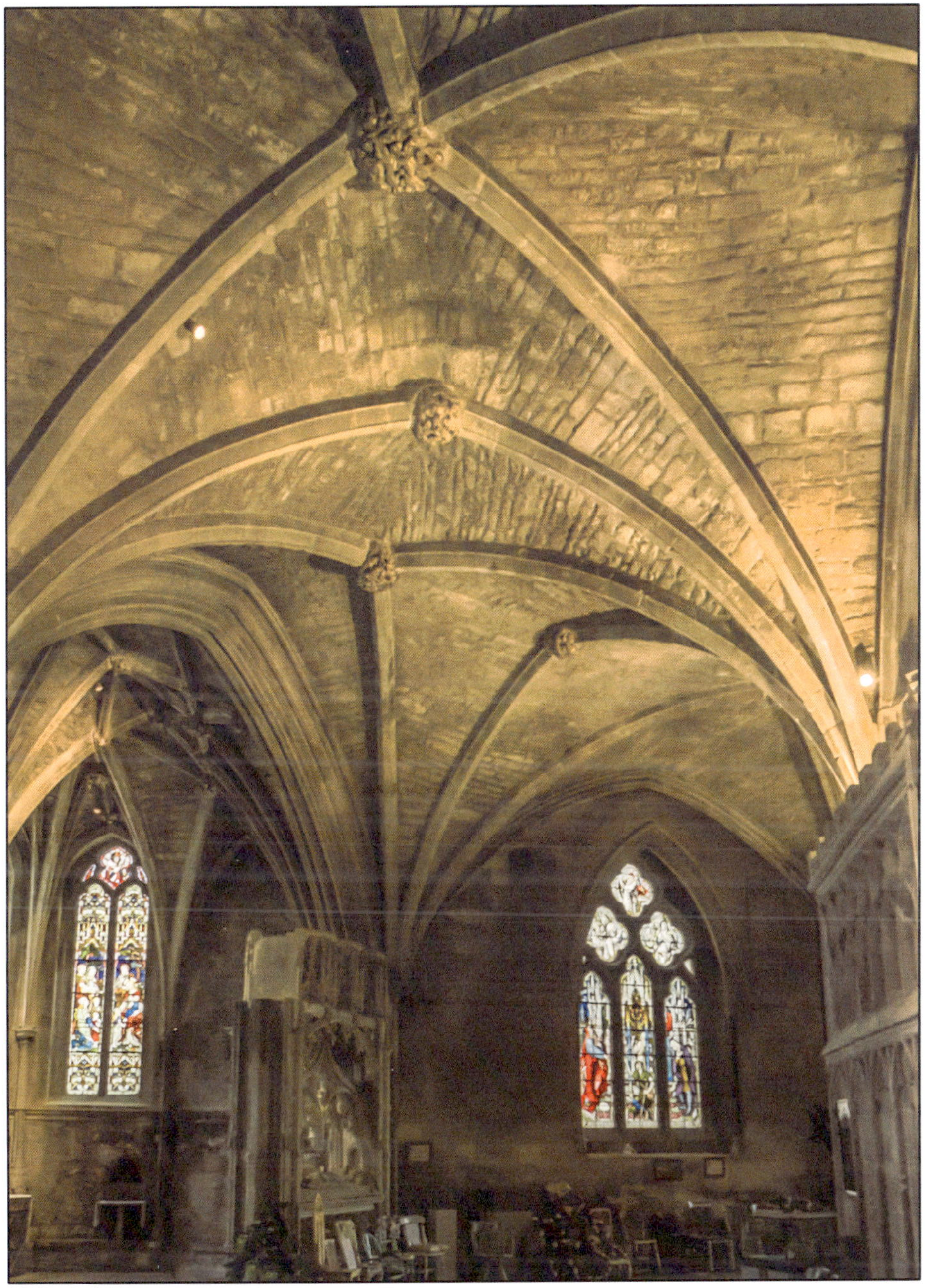

1/60sec f7.1 18mm ISO800 Fuji X-T1

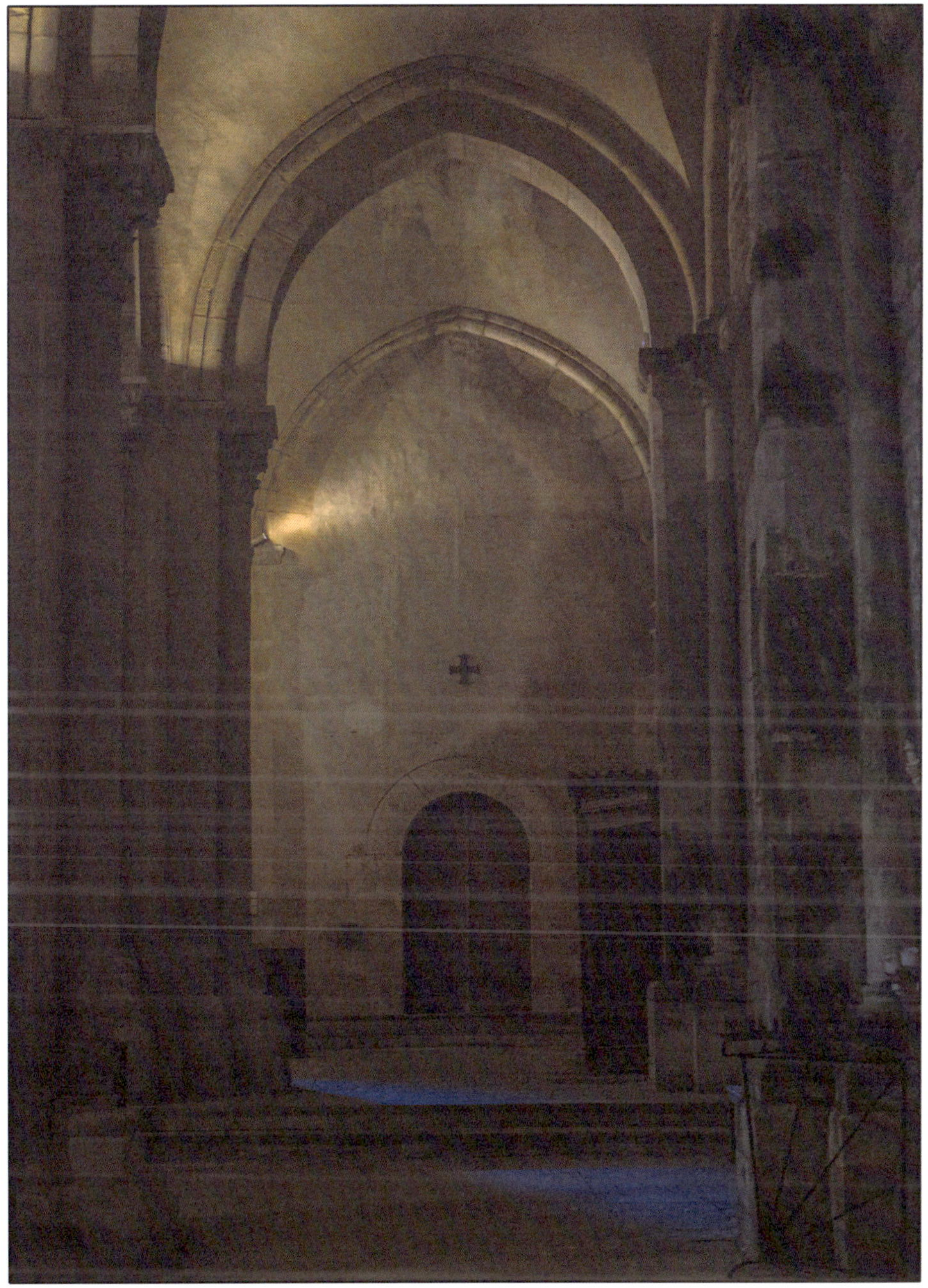

1/60 sec f5.6 36.6 mm ISO3200 Fuji X-T1

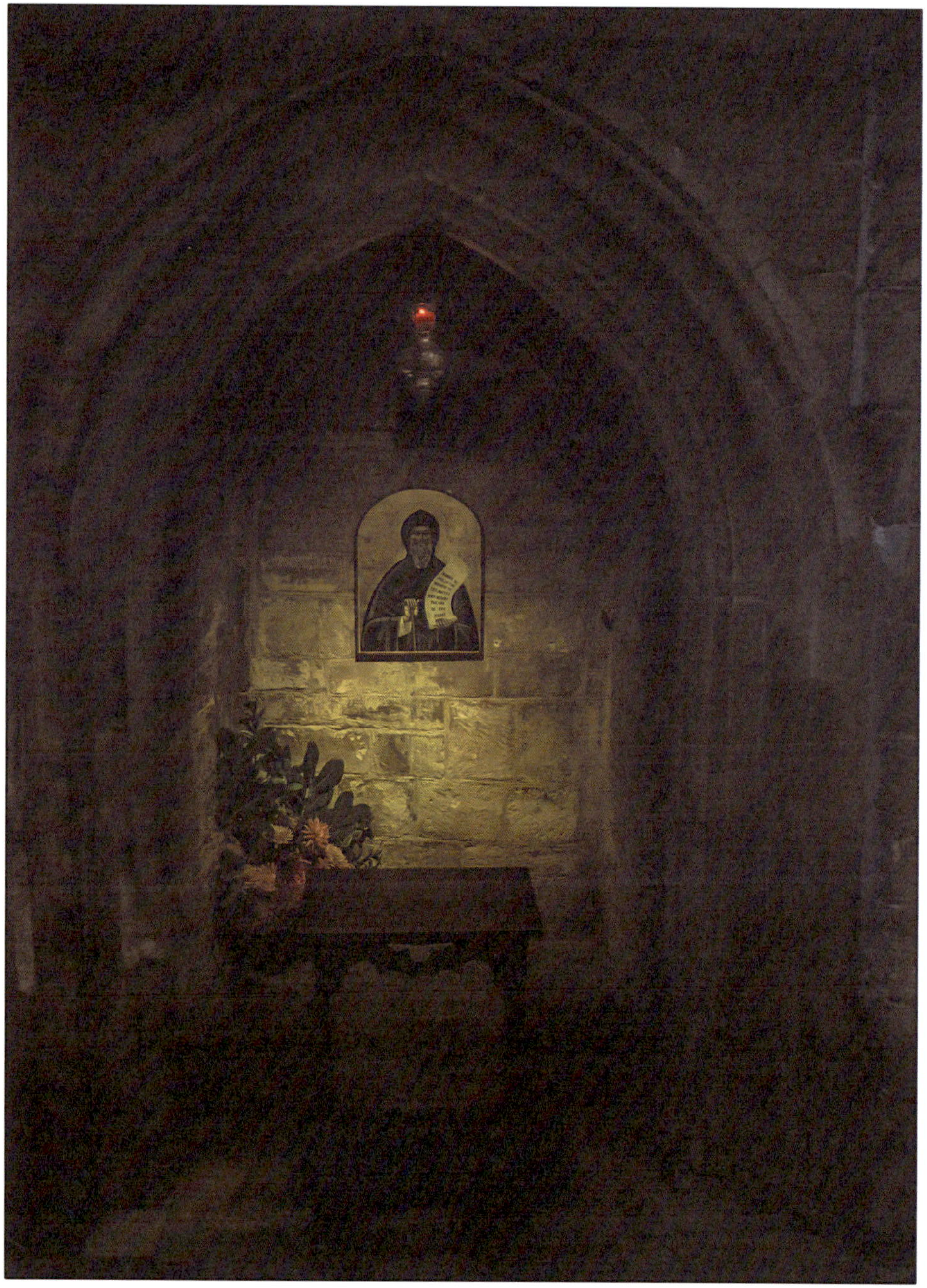

1/60sec f4 20.8mm ISO400 Fuji X-T1

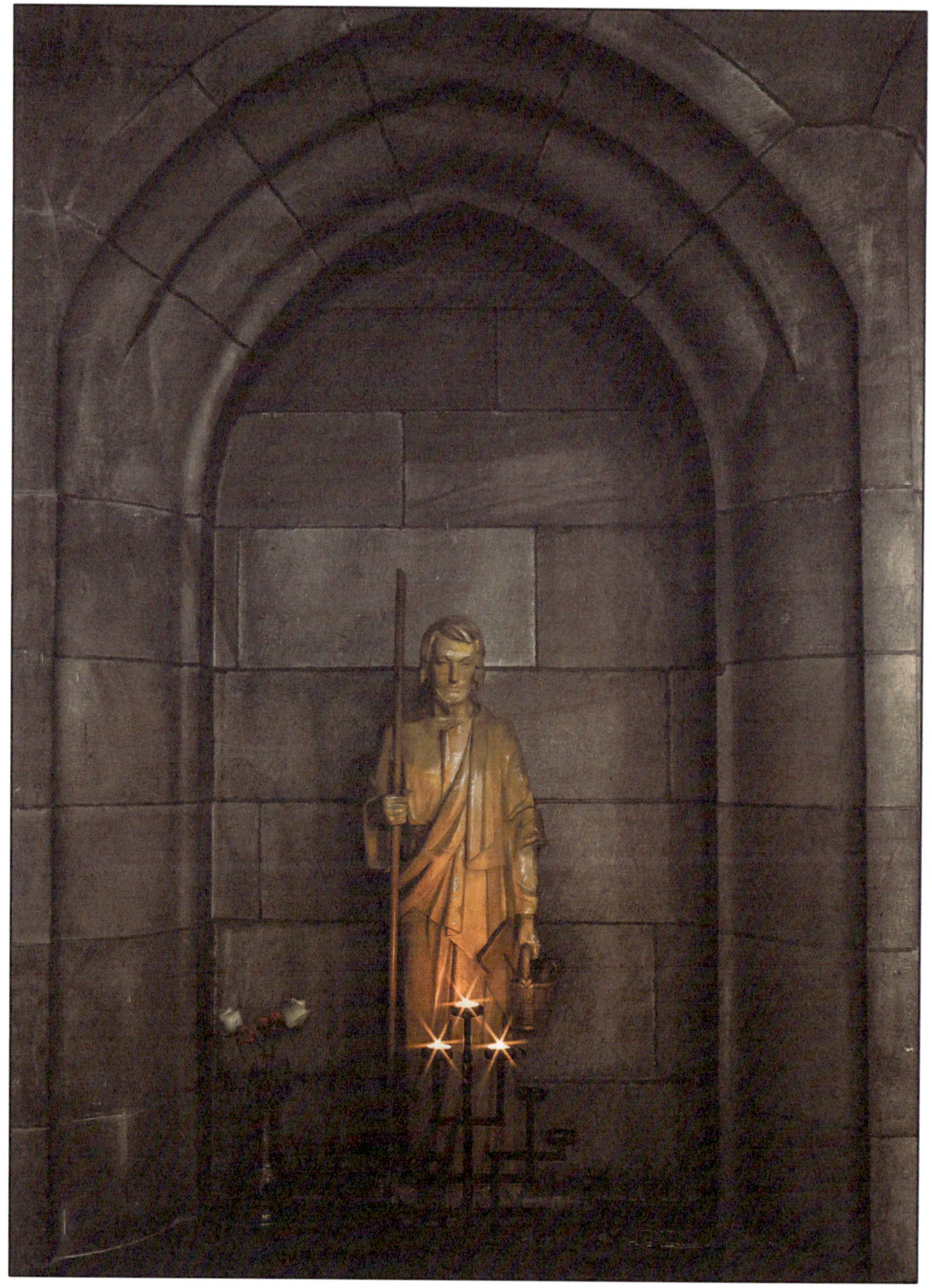

15sec f22 30mm ISO200   Canon 6D

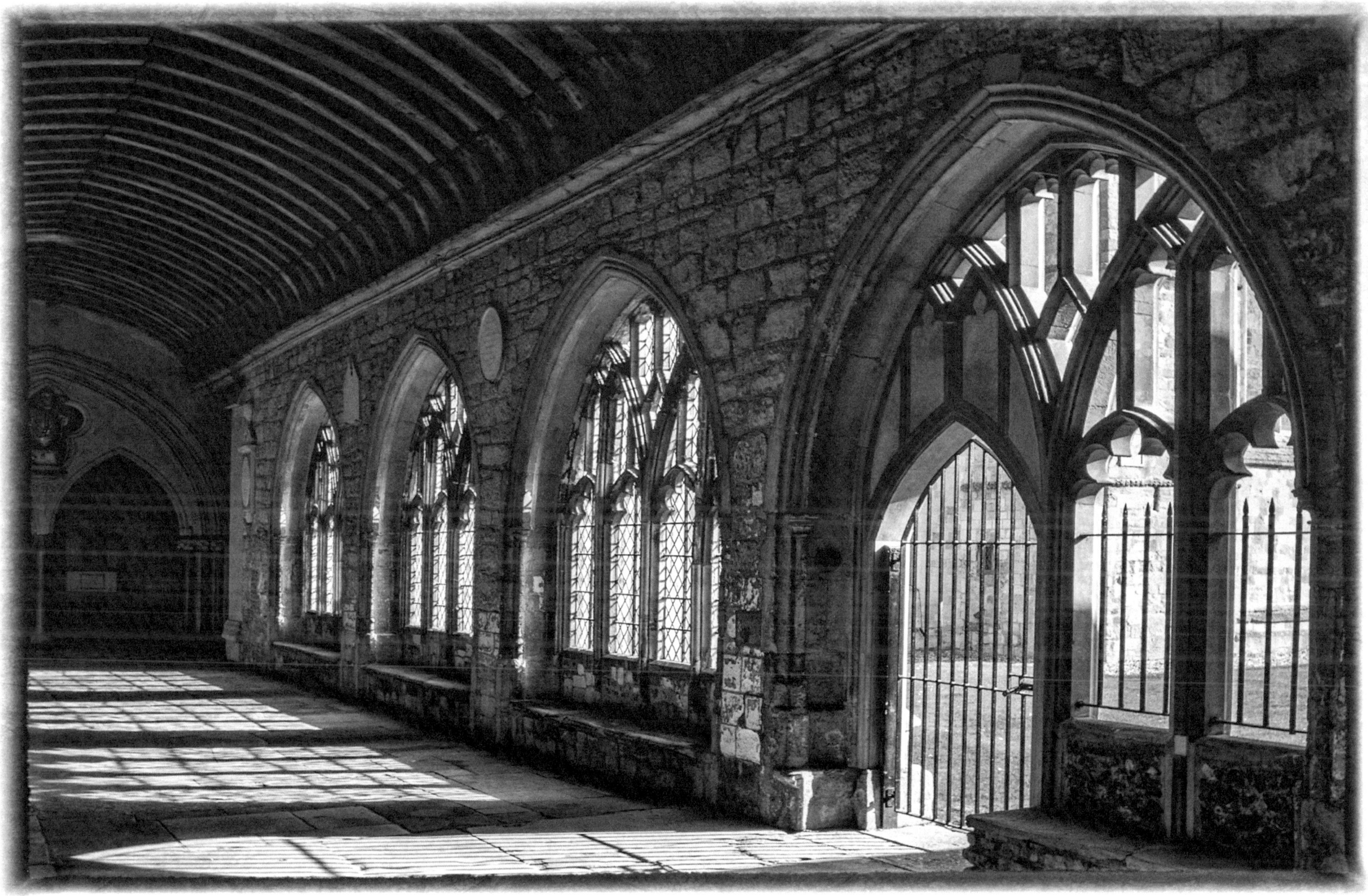

1.5sec f22 24 mm ISO100 Canon 6D

LIGHT OUT OF DARKNESS

Contrary to my **TIP 3** at the beginning of this book saying do not use flash, there is a way to introduce light into a dark corner, or to cast a shadow, or to highlight a feature. Your preparation is no different; camera settings will probably be **ISO100, f22** or **f32** with a **30second** exposure. Identify the area you want to cast additional light on. You can use a Speedlite (not attached to the camera) by pressing the **PILOT** light several times during the 30 second exposure pointed towards the area to be highlighted. This will be *'trial and error'* to begin with until you have the correct amount of light held for the desired effect. Try this at home before losing time on site. Use this technique if you are not comfortable with the Lightroom or Photoshop blending techniques.

Here are a some examples using a Speedlite.

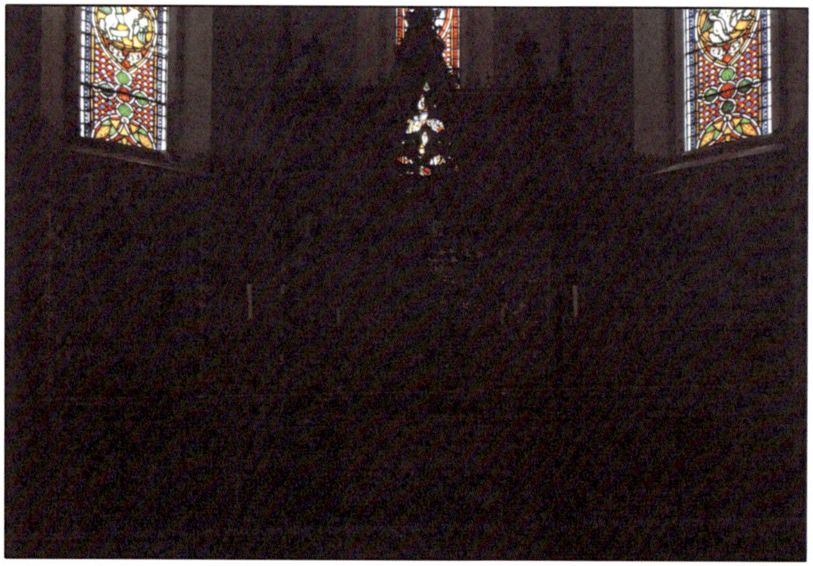

Fig.1

10sec f19 24mm ISO100

Ensure you take both images on a tri-pod without moving the camera between exposures.

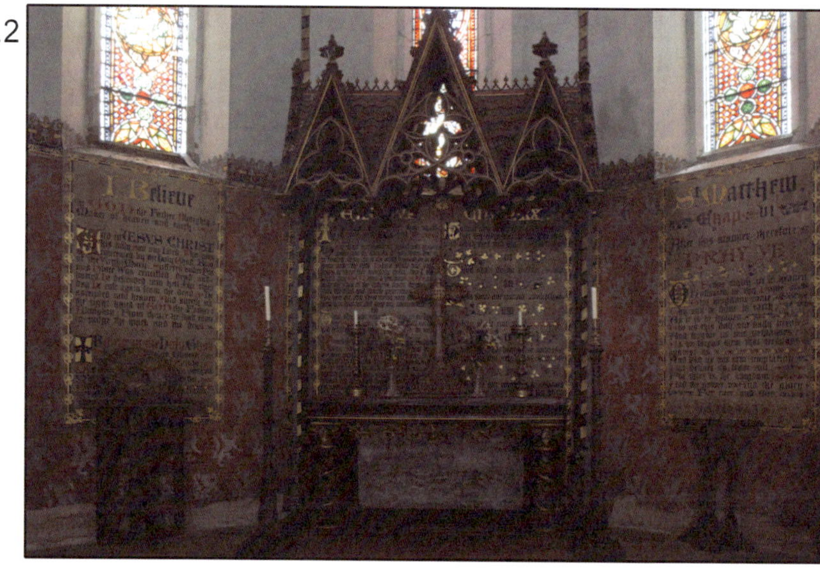

Fig.2

10sec f11 24mm ISO100 plus hand held Speedlite

The two images above were taken using the same time exposure and blended together as explained on page 36 to achieve the final image. Fig.3

Although you have added light to the image in Fig.2, blending the two images will enhance the detail in the stained glass

Final image using Lightroom HDR blend mode.

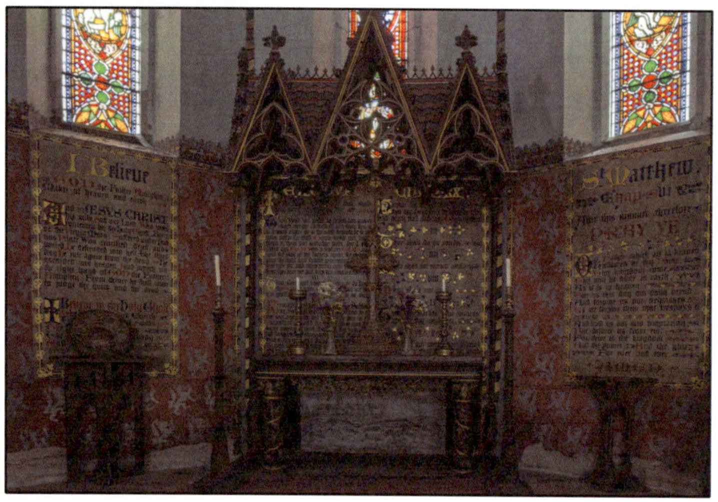

Fig.3

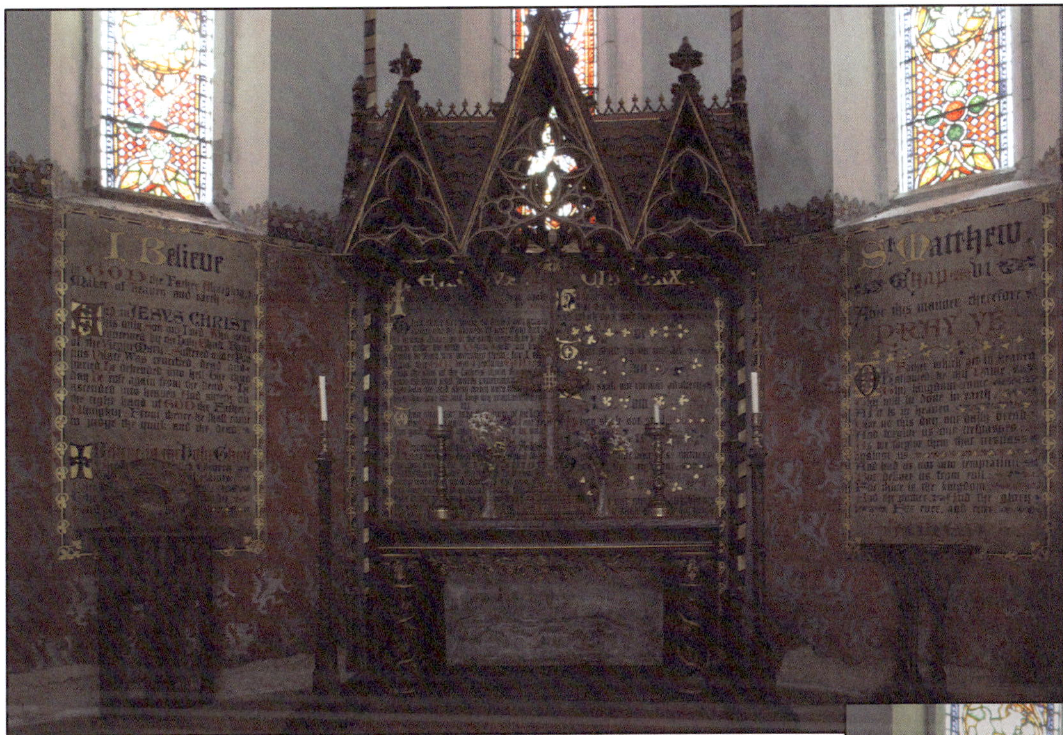

10sec f11 24mm ISO100 plus hand held Speedlite

Example of processing one image without using the blending mode.

(Left) This is the image that was given 10 seconds of light from my Speedlite by pressing the PILOT button continuously. The result gives a decent amount of light without the 'hard-flash' effect that would have been apparent and reflected off the glass.

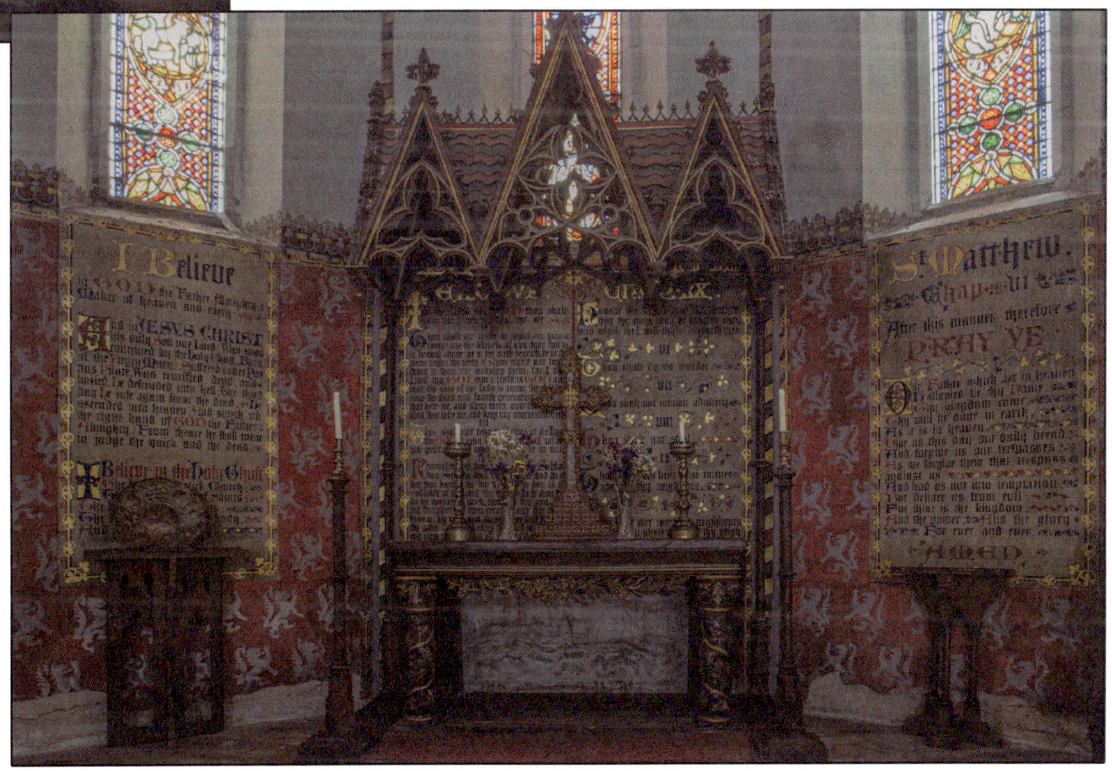

The Stained glass may not be as deep as the original colour, but some adjustments in software using '*whites*' and '*highlights*' give a satisfactory result.

In Lightroom, move the *Highlight* slider slowly to the left until the colours in the stain glass appear more natural. Likewise, move the *White* slider slowly to the left to remove any further under-exposed areas in the glass.

Use the *Radial Filter* in Lightroom to make local adjustments to darker areas.

EXAMPLES OF OVERLAYING TWO IMAGES TO PRODUCE A GOOD STAINED-GLASS VISUAL

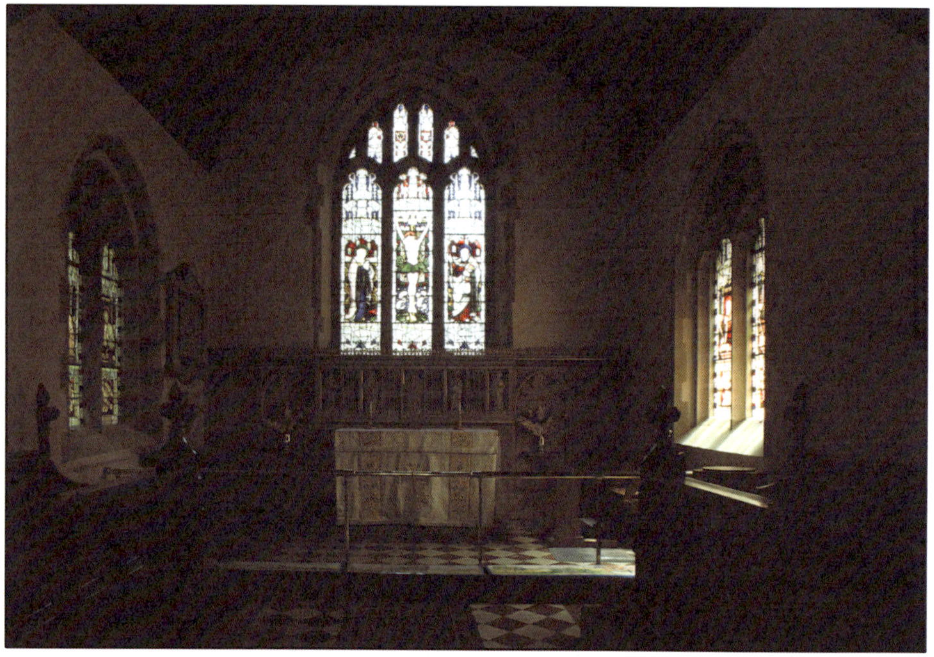

10sec f22 24mm ISO100

Window is under exposed at this setting. Without moving the tri-pod, adjust the Shutter speed to around 2sec

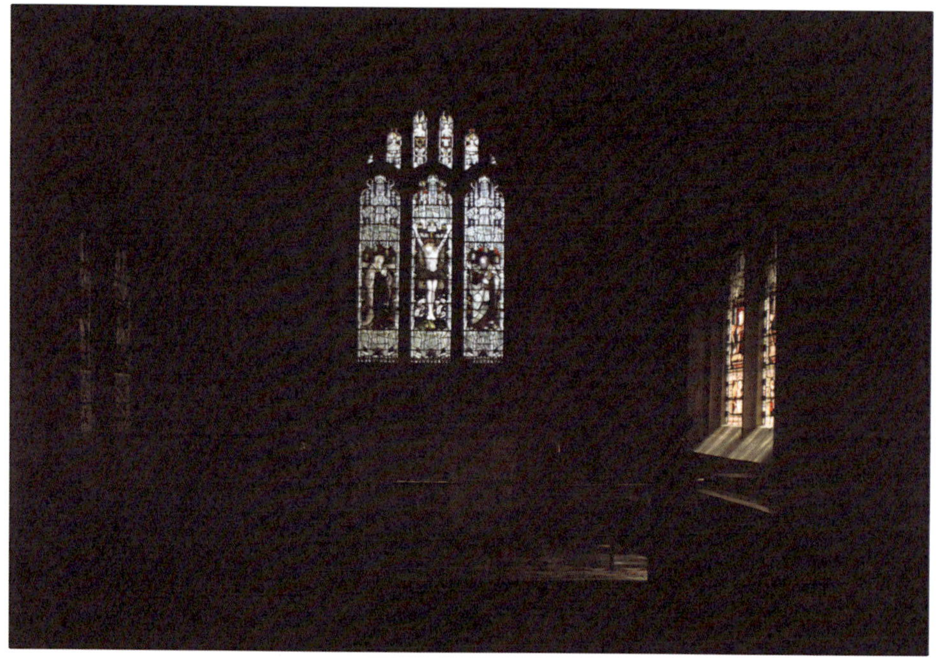

1.5sec f22 24mm ISO100

At this setting the window is at the correct exposure but the remaining area is not visible.

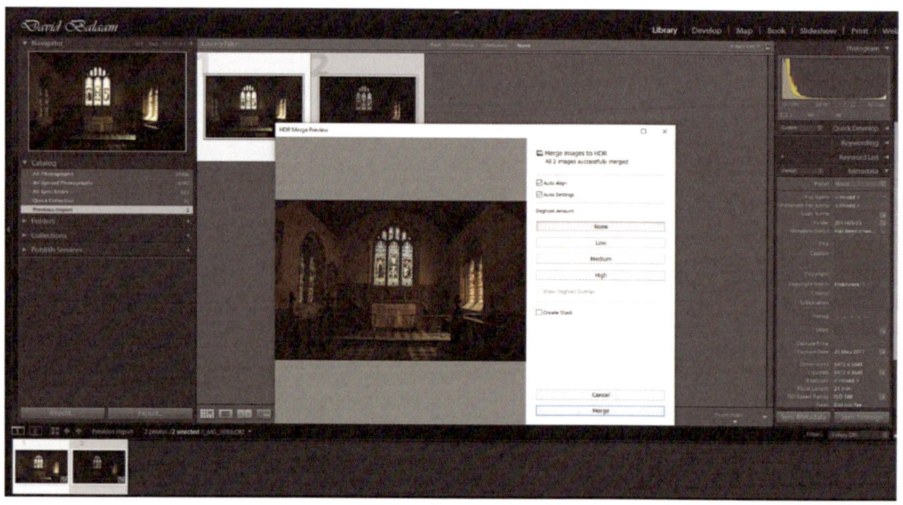

Fig.1

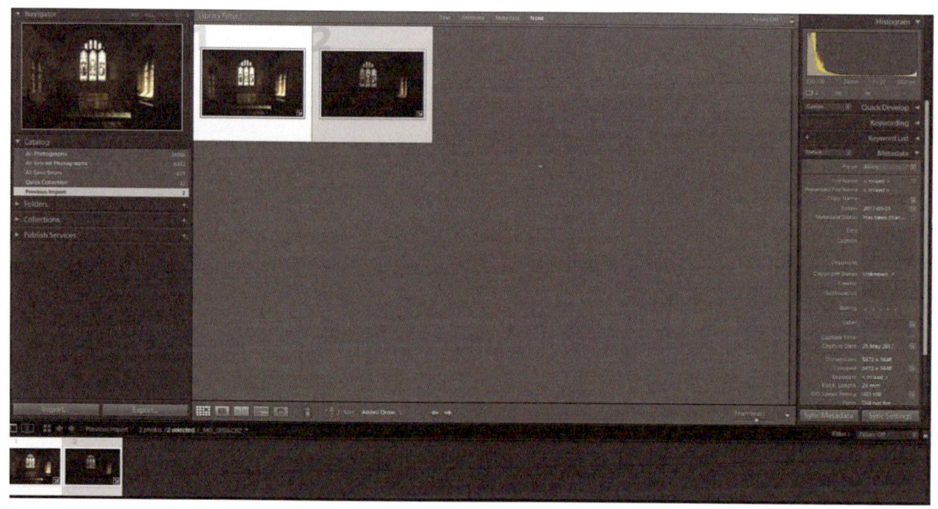

Fig.2

In Lightroom, select *'Photo'* from the top bar (Fig.1), then *'Photo Merge'*, then click HDR (Fig. 2). The two images will be overlaid, and if selected the software will *auto tone* the finished image, but you can always over-ride this and do it manually afterwards.

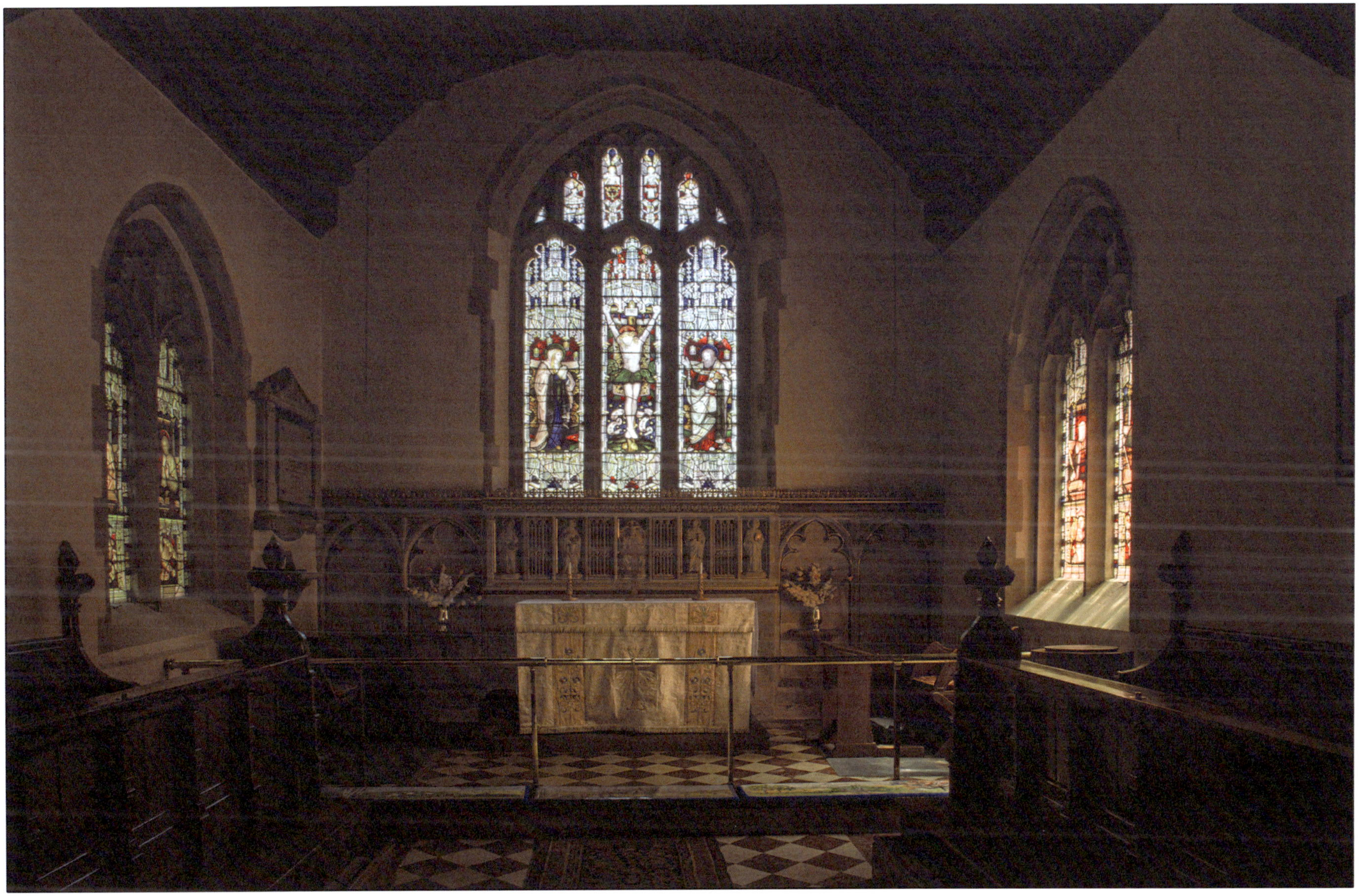

Final combined image using Lightroom.

The stained glass windows retain their colour, but the detail in the foreground and the side walls have now been merged satisfactorily to produce an atmospheric image.

STAINED GLASS

One of the major challenges in church photography is capturing the beauty of Stained Glass windows. As mentioned in my introduction, if the sun is bright the more difficult it will be to produce the perfect image. I have many examples of windows taken as *'close-ups'* in the right conditions, but they look best when photographed *'in situ;'* the largest usually being behind the altar. There is *a 'work around'* to producing an acceptable window shot, which I explain on the following pages. Here, however, are some fine examples of stained glass to be found in the UK.

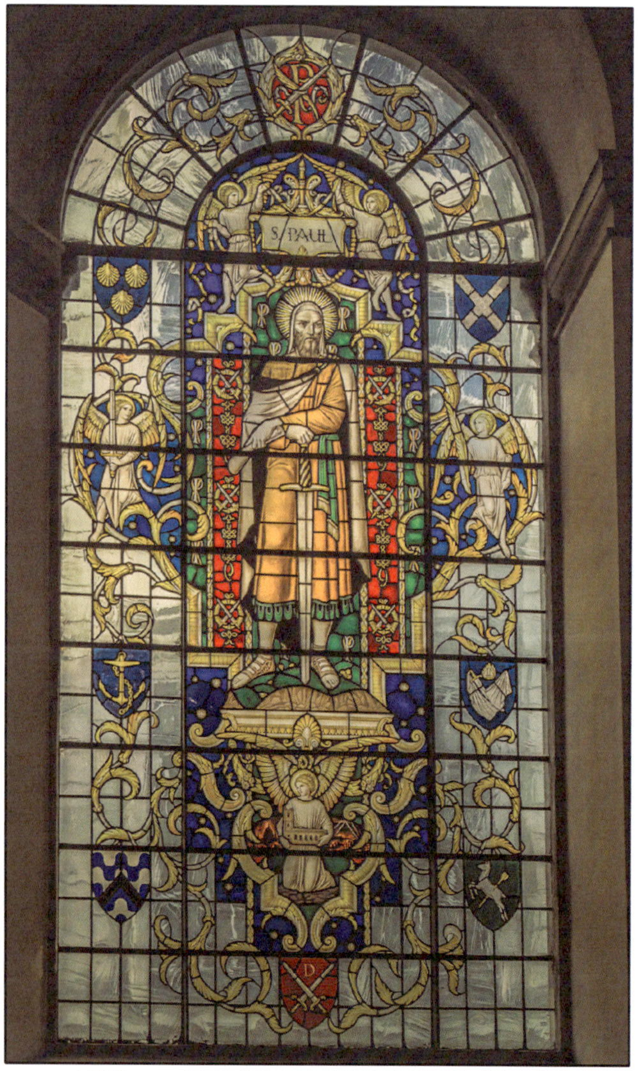

1/60sec f10 40mm ISO400 Fuji X-T1

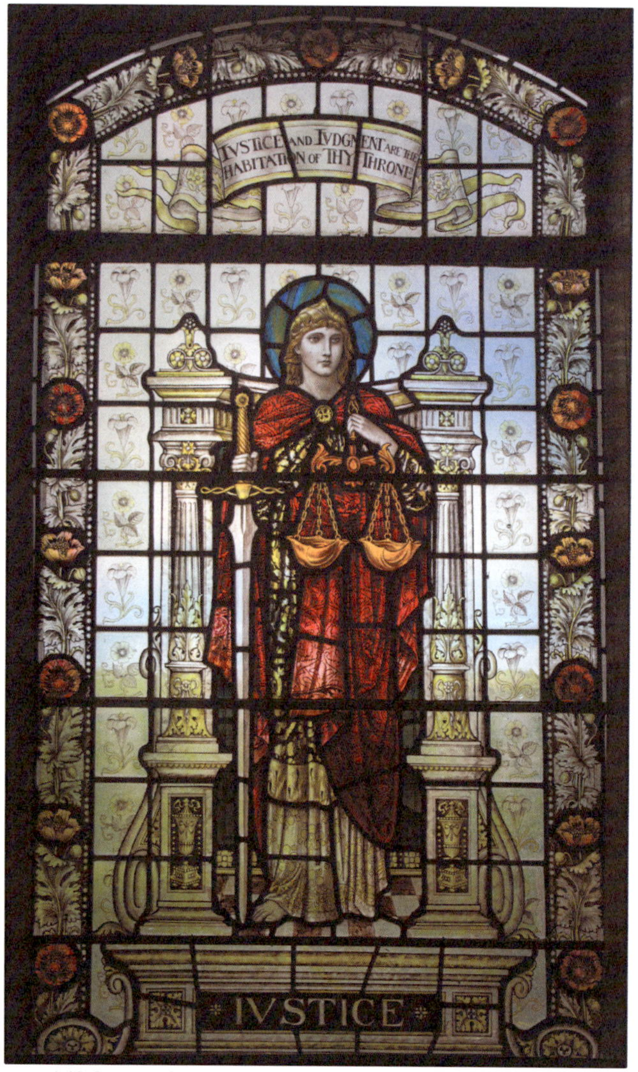

1/30sec f19 44mm ISO 200 Fuji X-T1

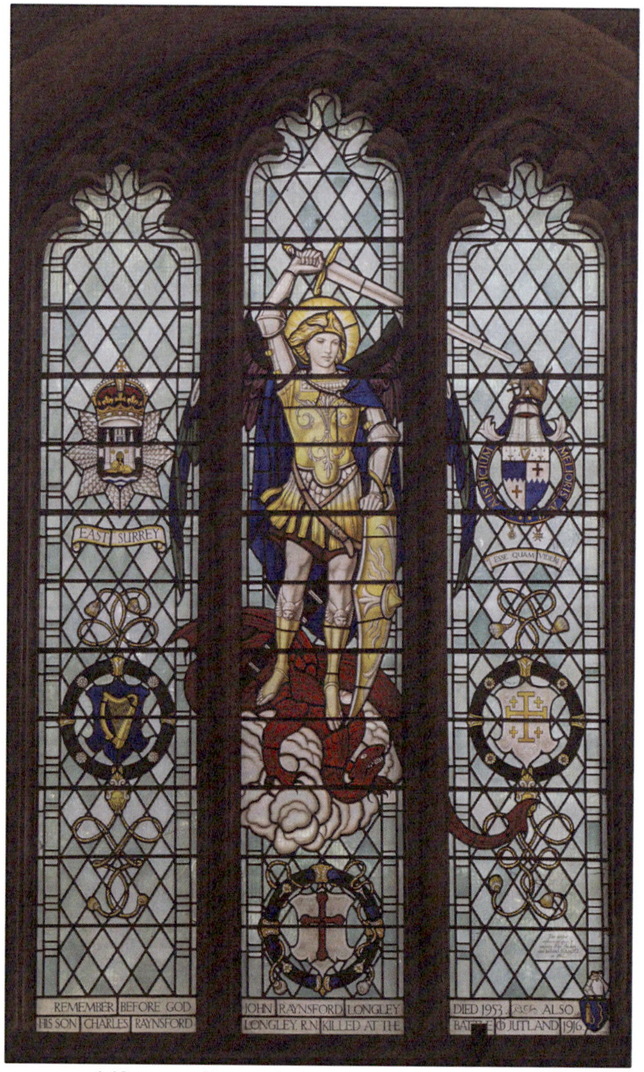

1/3sec f27 ISO200 Canon 6D

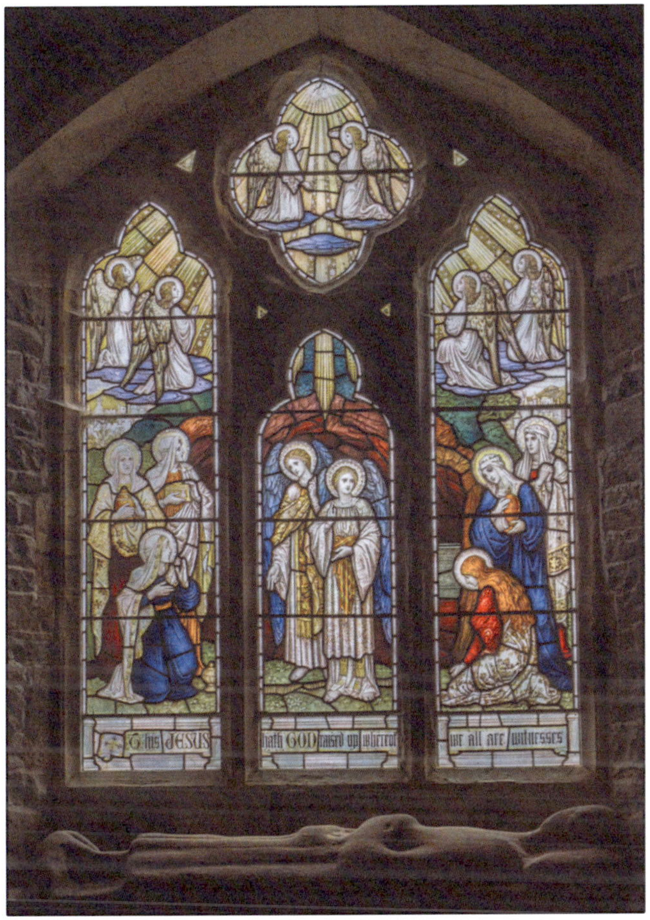

1/8sec f9 52 mm ISO100 Canon 6D

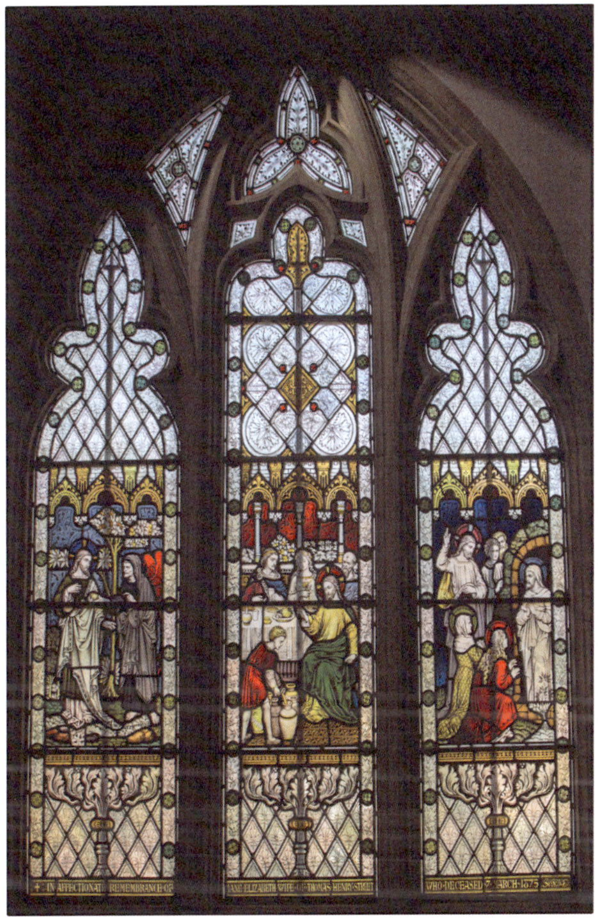

1/6sec f16 28mm ISO100 Canon 6D

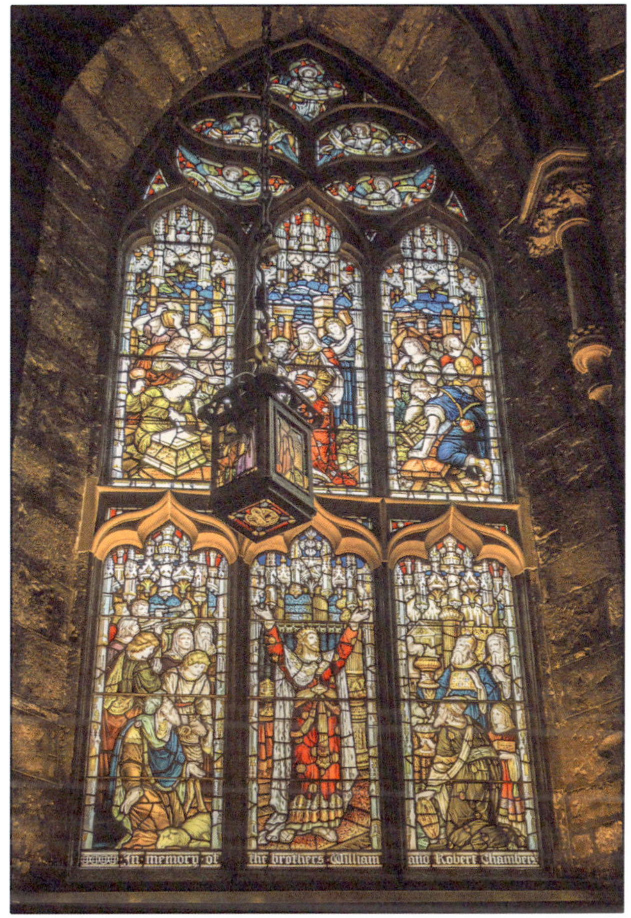

1/60sec f5.6 20.8mm ISO800 Fuji X-T1

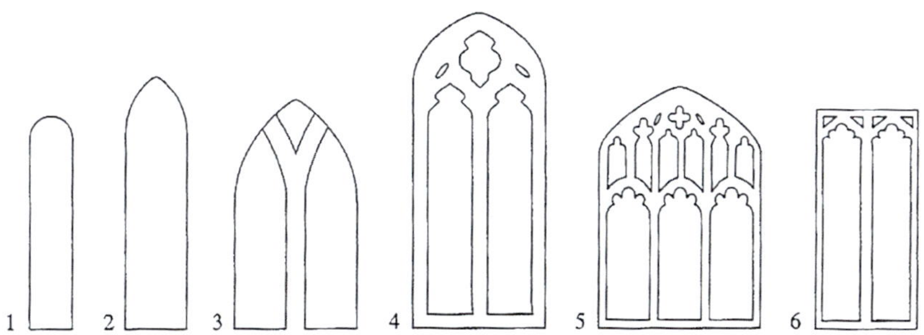

Examples of window styles from 12c to 16c

1. 1100 Norman
2. 1250 Early English
3. 1300 Geometrical
4. 1330 Decorated
5. 1400 Tudor
6. 1580 Elizabethan

REMOVING UNWANTED OBJECTS AND OTHER ANNOYING BLEMISHES

Even in an older church you will find *'modern'* objects which are not in keeping with the ambience of the surroundings; Light-fittings, loud speakers and radiators are just a few irritating examples. I prefer to use the *Spot Healer* in Photoshop, but there is also a tool in Lightroom.

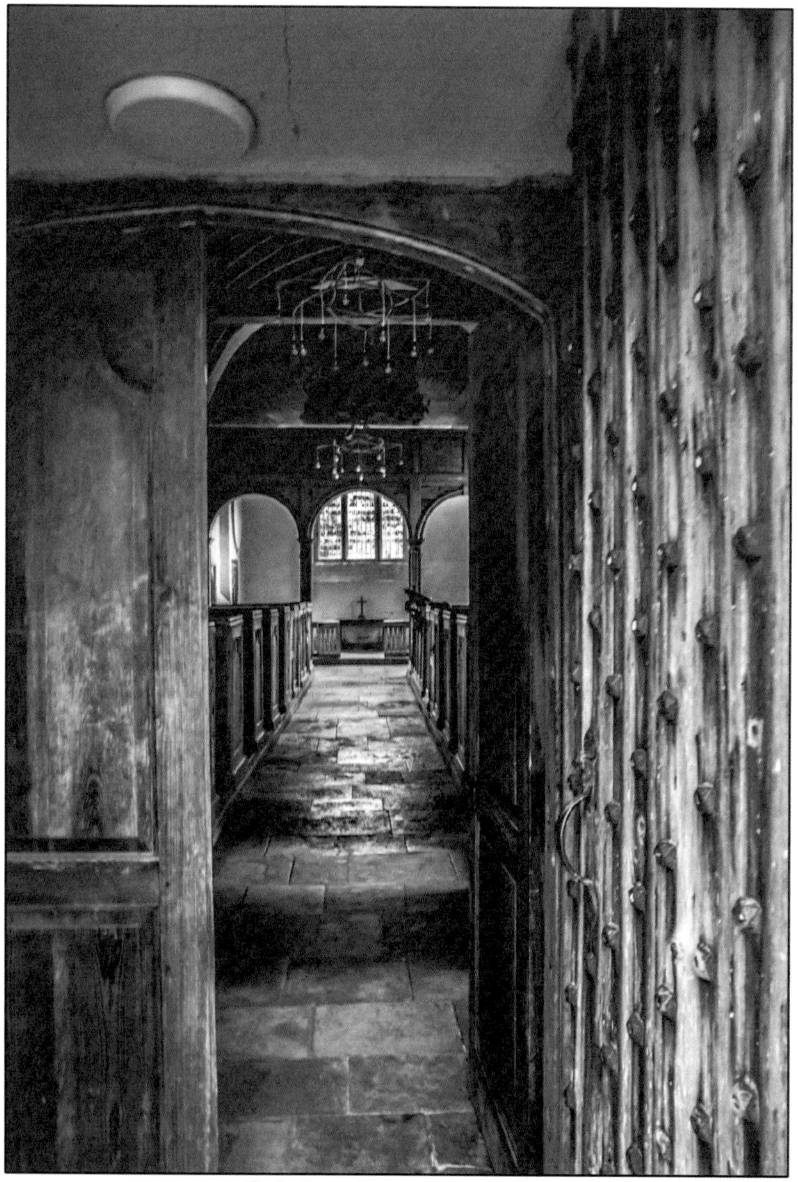

Original image

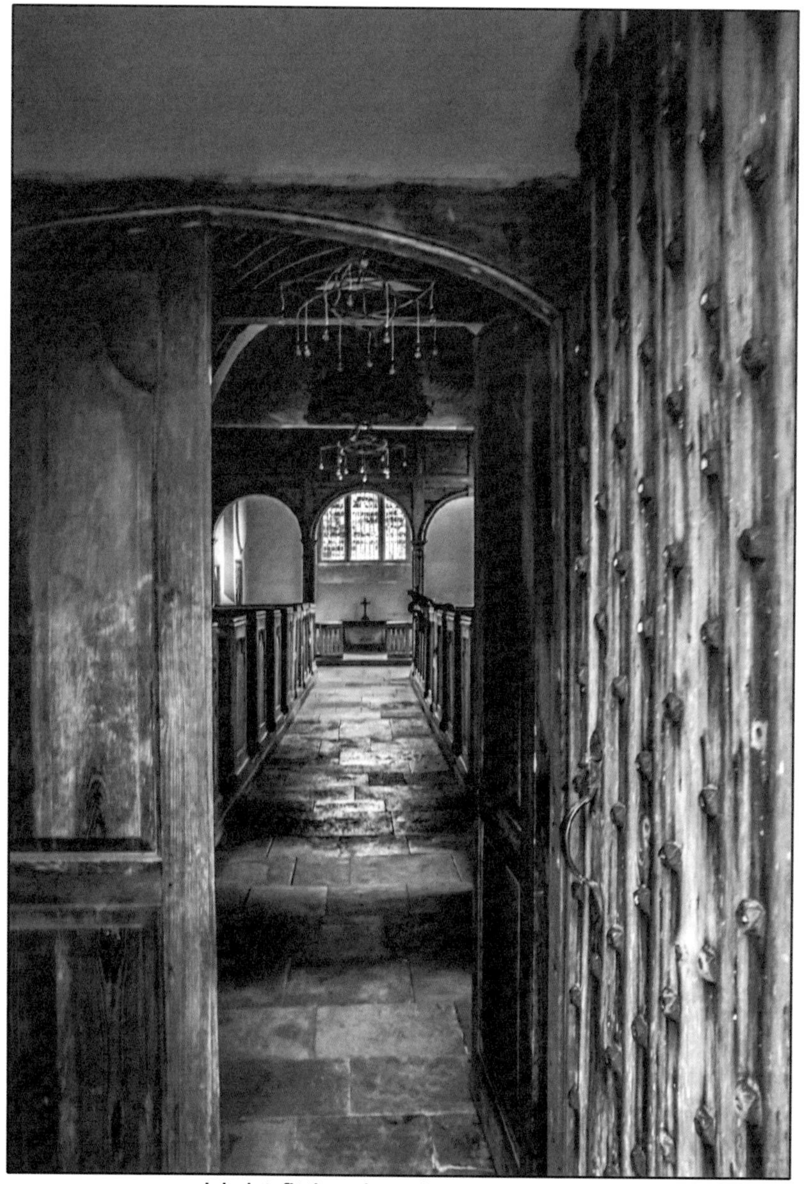

Light fitting has been removed

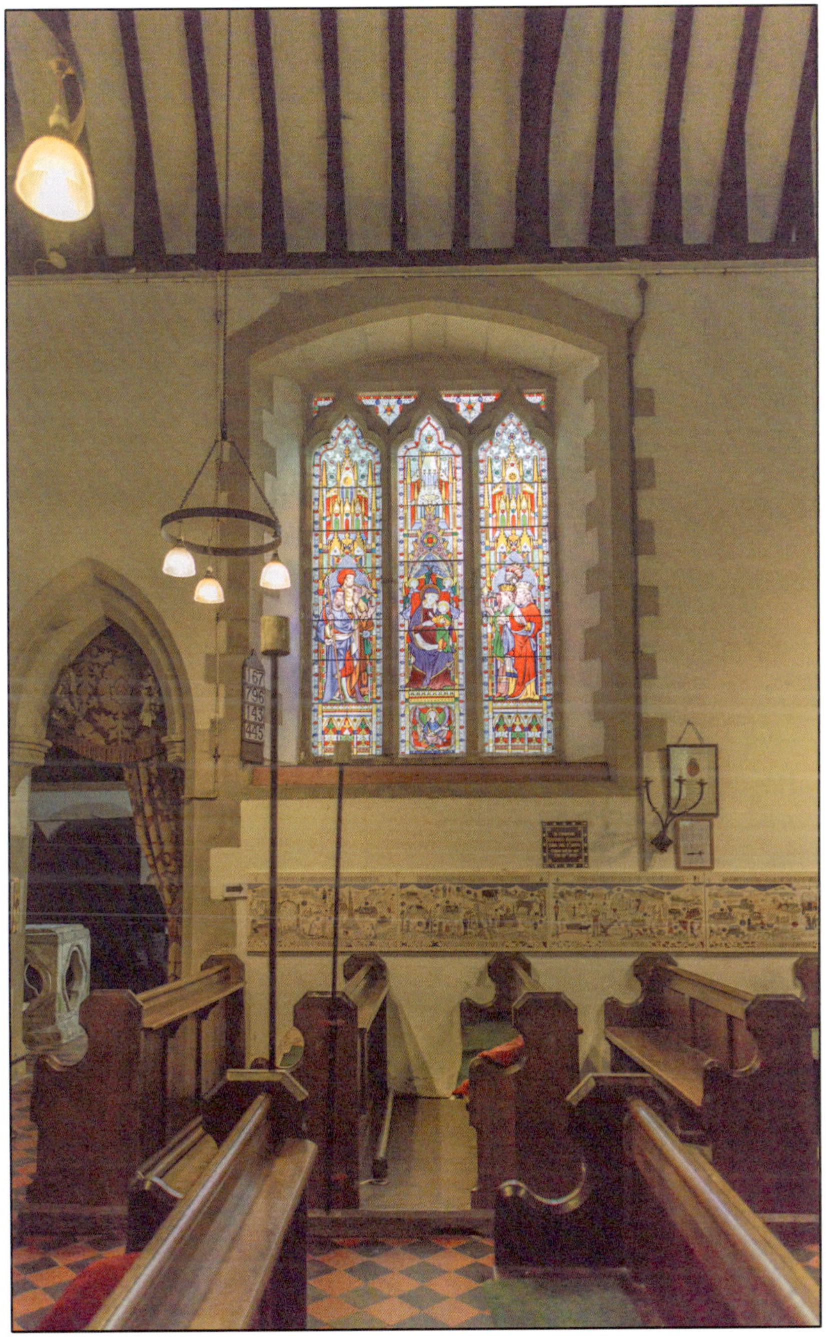

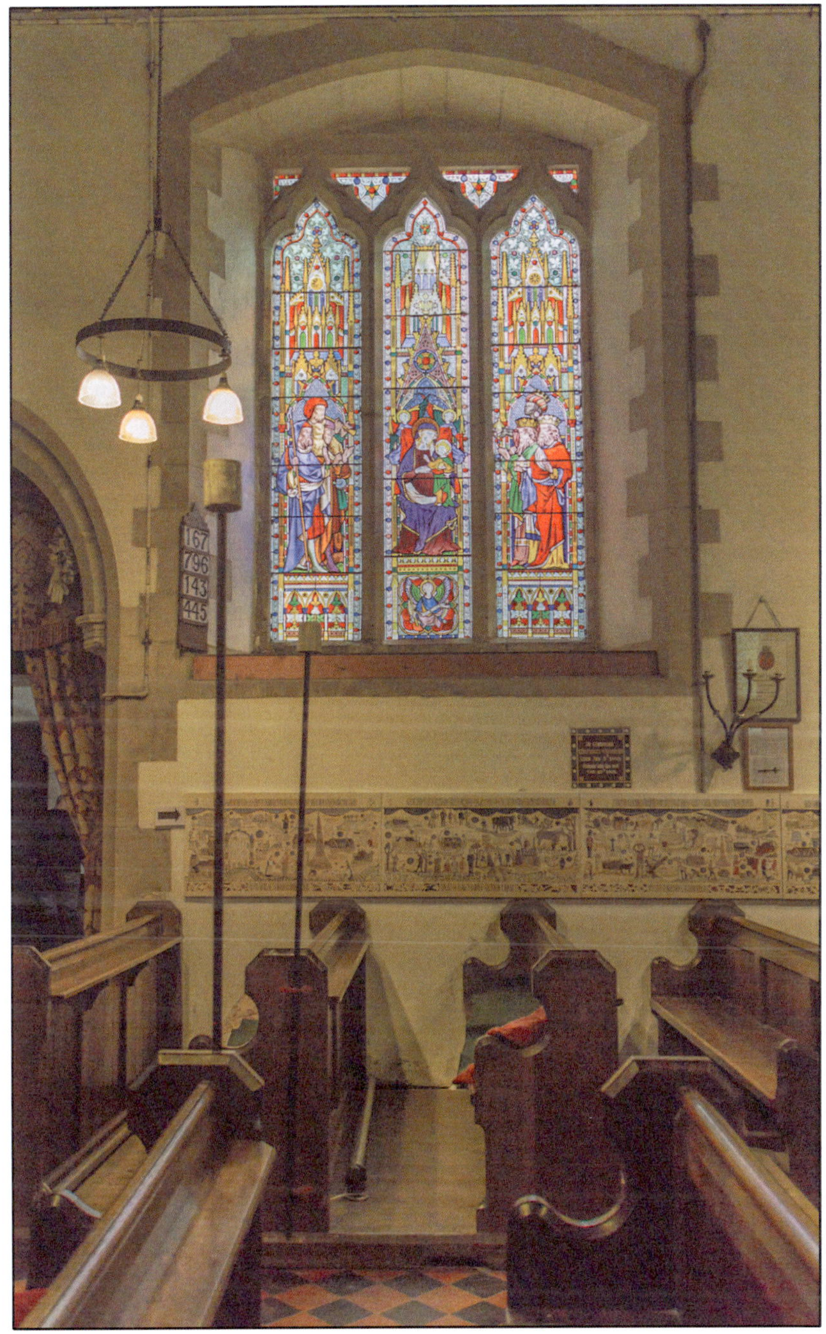

Cropping an image will also remove unwanted objects without the need to use the *Healing Brush*, as shown above, right.

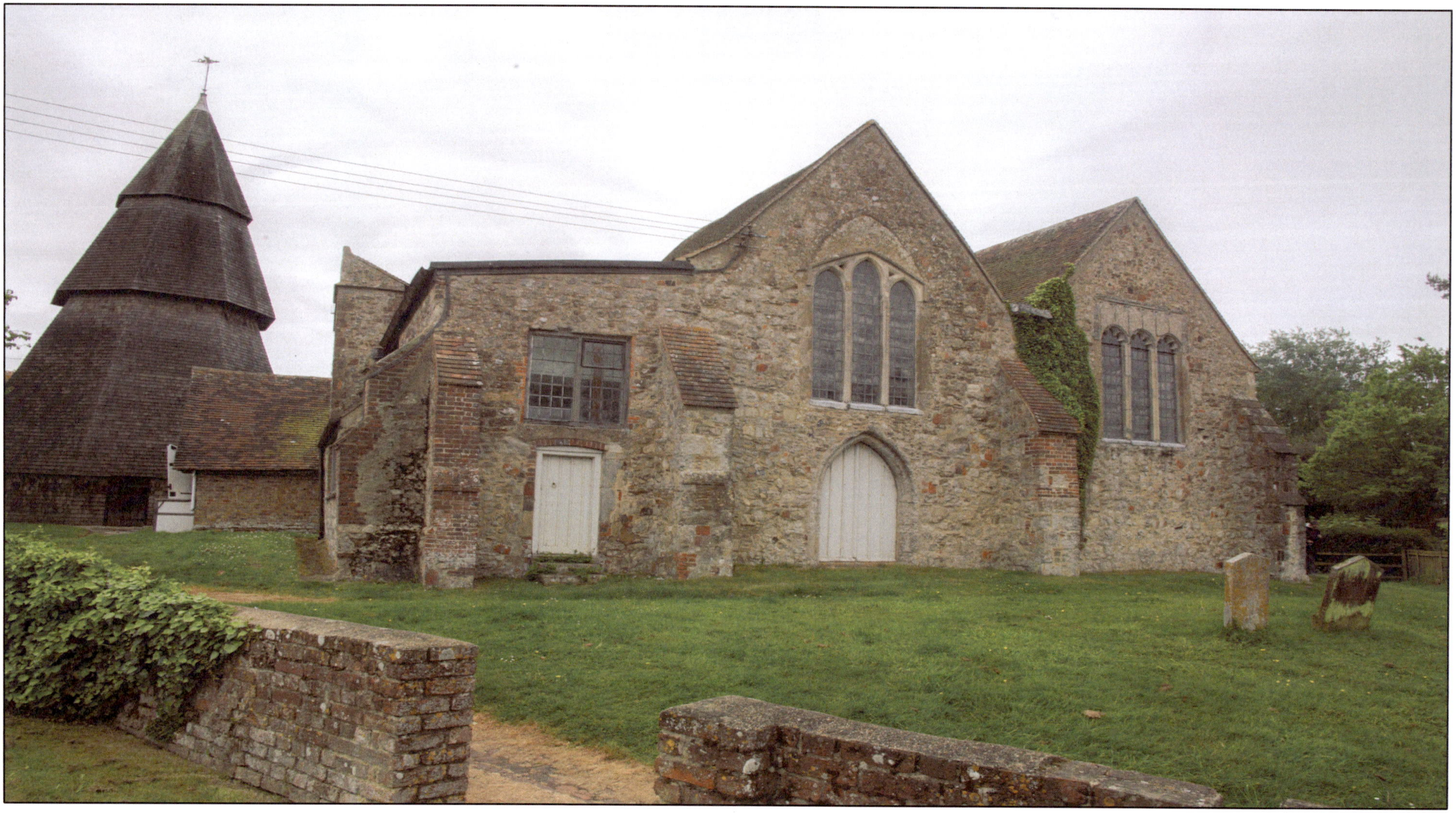

In this example there are *'dust spots'* in the sky and several other objects that need to be removed. Firstly, in Lightroom, I *straighten* the image and apply *tone and texture* as required.

In Photoshop use the *Healing Tool* to remove the telephone lines, dust spots and other areas that are unsightly. See next page.

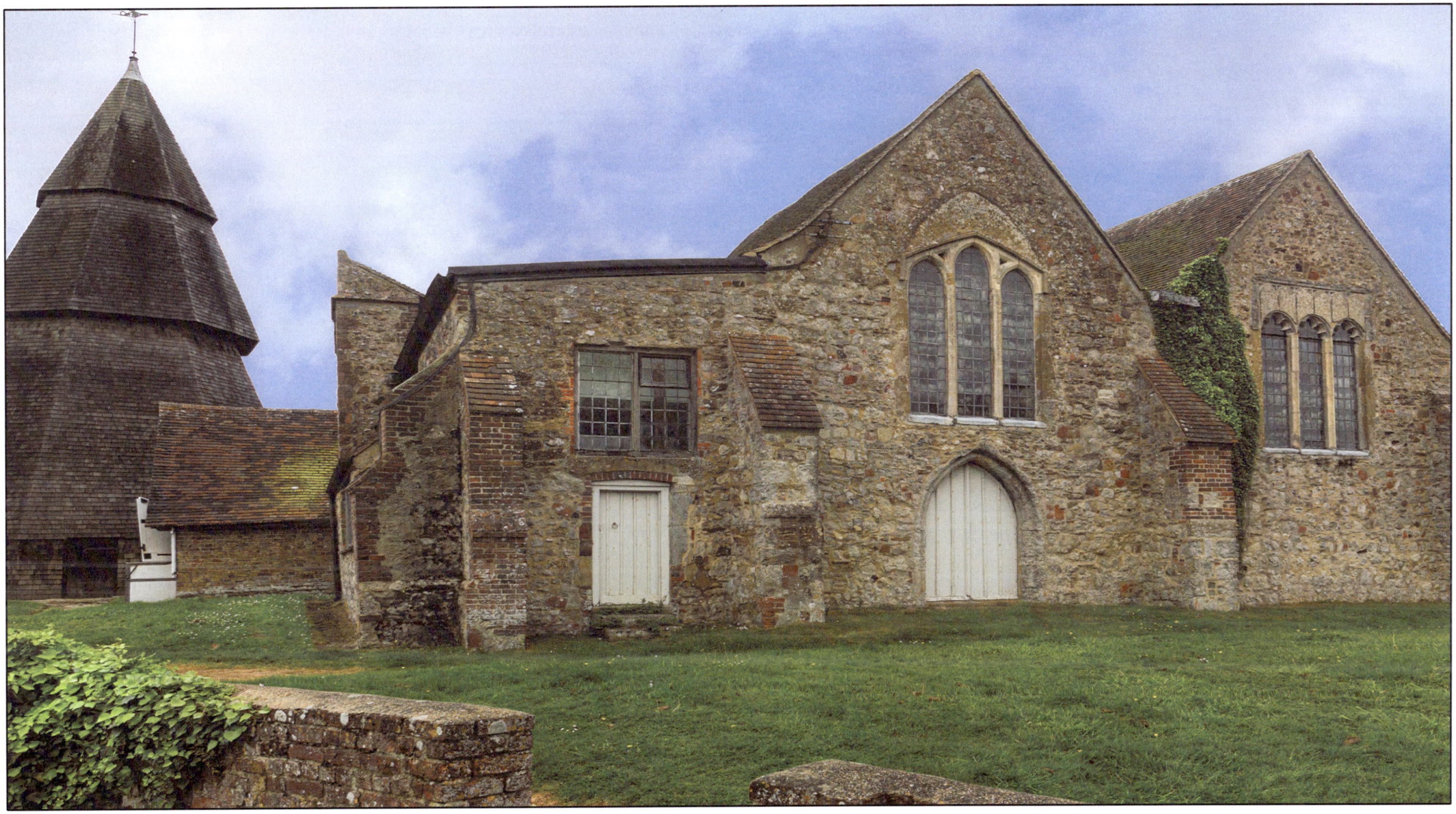

Some colour adjustment and the image looks a lot better. **TIP**: Do not overuse the *vibrance* slider in Lightroom as this will add even more spots as well as unwanted *halos* around the edges of buildings and trees.

I have also replaced the sky as the original was too flat and uninteresting, and a final crop now gives me a presentable image.

FONTS

Like Pulpits, there are many different designs of Fonts spanning the centuries. From simple plain stone Norman fonts to highly decorative Victorian centre pieces.

TIP: Photograph at same level as the font, and crop in to show off the stonemason's or carpenter's fine detail.

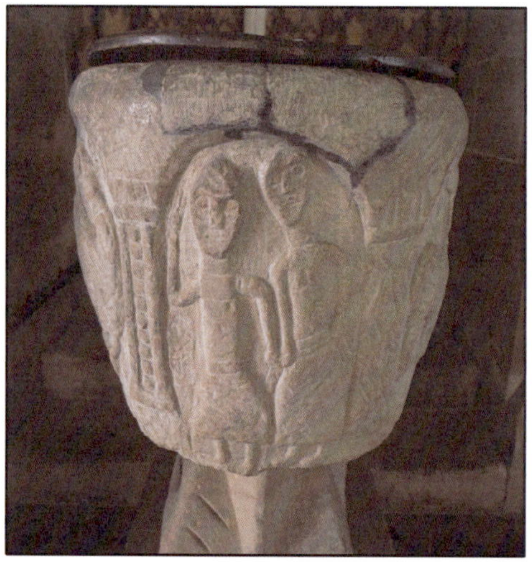

0.5sec f 4. 24 mm ISO100 Canon 6D

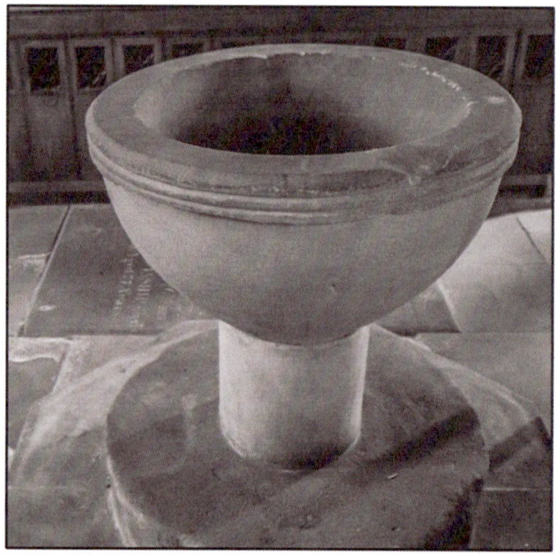

1/60sec f4 22.4 mm ISO800 Fuji X-T1

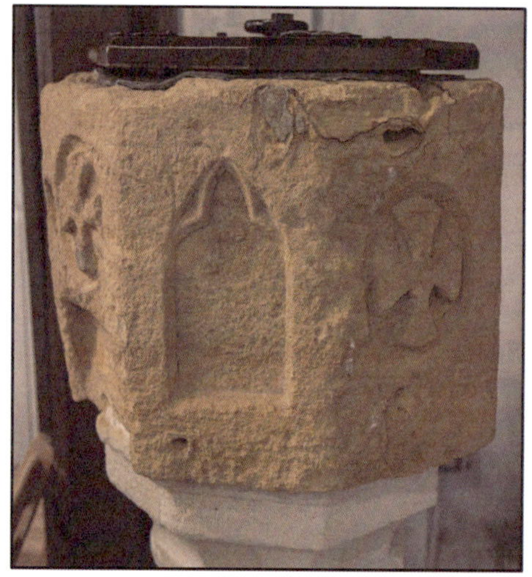

0.3 sec f 5.6 46 mm ISO100 Canon 6D

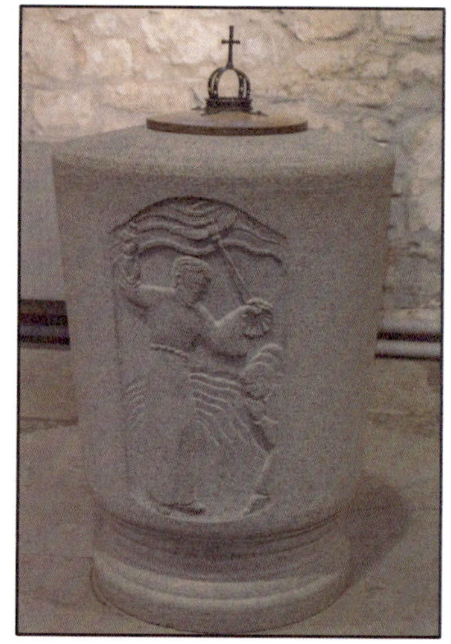

1/60sec f4.3 30.9 mm ISO400 Fuji X-T1

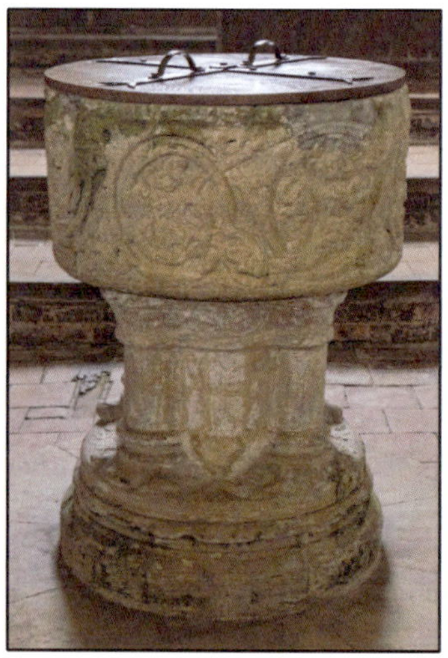

1/125sec f5.6 36.6 mm 33-100 ISO3200 X-T1

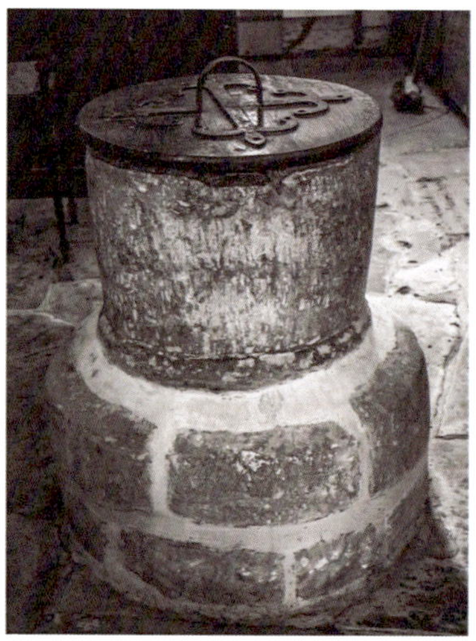

15sec f9.5 58mm ISO100 Canon 6D

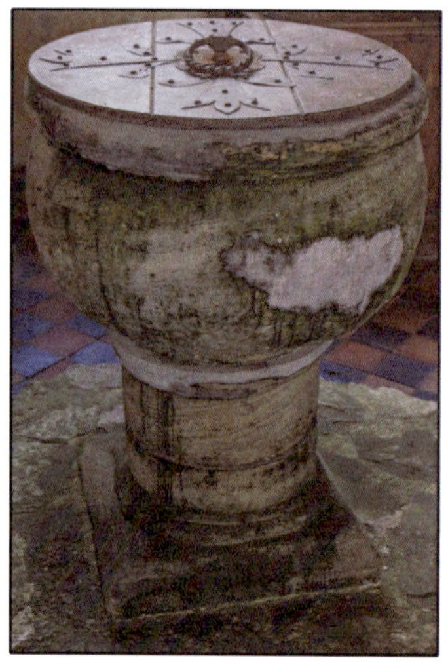

1/80 sec f4.3 34.5 mm ISO 400 Fuji X-T1

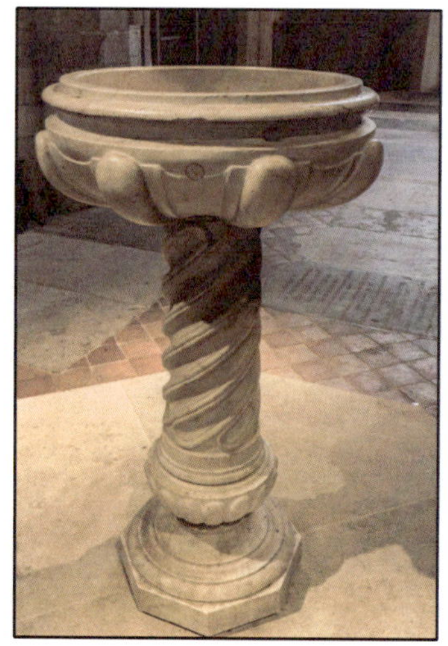

3.0sec f19 33 mm ISO 100 Canon 6D

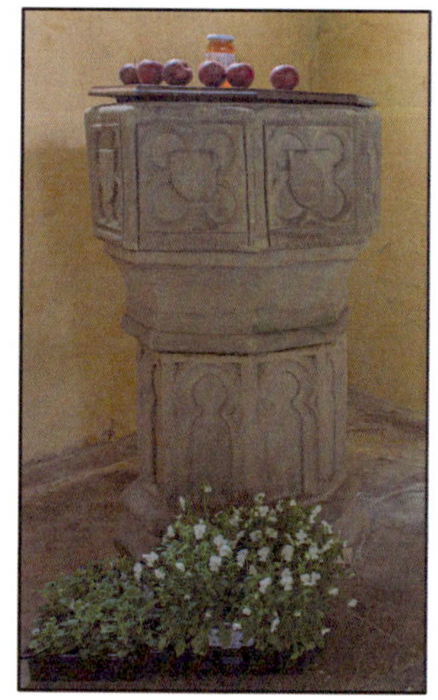

2.5sec f13 ISO100 24mm ISO100 Canon

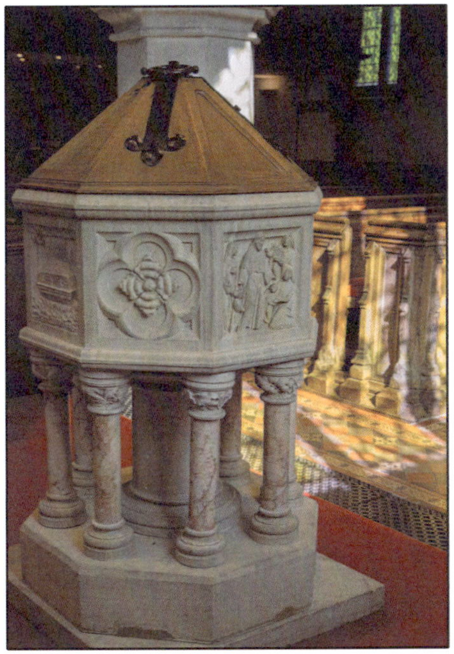
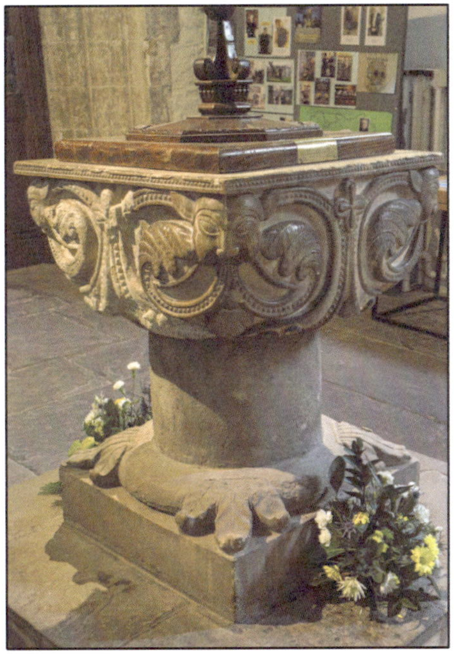
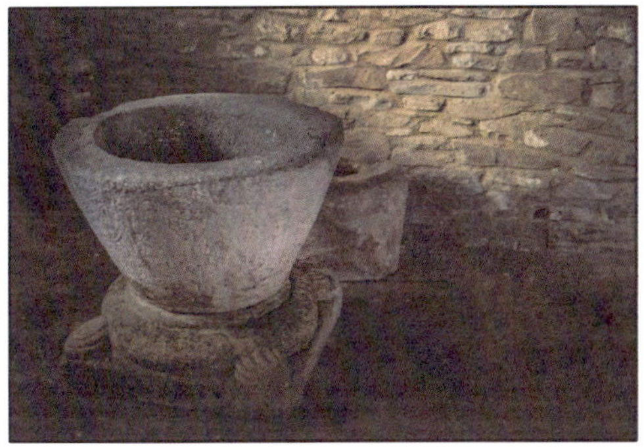
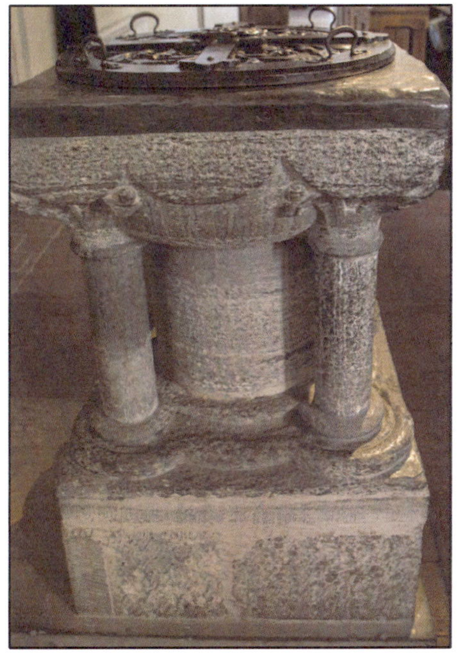
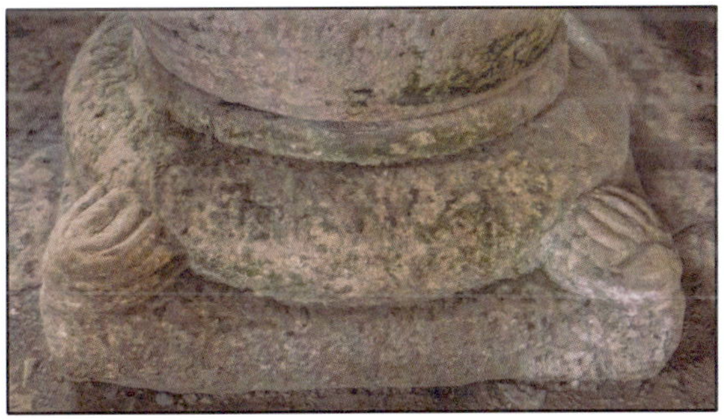
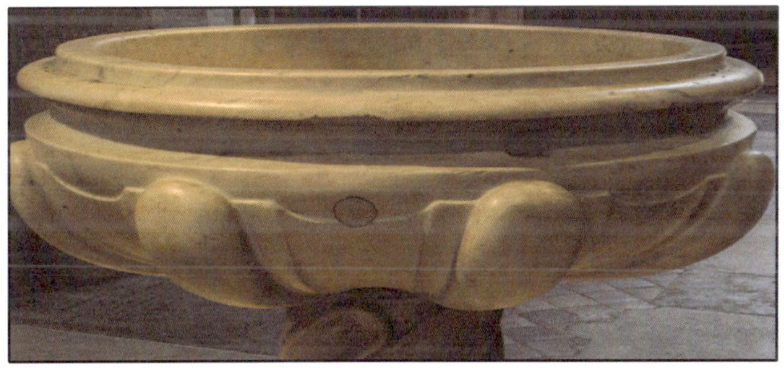

Don’t forget the detail in these beautifully made old Fonts.

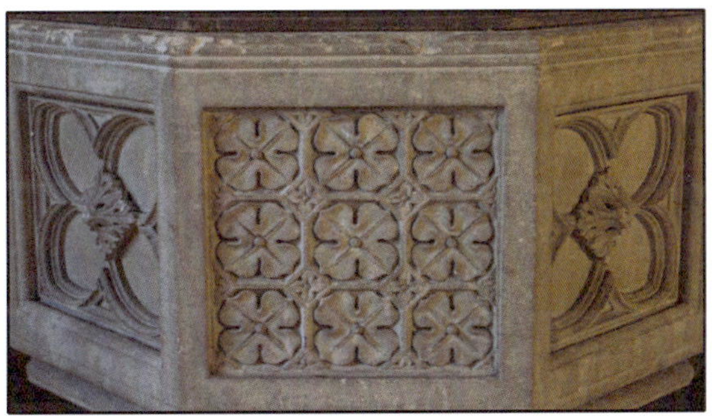
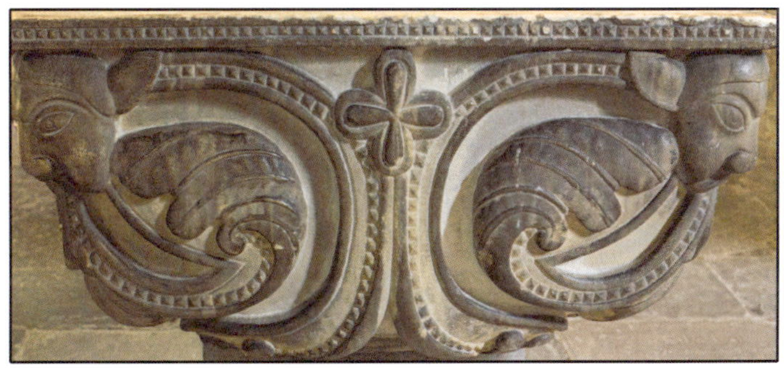

THE CHURCH ORGAN

Many organs have been replaced over the years, especially in the Victorian era. To say which is the oldest organ still in use in the UK depends if we are talking about the pipes, the wind chest or original case and keyboard. Nevertheless, many organs make a proud statement in the smallest of churches; usually placed in a prominent position and adorning highly decorative pipes.

Try close-ups of the colourful pipes to show-off the hand painted designs.

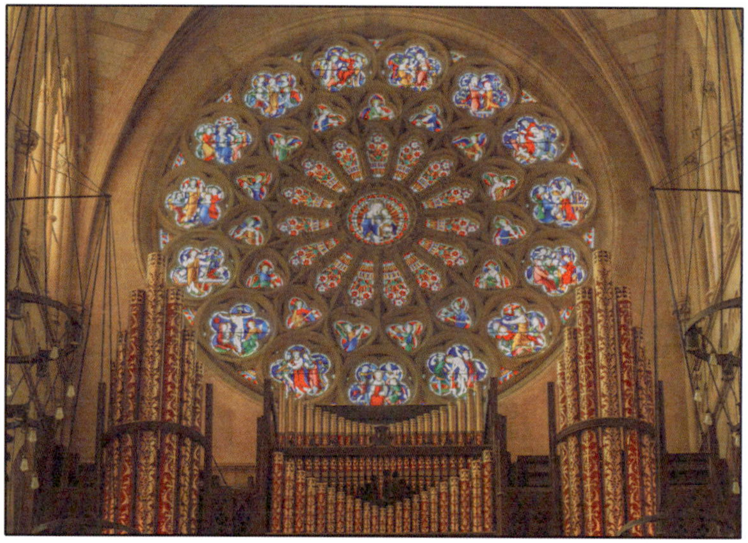

1.0sec f 32 70mm ISO100 Canon 6D

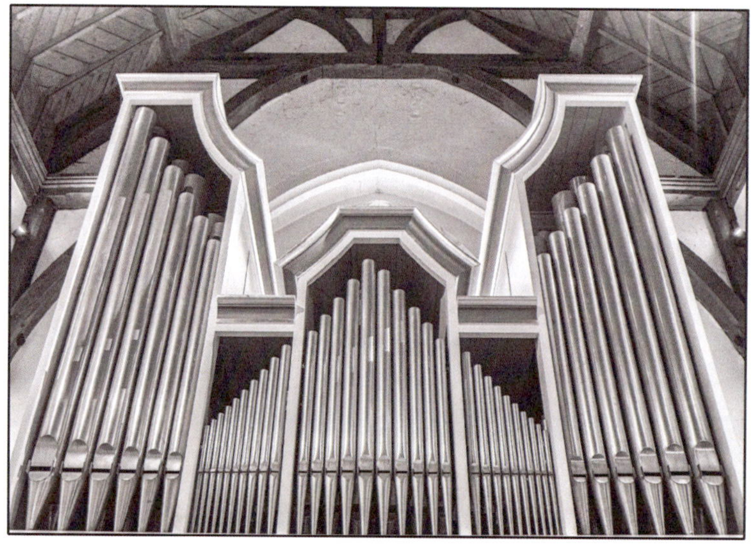

1/40sec f 3.6 19mm ISO800 Fuji X-T1

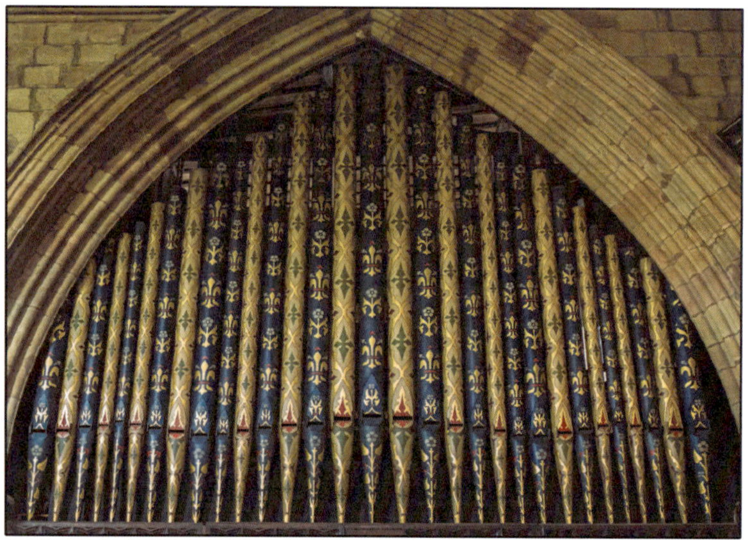

20sec f8.0 24mm ISO100 Canon 6D

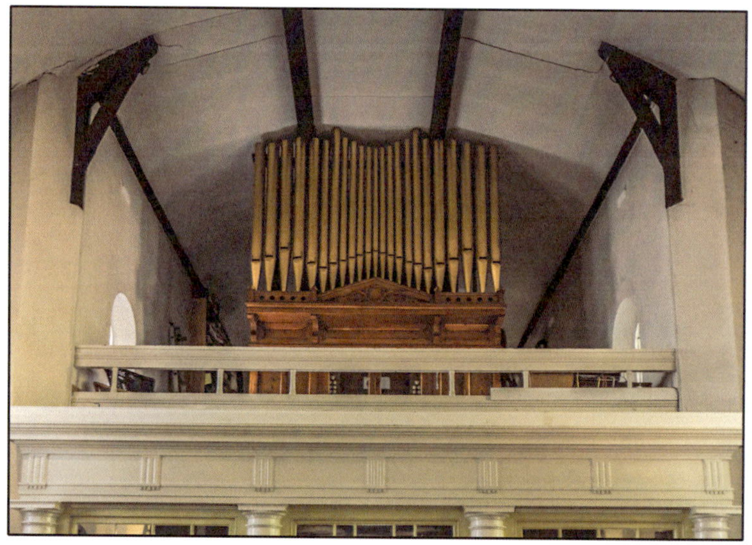

1/30 sec f 3.6 20mm ISO2000 Fuji X-T1

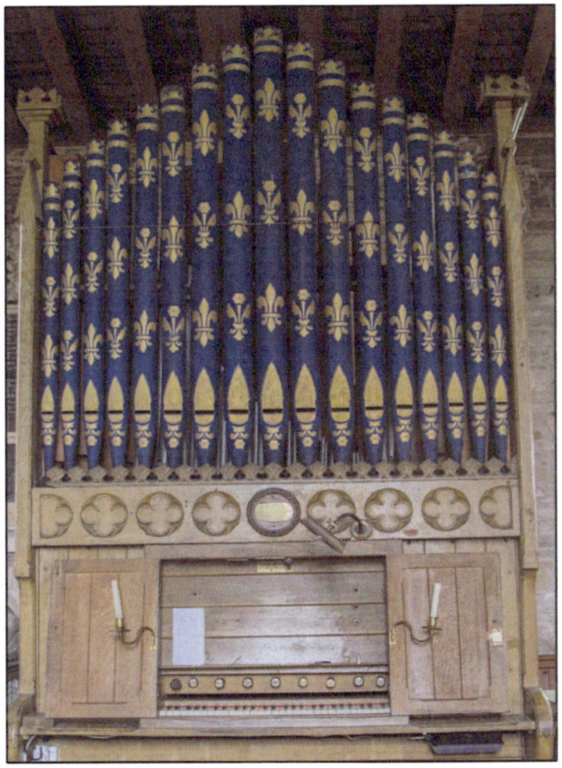

0.5sec f 4 24 mm ISO100 Canon 6D

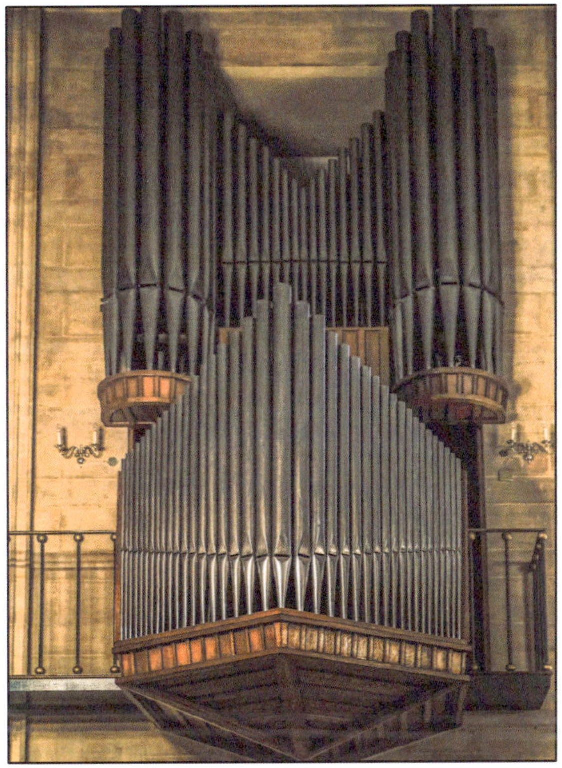

1/40sec f5.6 34mm ISO1000 Fuji X-T1

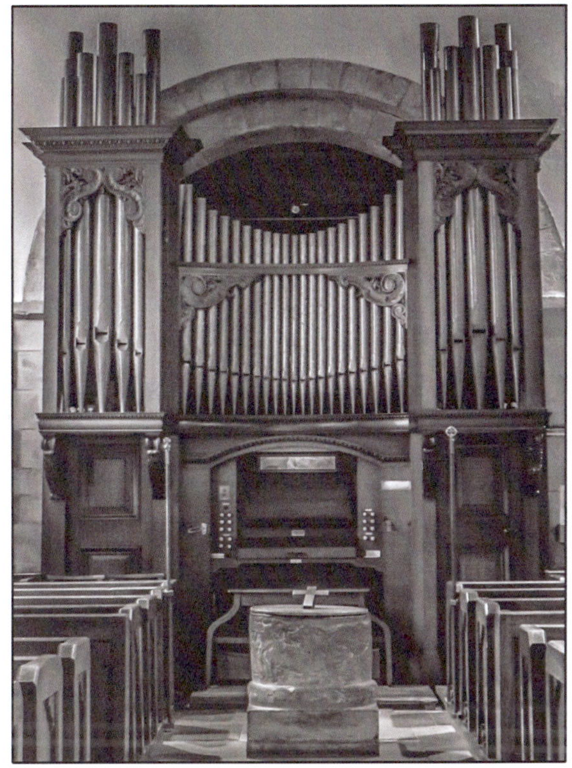

8sec f 4 24 mm ISO100 Canon 6D

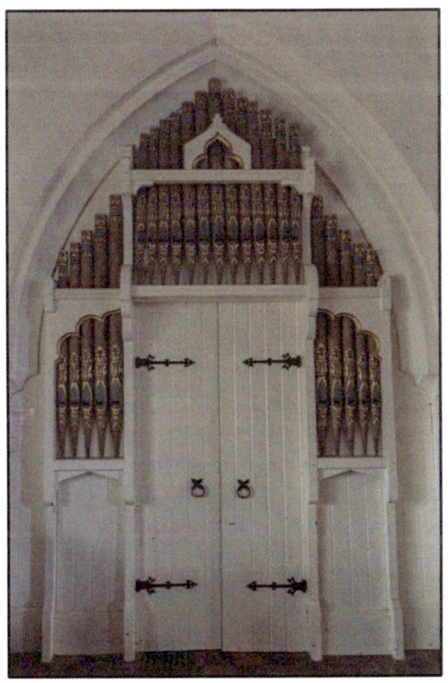

1.0sec f 4.0 24mm ISO100

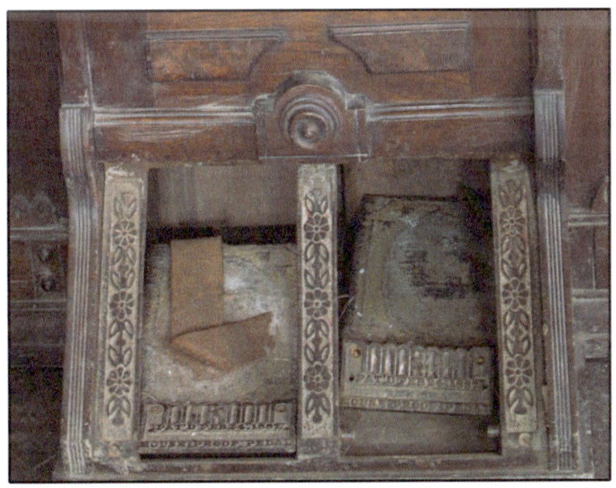

4sec f9.5 37mm ISO200 Canon 6D

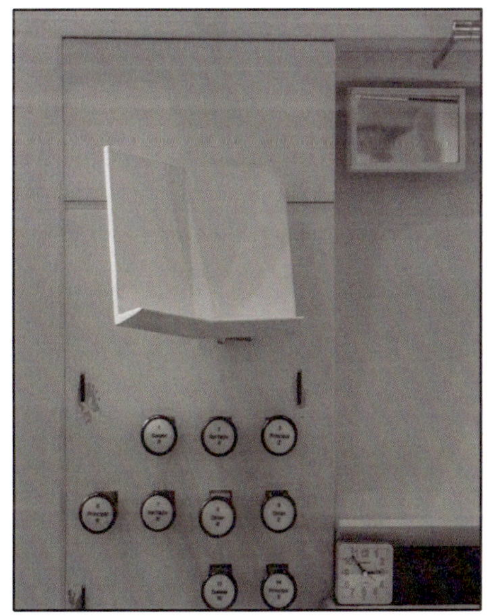

1.5sec f 6.7 54mm ISO100

FLOWER ARRANGEMENTS

Every church I have visited does have one thing in common – *flowers*. From a small posy on an ancient windowsill, to gorgeous over-the-top bouquets adorning the altar. They can make an interesting subject, but ensure your field-of-view is correct otherwise you will have only the nearest buds in focus, unless you attempt *'stacking'* (taking multiple images at the same exposure but moving the focus point manually to capture many focus points and combining in Photoshop) unless you have a camera with built-in focus-stacking, like the Fuji X-T3.

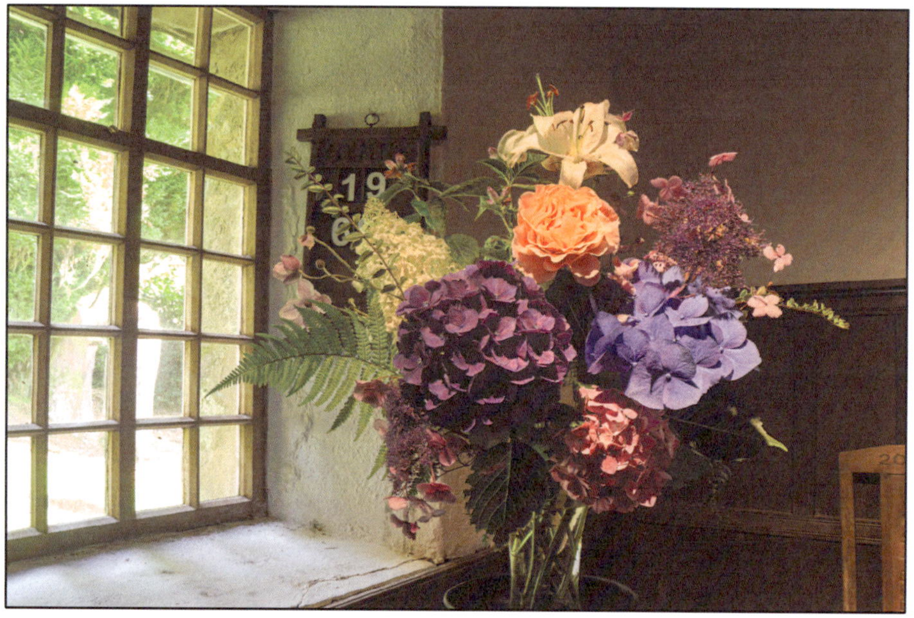

6sec f19 24mm ISO160 Canon 6D

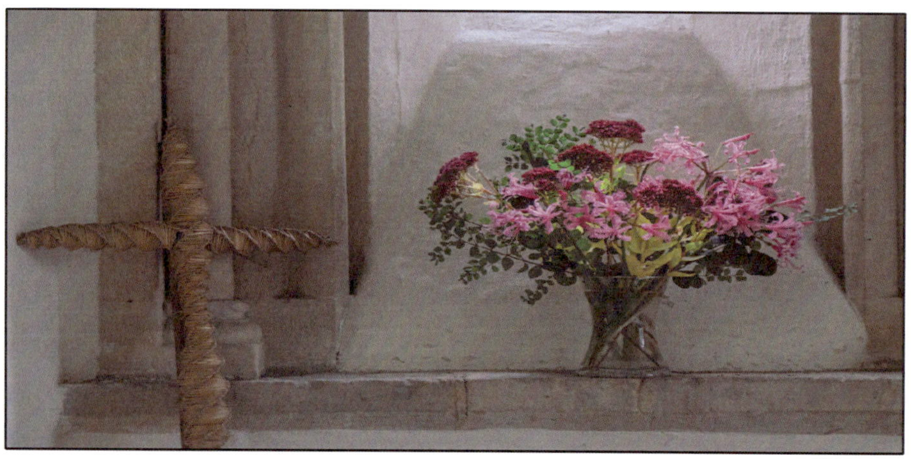

1/30sec f4.7 43.9mm ISO800 Fuji X-T1

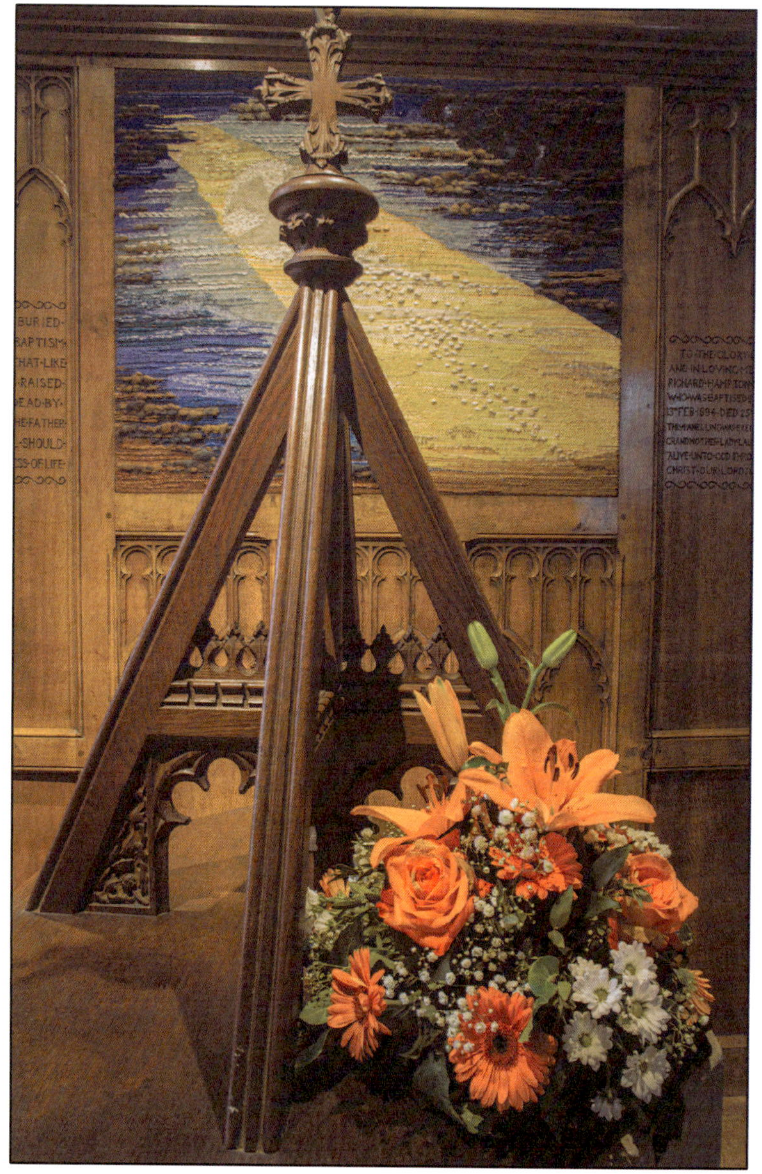

8sec f 22 24mm ISO200 Canon 6D

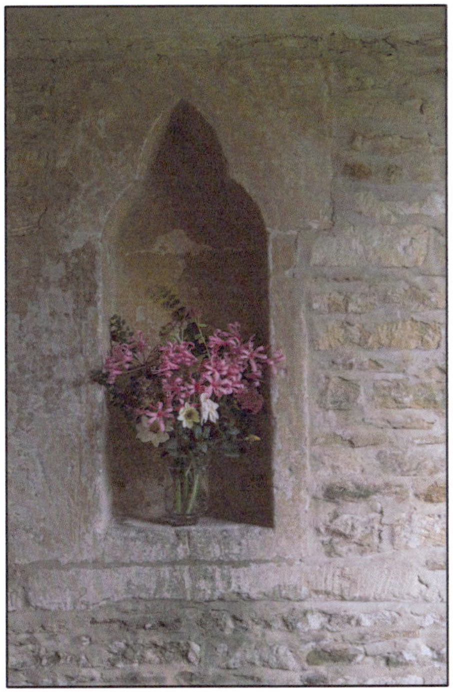

1/6 sec f4.2 27.9 mm ISO400

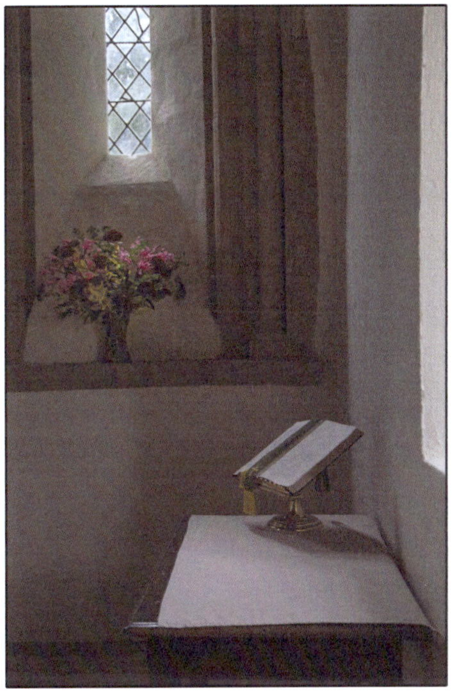

1/60sec f 4.2 27.9 mm ISO800

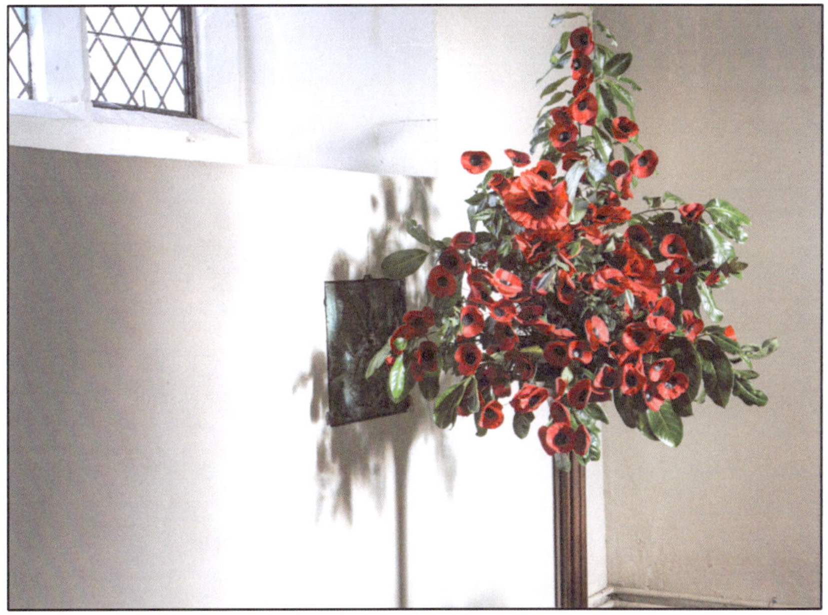

15sec f19 58mm ISO100

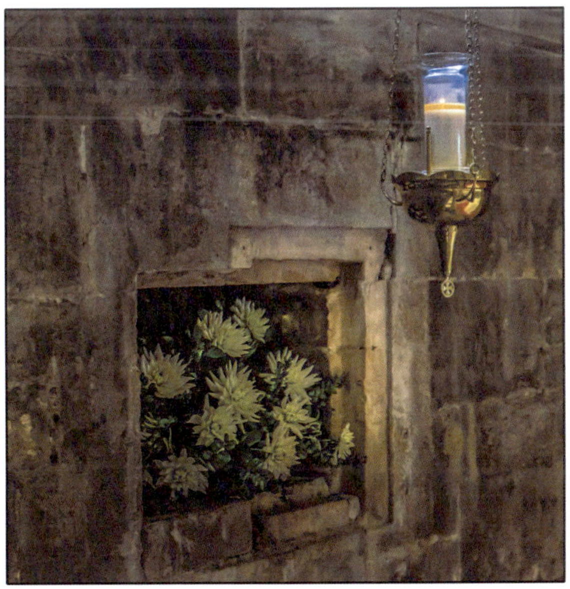

1/60sec f 4.3 34.5 mm ISO400

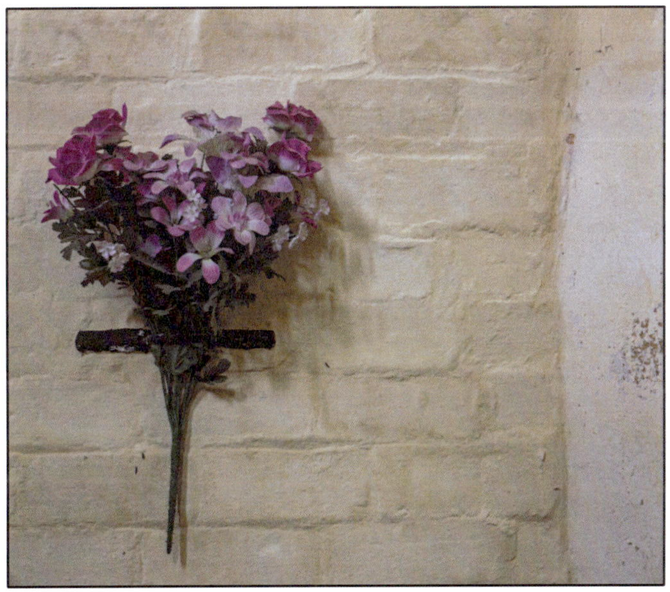

20sec f27 58 mm ISO100

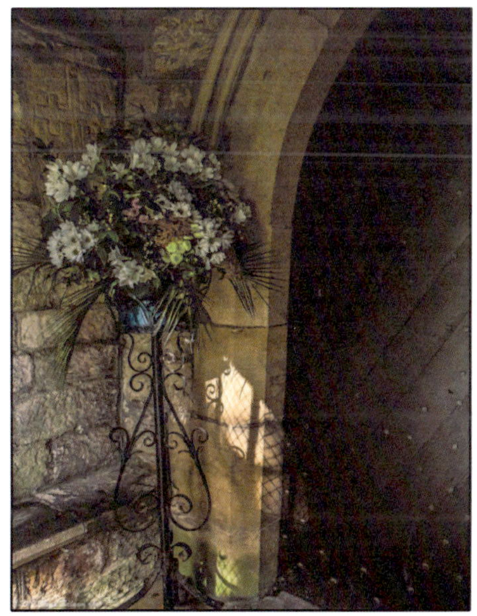

1/60sec f3.5 18.5 mm ISO320

BEHIND CLOSED DOORS

Many old churches have a Vestry. Some are now used as a store cupboard for old artefacts or lost property. If you find one try the handle (but don't force it). I have found many a splendid item of days of old.

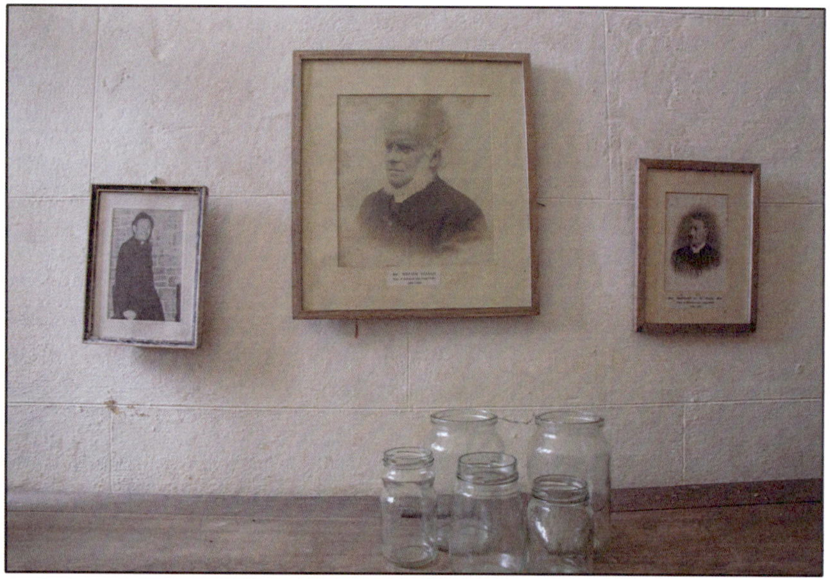

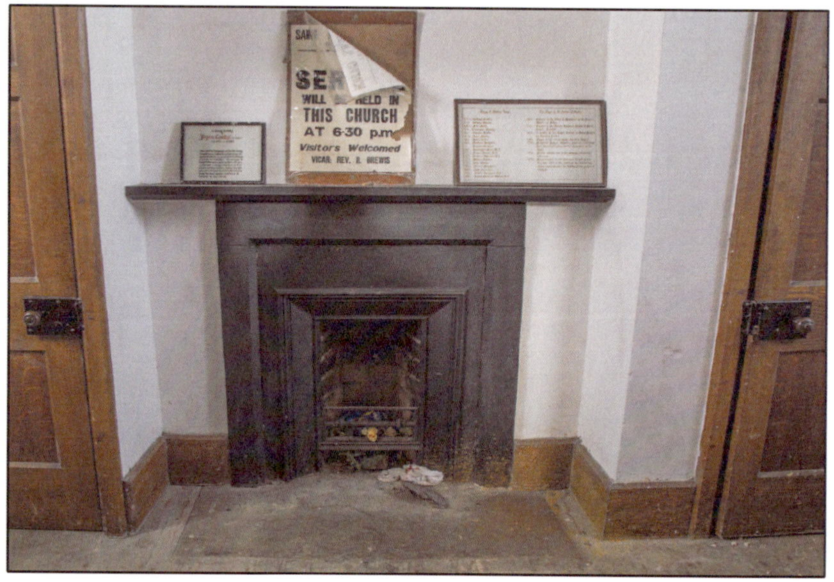

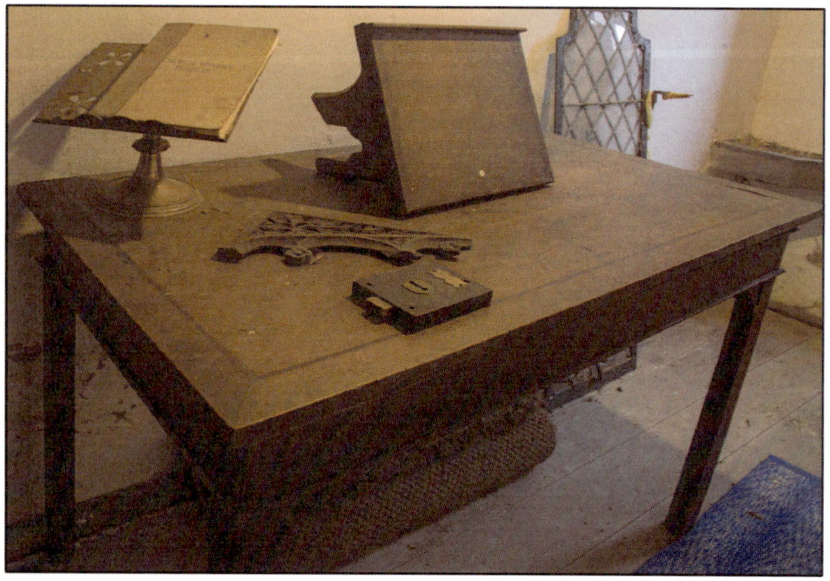

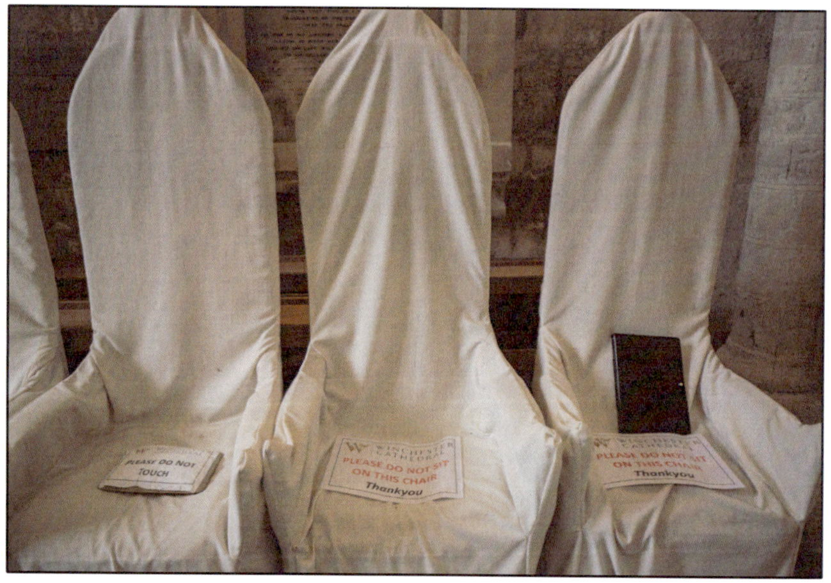

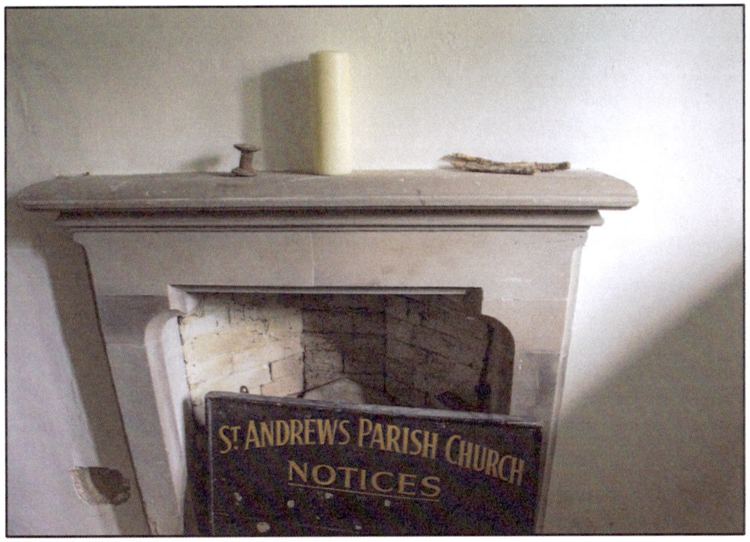
St. ANDREWS PARISH CHURCH
NOTICES

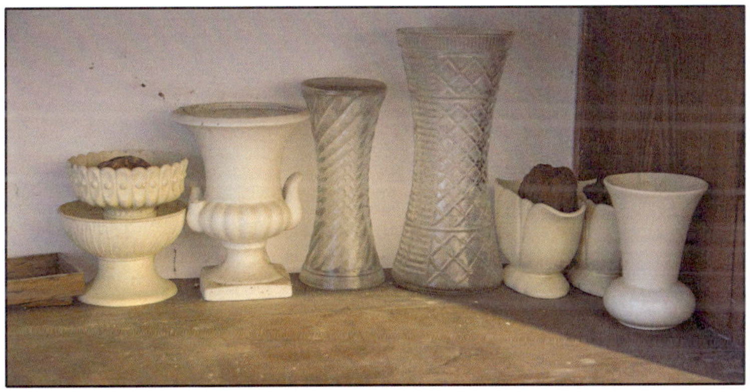

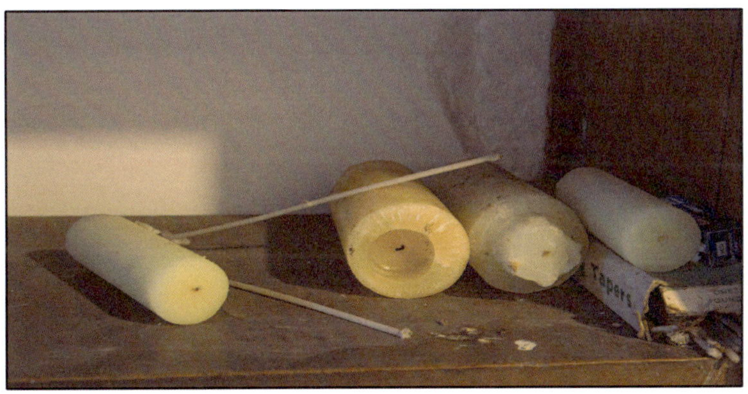

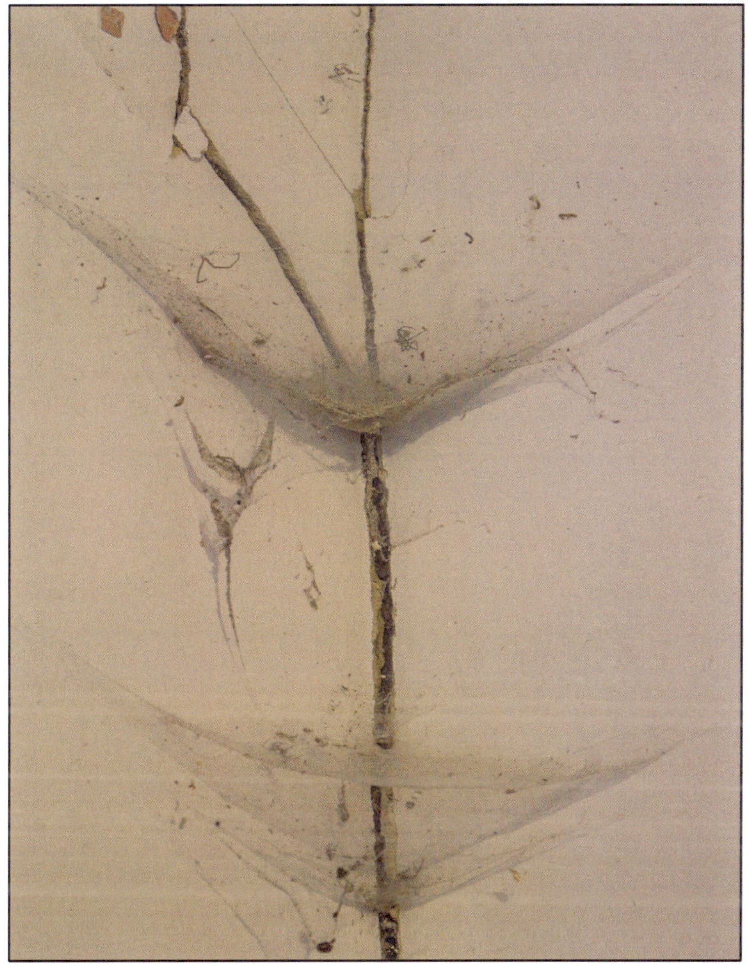

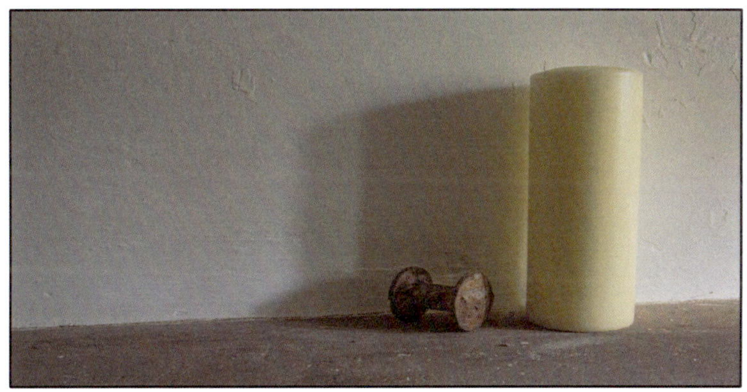

THE SQUINT

Many of these ancient features have been bricked up over time, but some still exist. They were for a person to *'view or squint'* at the Mass behind the rood screen that the congregation could not see. That person would then indicate to the congregation when a certain point of the Mass had been reached. I have only seen these two in all my travels.

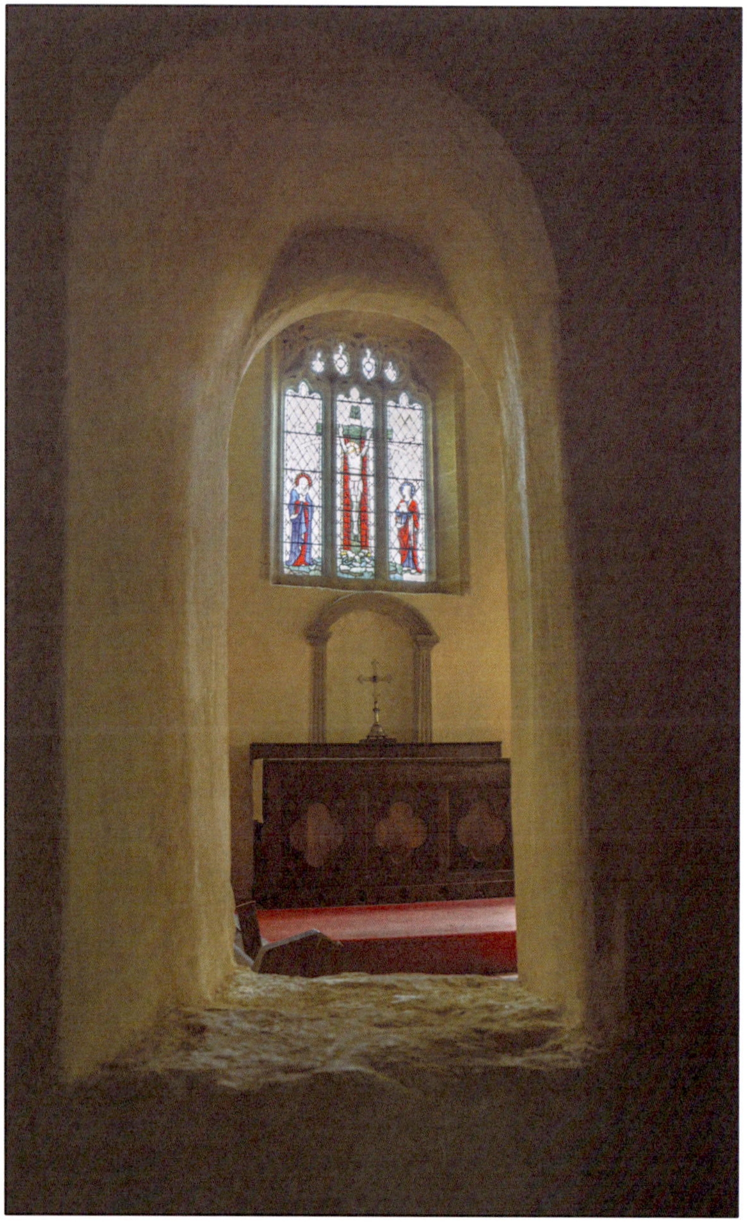

1/3sec f13 30mm ISO200 Canon 6D

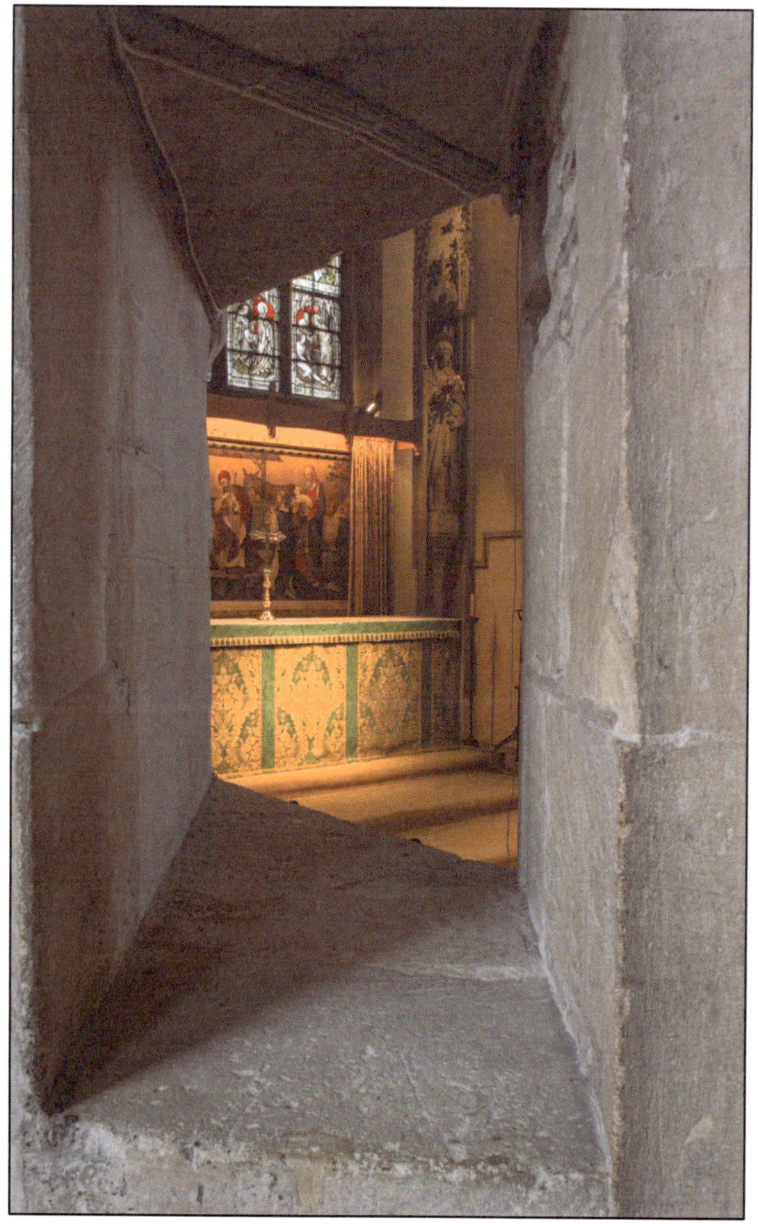

6sec f20 24mm ISO 100 Canon 6D

THE PISCINA

Piscinas are found near the altar and were used for washing communion vessels. They originally had a hole and pipe to drain the used water. They became more prevalent in English churches from the century. There is usually one in most churches and sometimes a double, but a triple is rare.

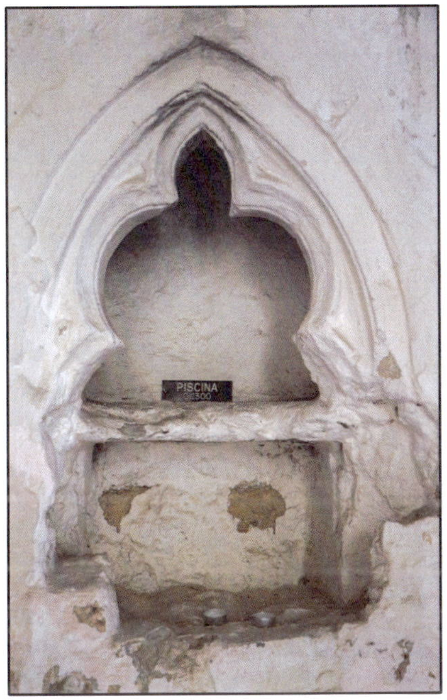

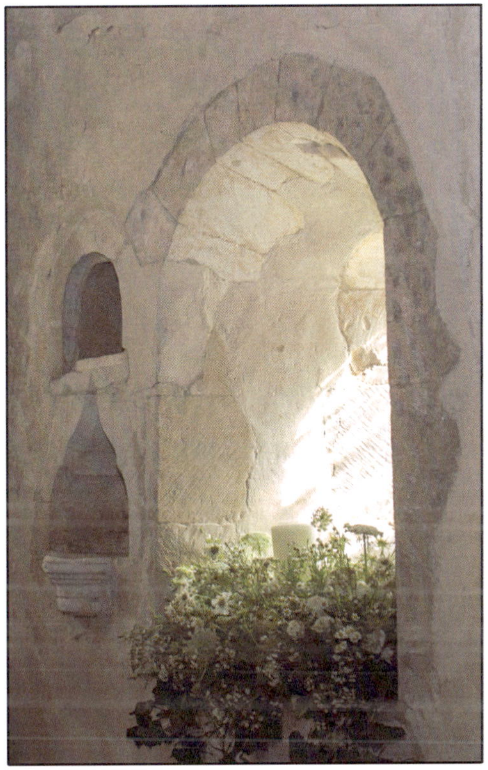

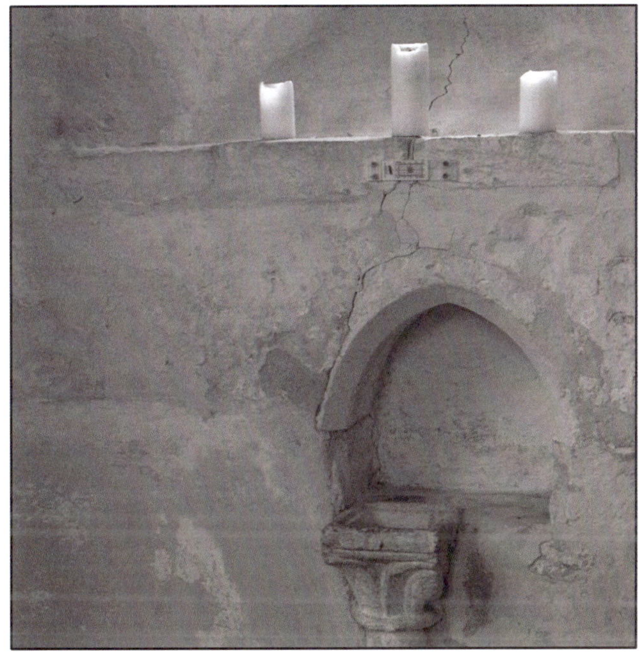

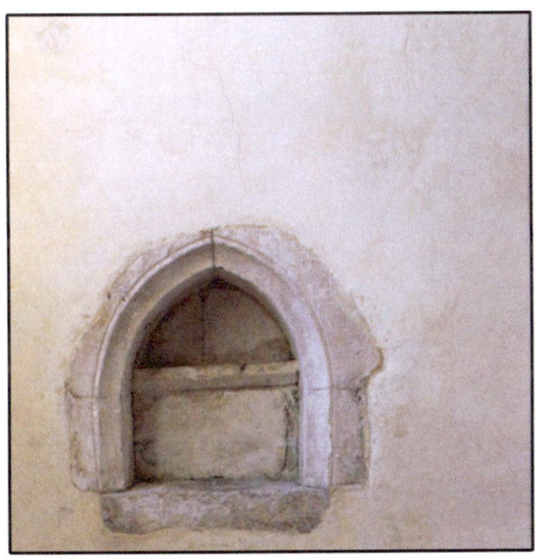

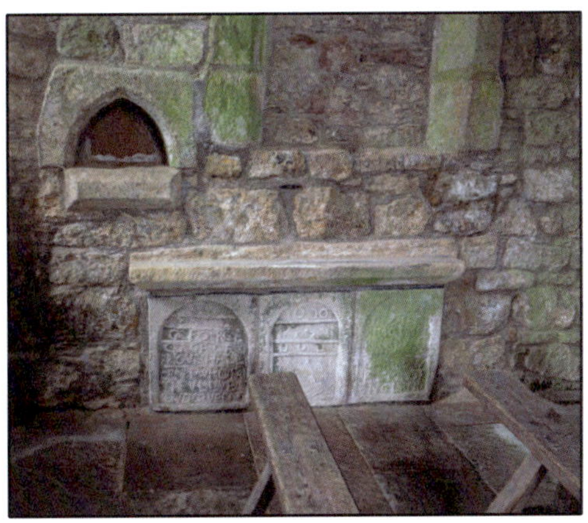

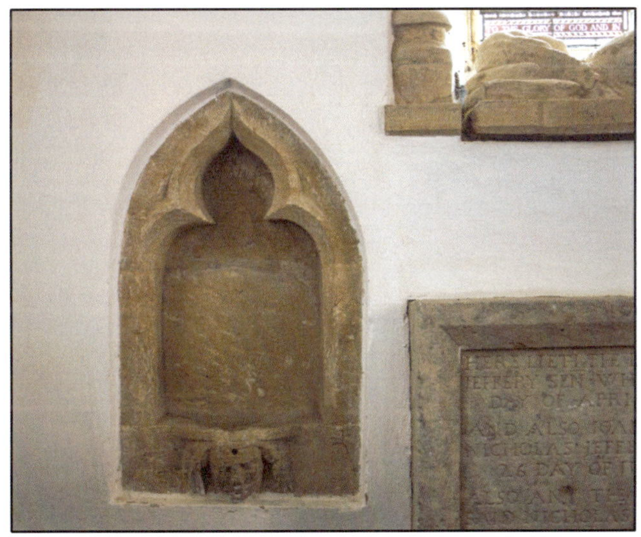

STOUP

A stoup is a vessel containing holy water which is positioned near the entrance of a church for worshippers to use to cross themselves. They differ from a Piscina as they do not have a drain hole.

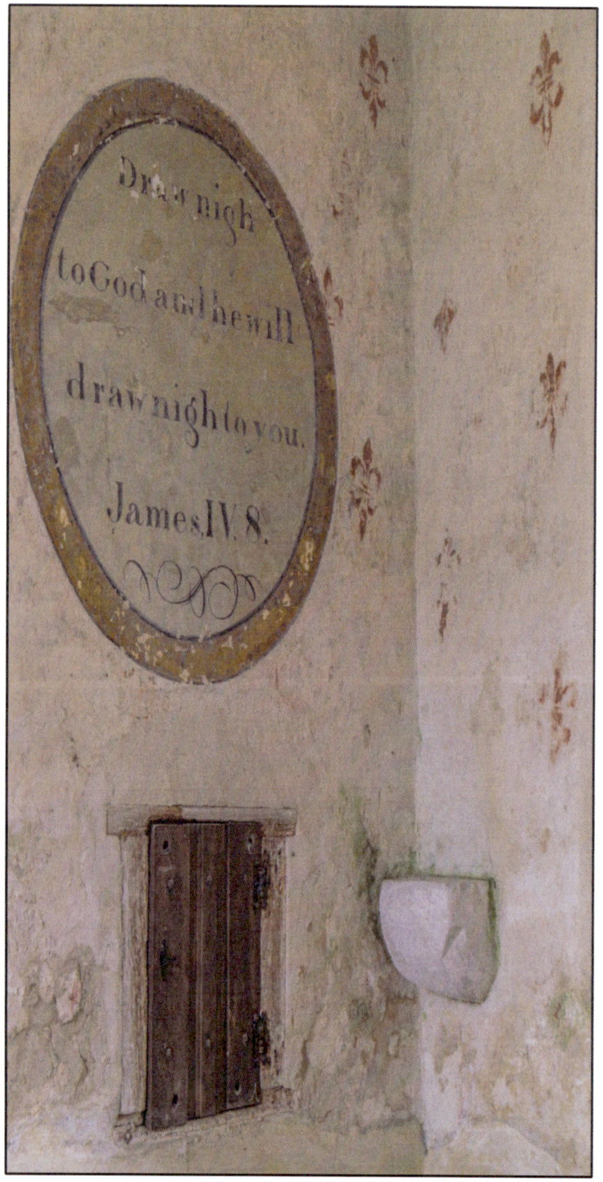

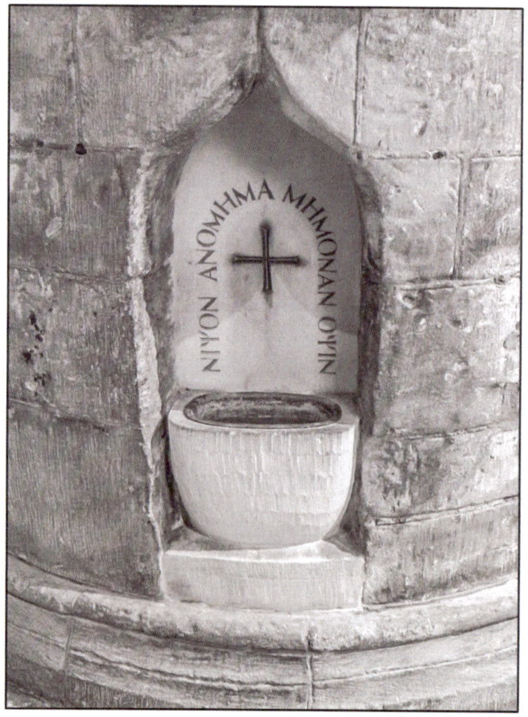

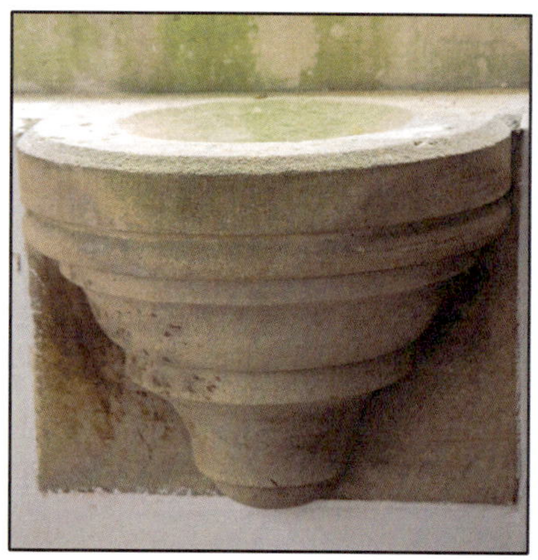

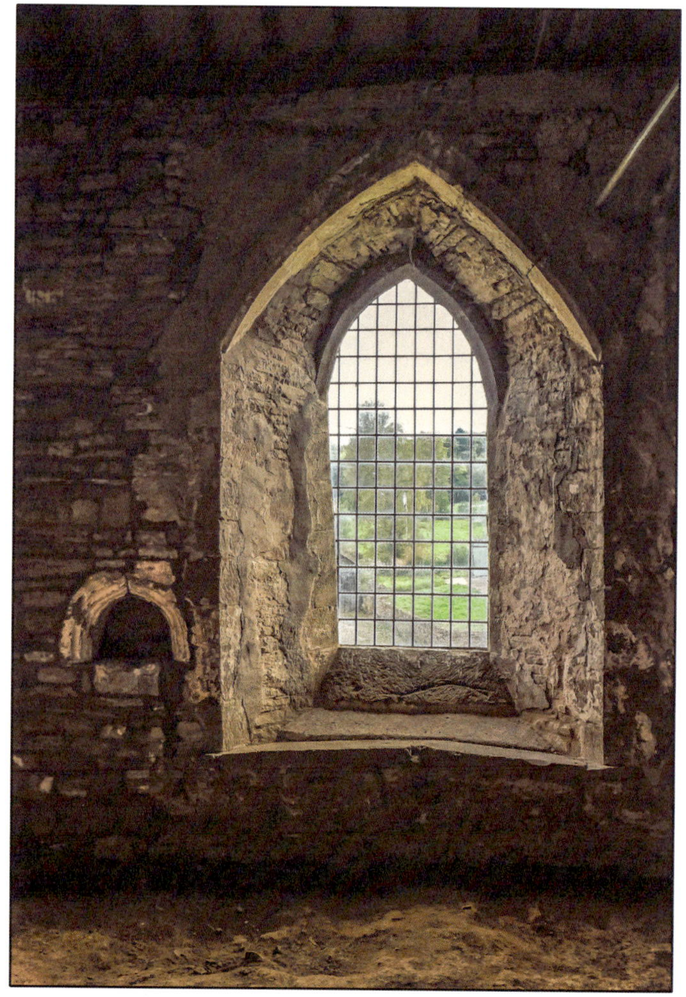

1/60sec f13 18.5mm ISO1000 Fuji X-T1

THE SEPULCHRE

This is a stone or wooden recess chamber where Christ's body was laid between burial and resurrection. In churches today they usually contain an elaborate tomb of the local benefactor.

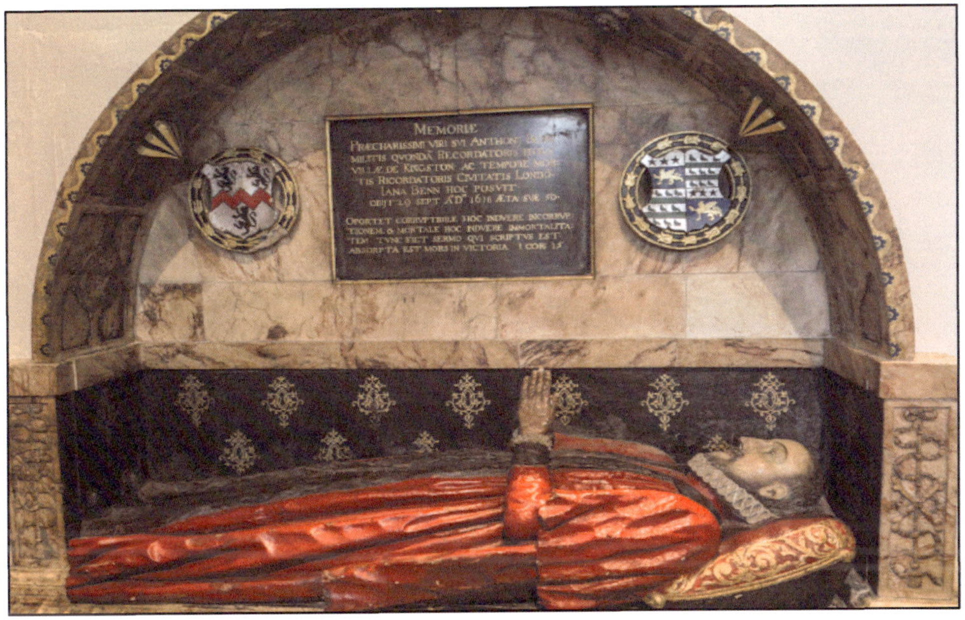

6sec f22 28mm ISO200 Canon 6D

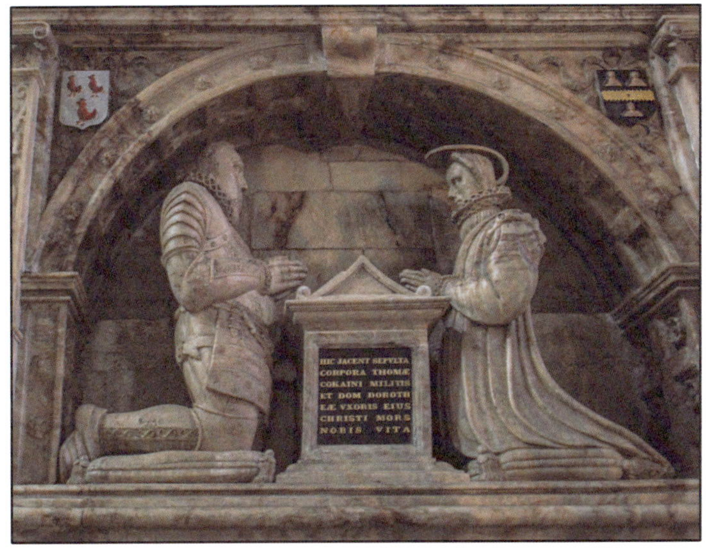

0.6sec f3.2 24mm ISO100 Canon 6D

Sepulchre (also spelled sepulcher) first appeared in Middle English around the beginning of the 13th century. It was originally spelled sepulcre, a spelling taken from Anglo-French. Like many words borrowed into English from French, sepulchre has roots buried in Latin. The word arose from Latin sepulcrum, a noun derived from the verb sepelire, meaning "to bury."

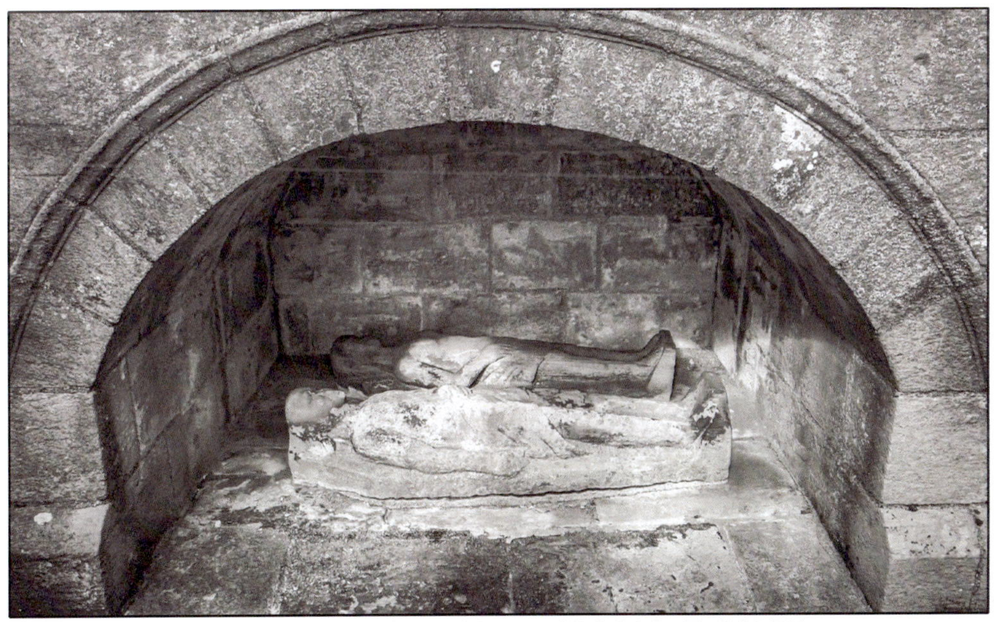

1/125sec f5.6 20mm ISO200 Fuji X-T1

SEDILIA

Found on the south side of the altar and usually made of stone. Early examples were one seat set into the wall, but the more usual number is three, and sometimes up to five. They became common in English churches by the 12th century.

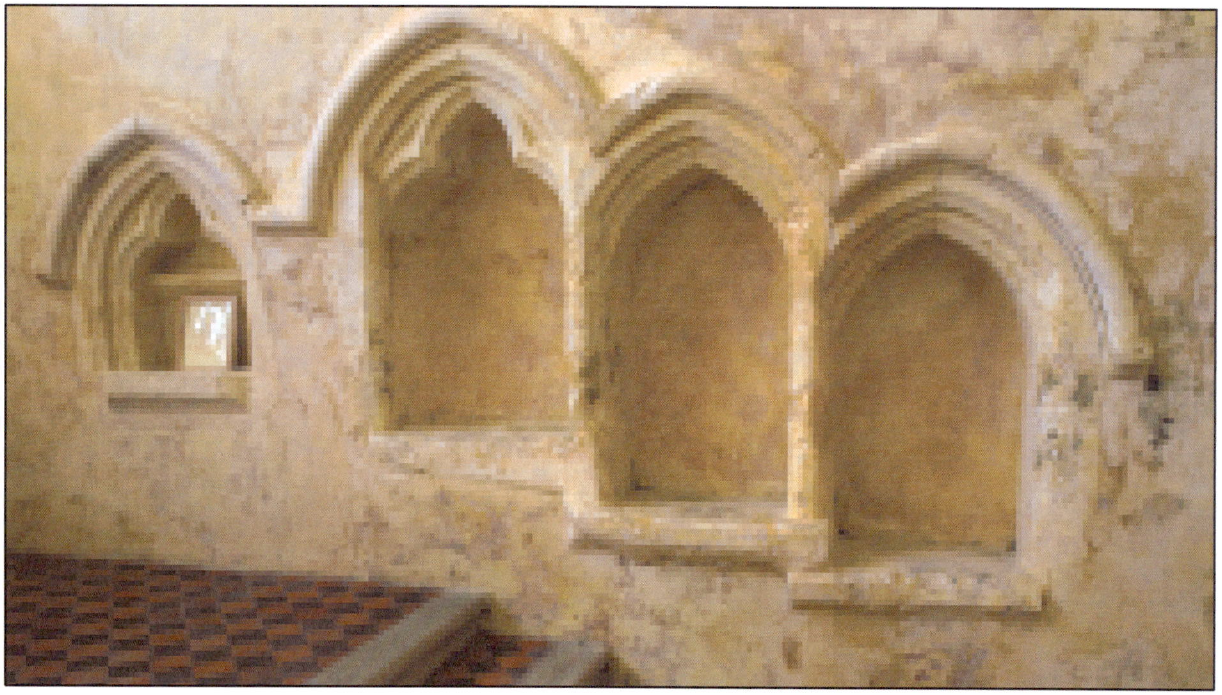

0.7sec f22 24mm ISO100 Canon 6D

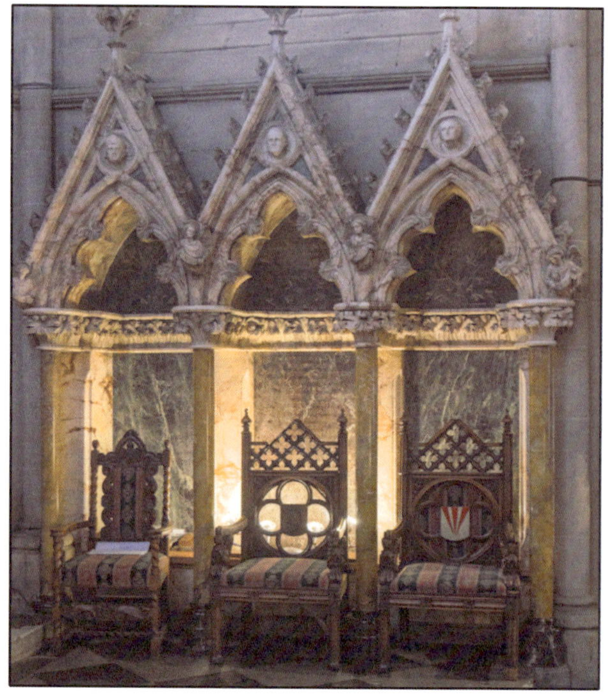

1/30sec f4 23mm ISO400 Fuji X-T1

Used primarily for the celebrant and ministers to sit at during certain points of High Mass.

Not all sedilia are stone; there is a timber one thought to be 15th century in St Nicholas' Church at Rodmersham in Kent.

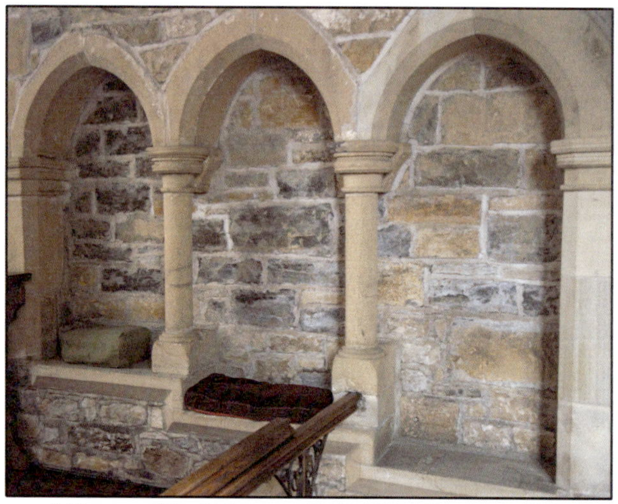

1/2sec f4 37mm ISO100 Canon 6D

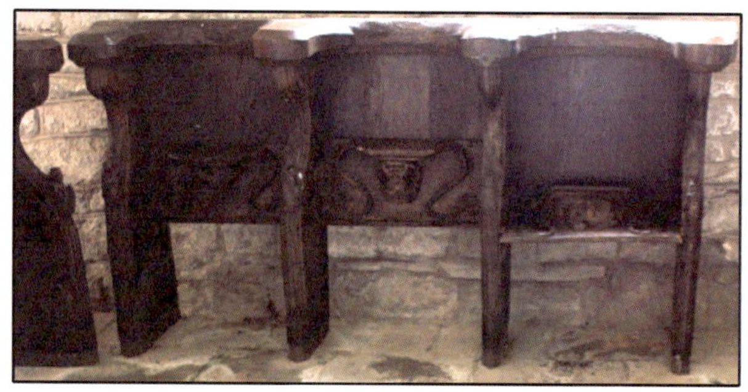

1.3sec f7.1 24mm ISO100 Canon 6D

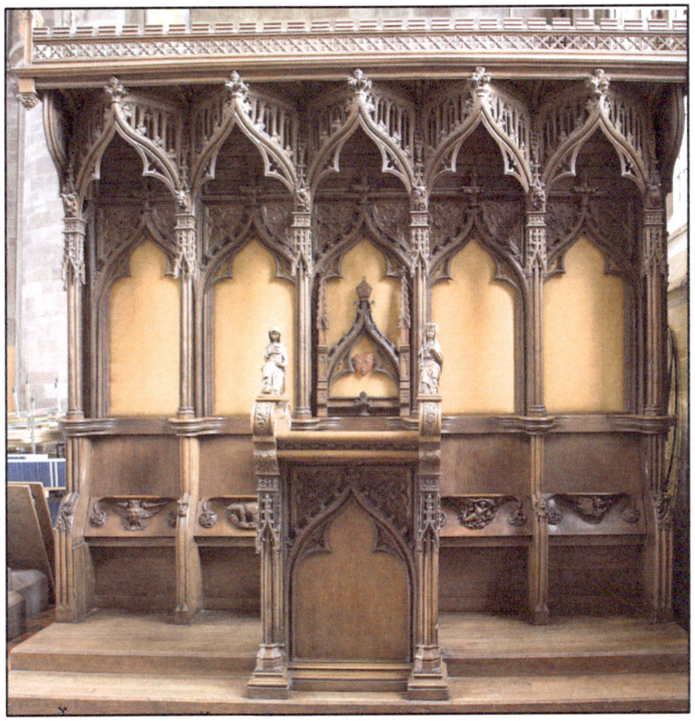

1sec f5.6 28mm ISO200 Canon 6D

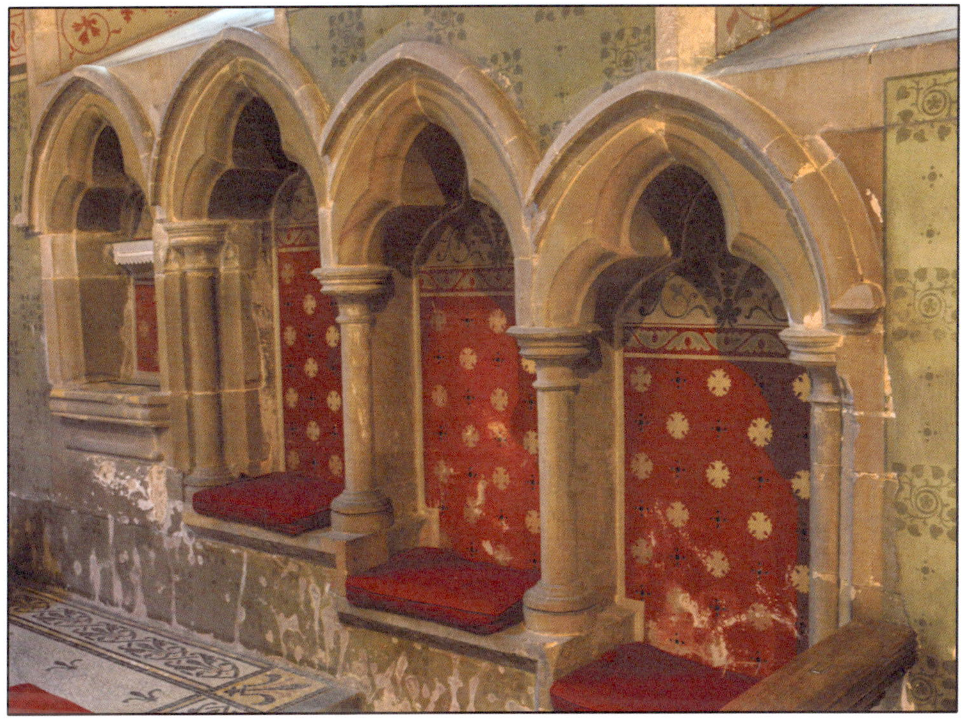

1.5sec f13 35mm ISO200 Canon 6D

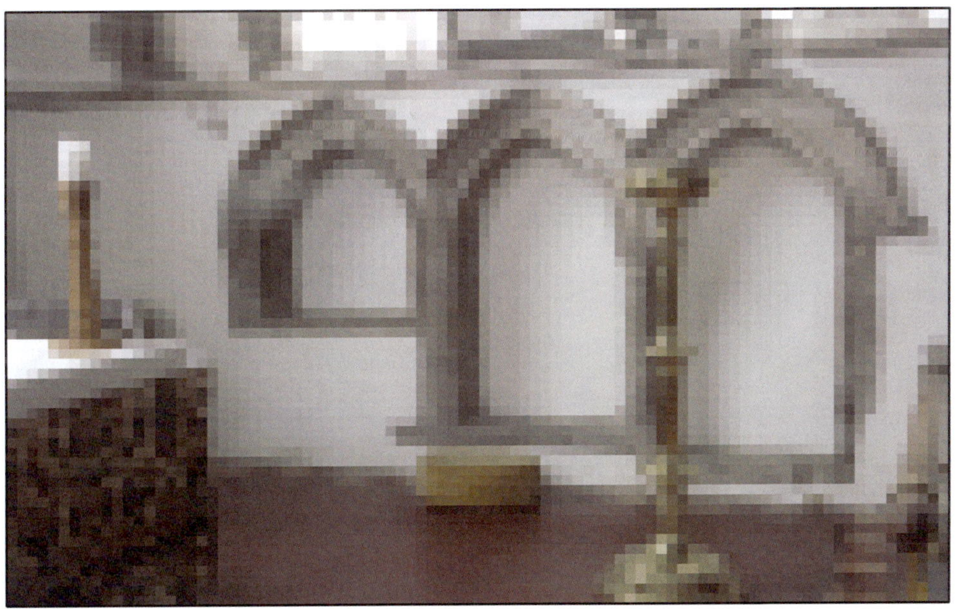

1sec f22 46mm ISO100 Canon 6D

STONE ARTEFACTS and CORBELS

There probably needs to be a separate book covering just the vast number of different carved artefacts and wall adornments found in our churches. Many older Corbels, which support a weight above it, have decorative stone work including heads of a prominent people, flowers, pagan faces or other artistic designs created by the stonemason. Some close-up work is required here so ensure you are working with an aperture around f2.8 – f3.5, so the background is softer.

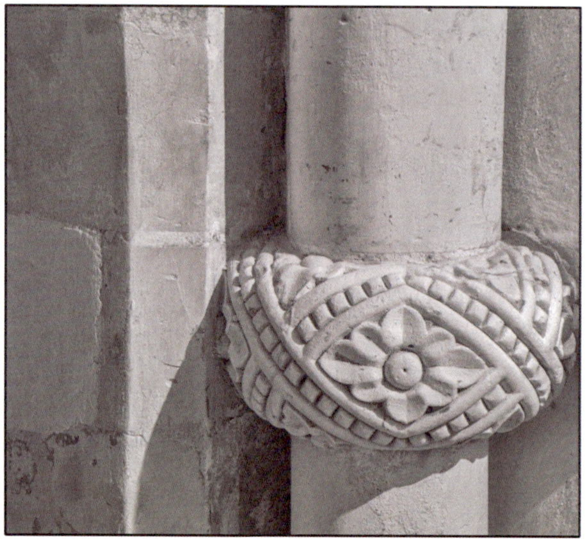

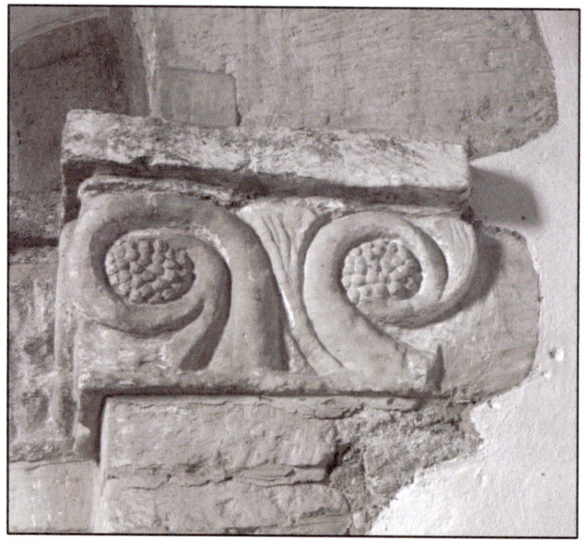

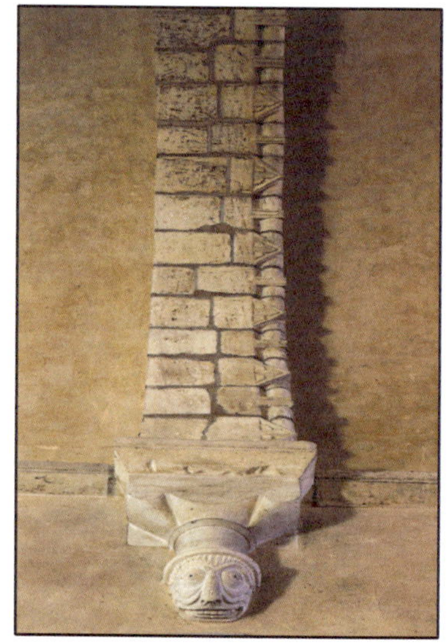

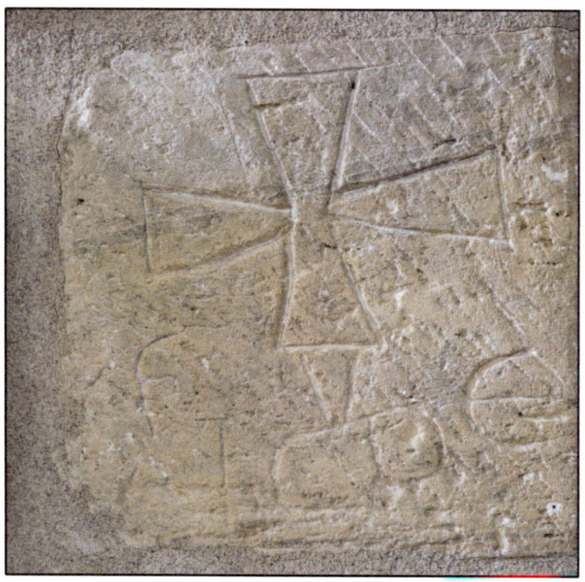

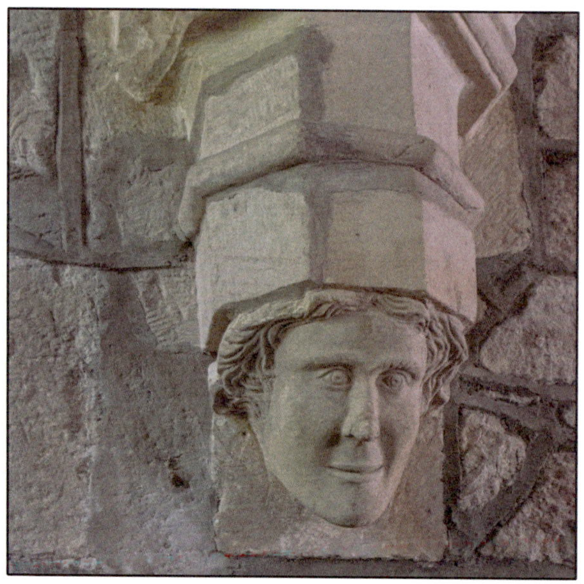

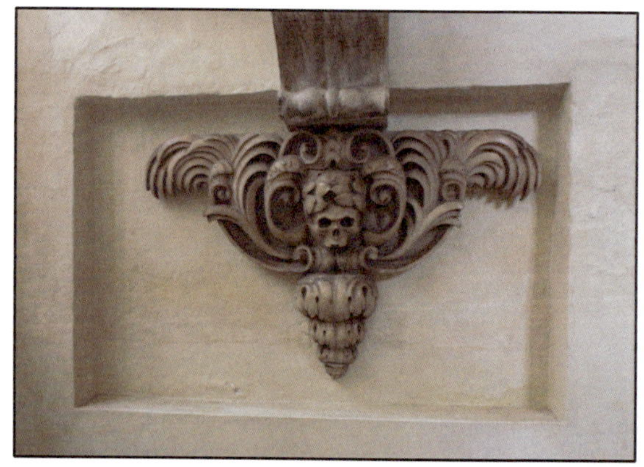

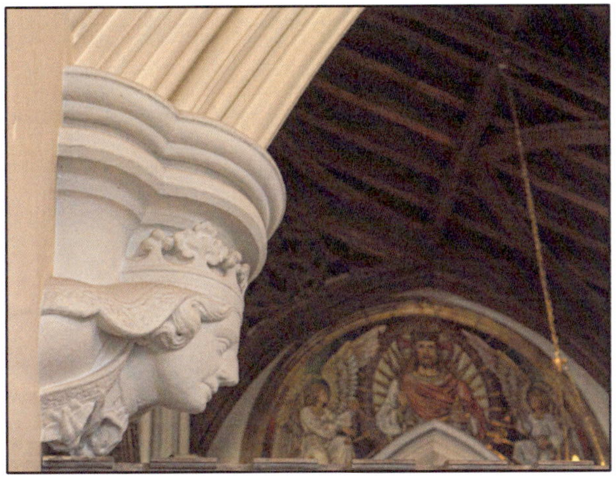
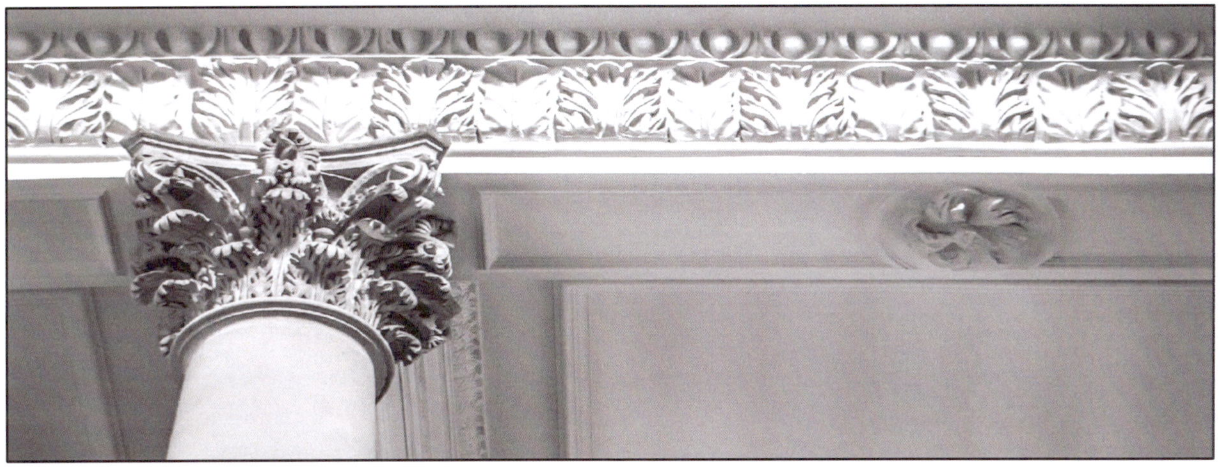
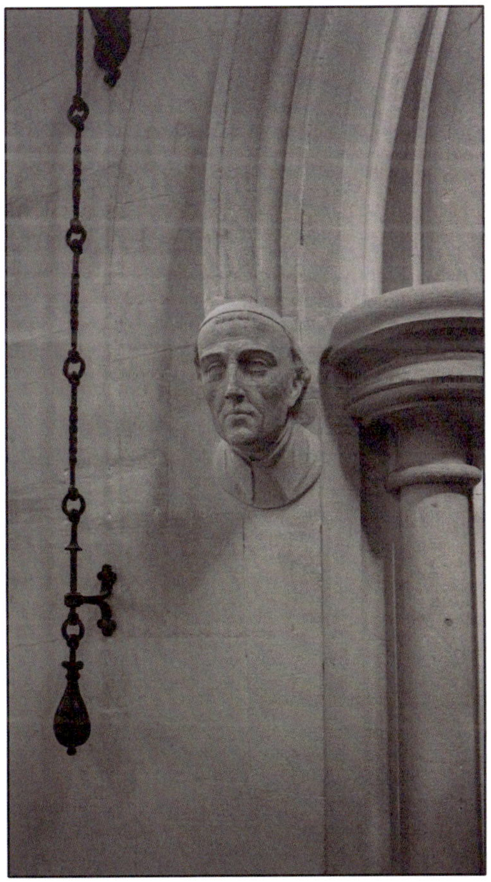
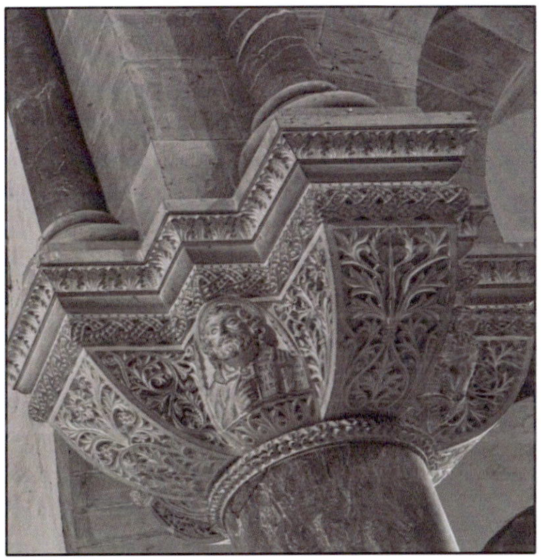
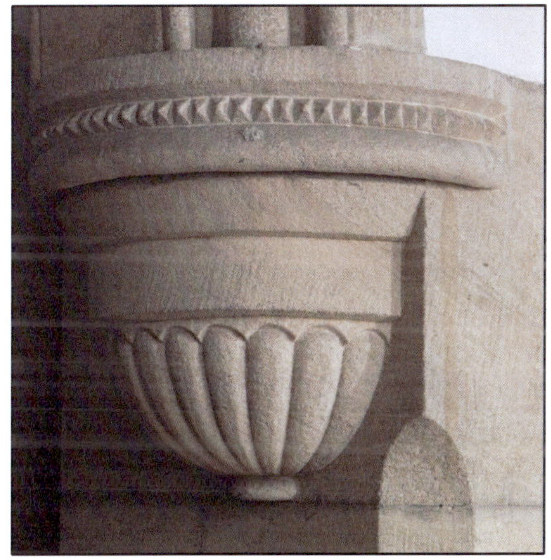
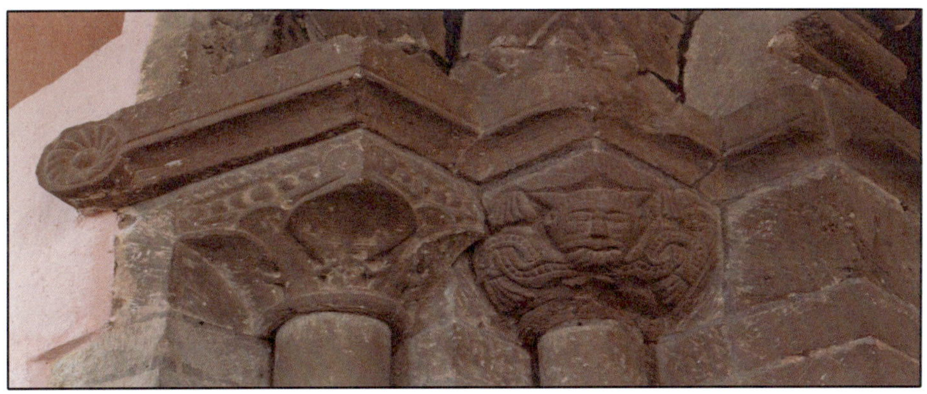

HATCHMENTS and HERALDRY

The Hatchment was usually placed over the entrance door of the deceased's residence at the level of the second floor, and remained *insitu* for six to twelve months, after which it was removed to the parish church. The practice developed in the early 17th century from the custom of carrying a heraldic shield before the coffin of the deceased, then leaving it for display in the church. You will find hatchment shields in almost every country church.

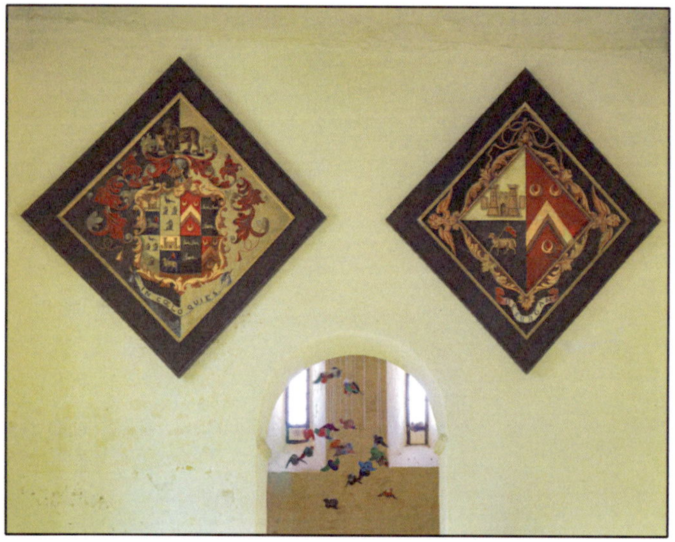

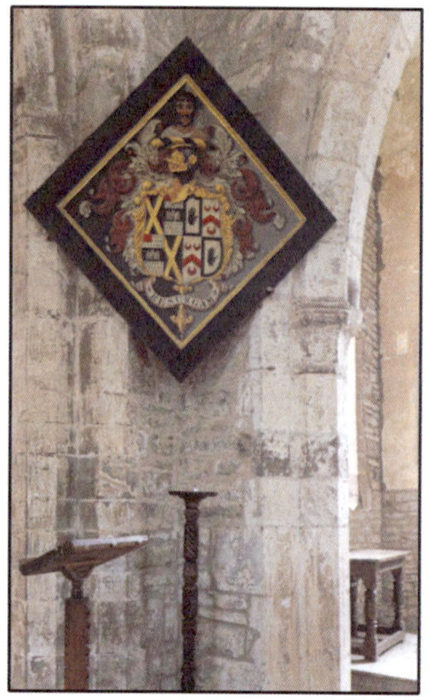

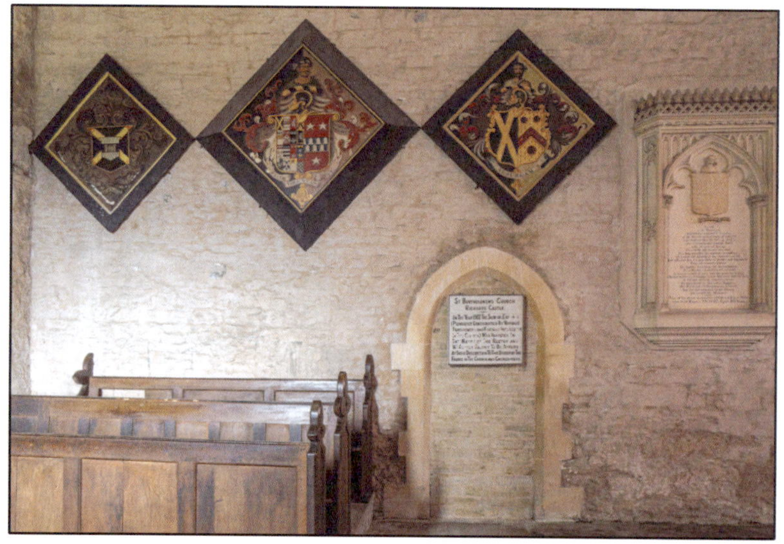

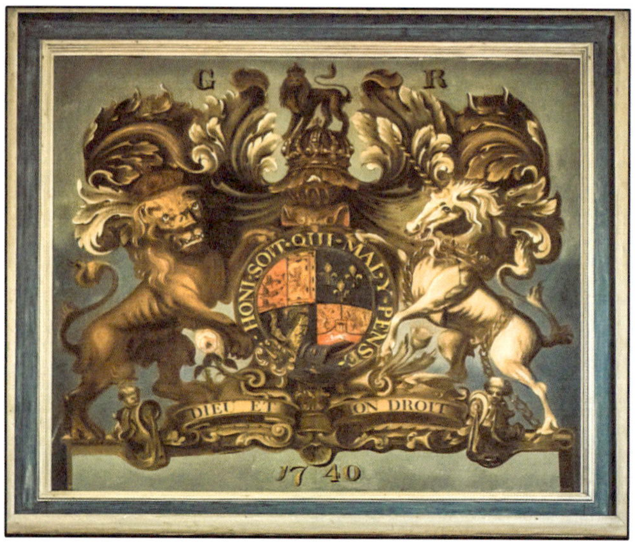

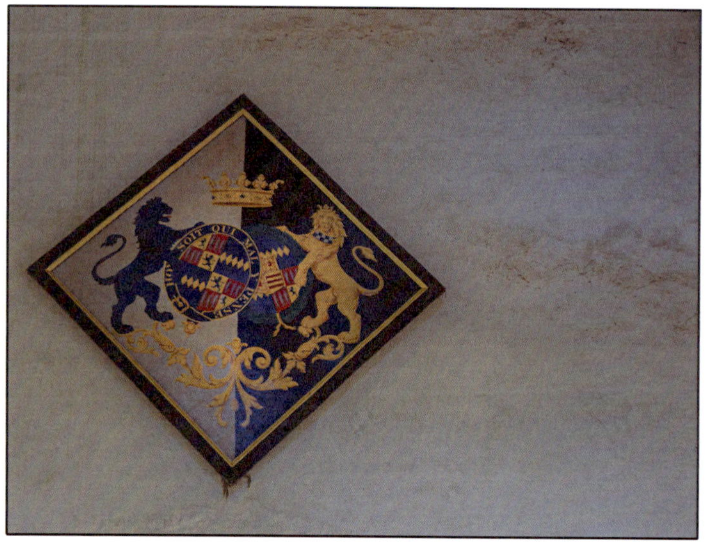

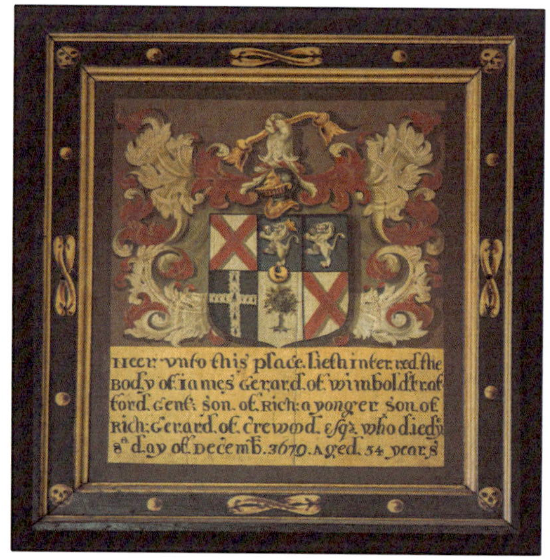

PERSPECTIVES

'A point of view.' Yes, but in photography it means something different. There are many long explanations in photographic handbooks, but to sum it in a sentence; *the effect of relative distance and position.* I have tried to give some samples here *(which may help or hinder your understanding of perspectives)*

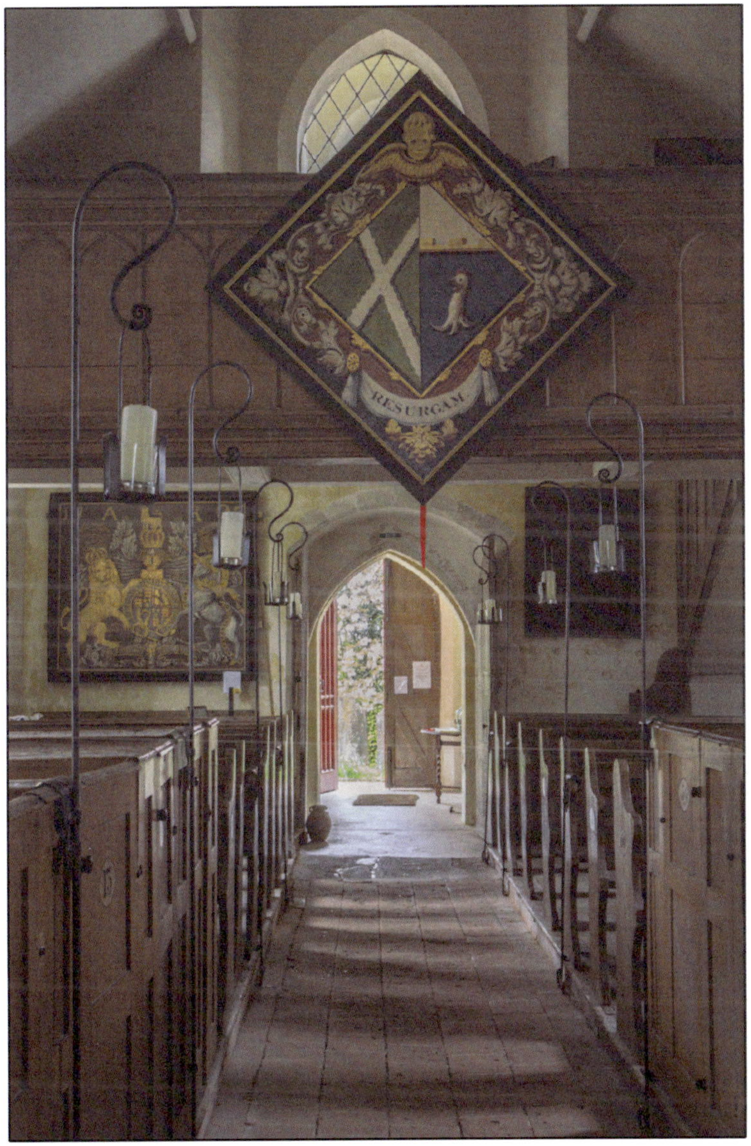

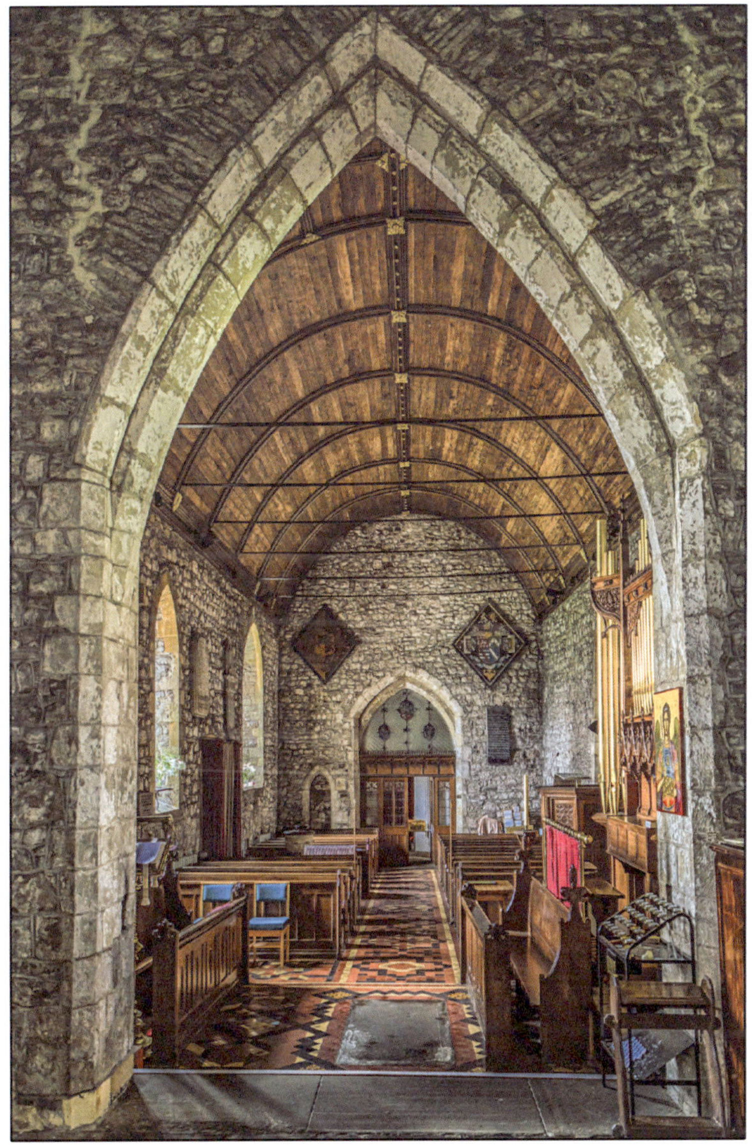

These *'leading lines'* give a perspective of distance with an insight to what is beyond.

Take the viewer on a journey through your photograph.

Examples of Perspectives in photography

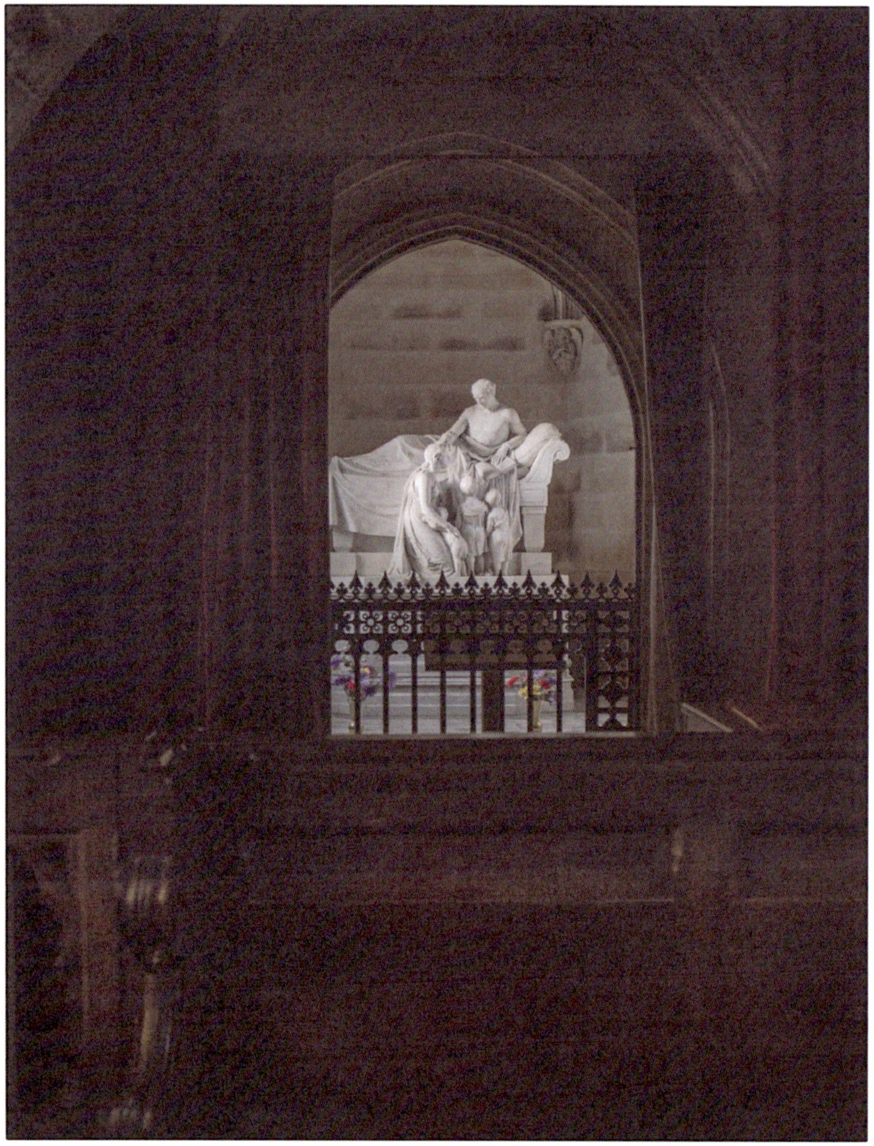

1/10sec f3.5 24mm ISO100 Canon 6D

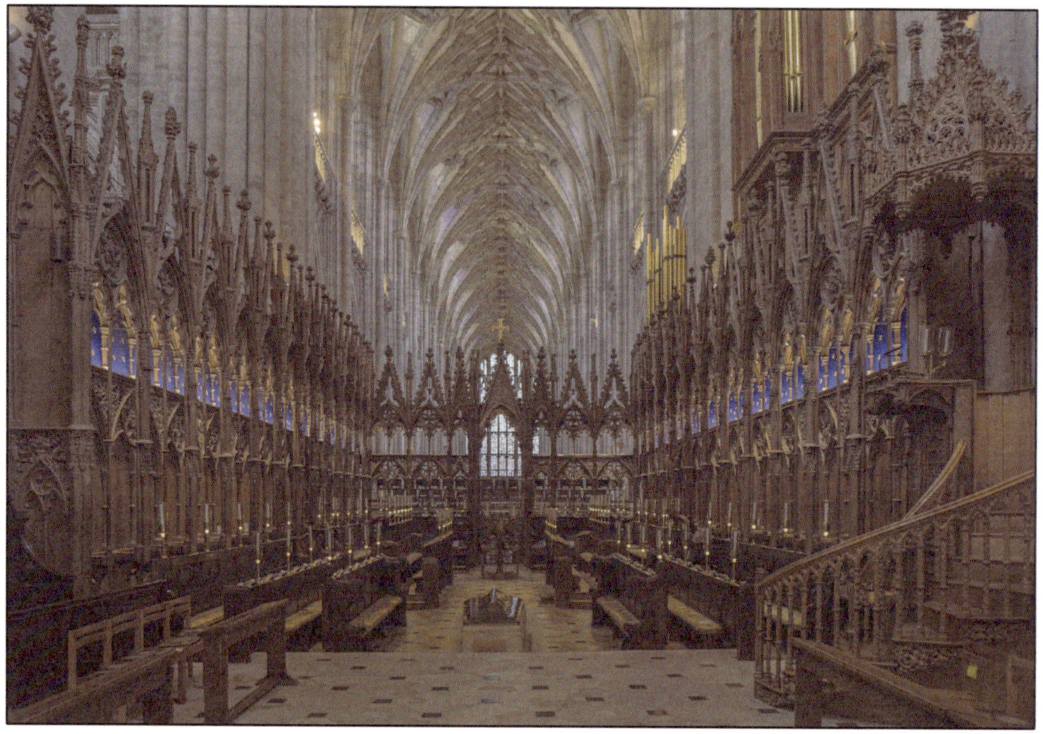

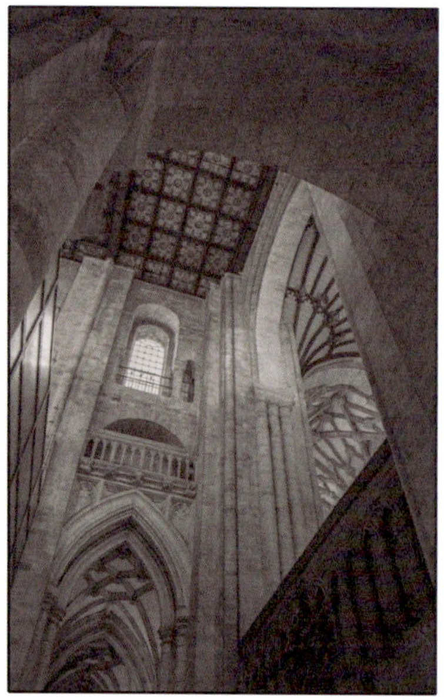

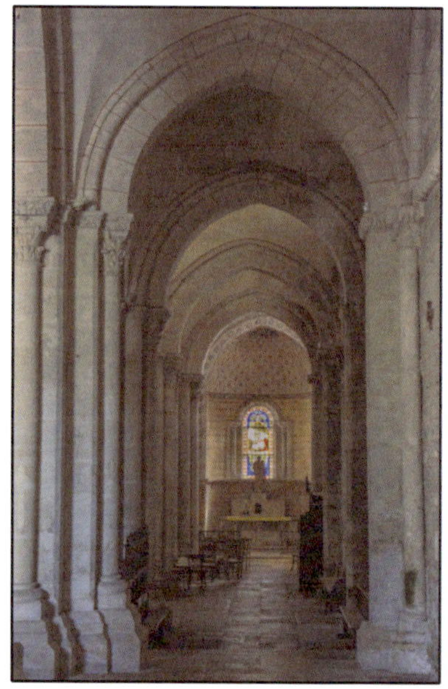

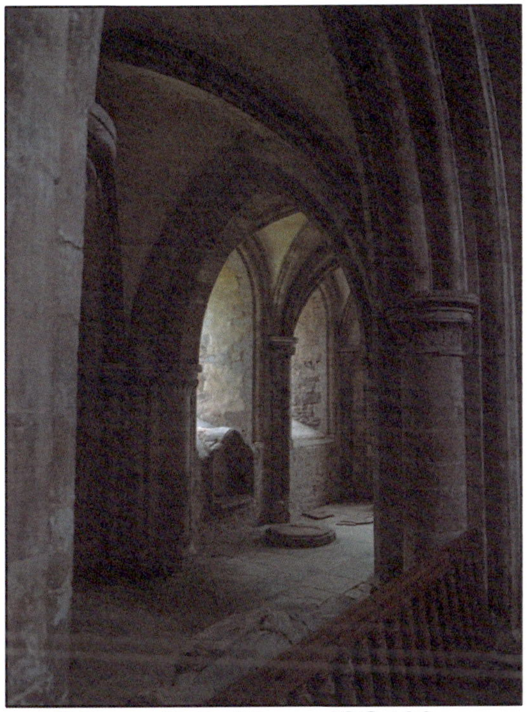

1/30sec f3.5 18mm ISO400

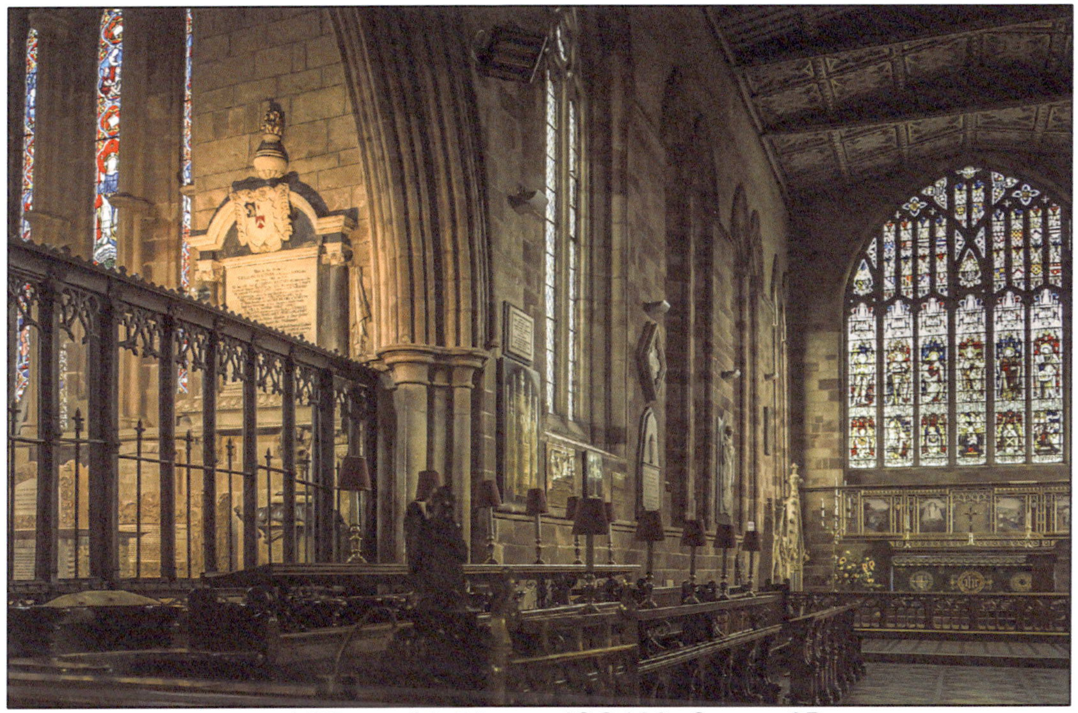

1/20sec f 3 24 mm ISO100 Canon 6D

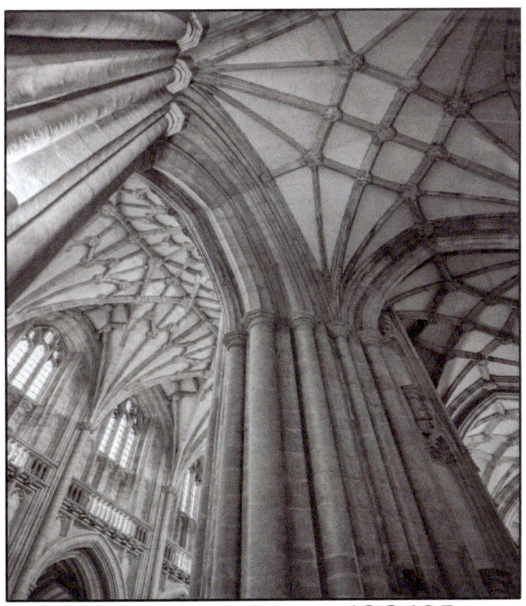

1/8sec f3.5 24 mm ISO125

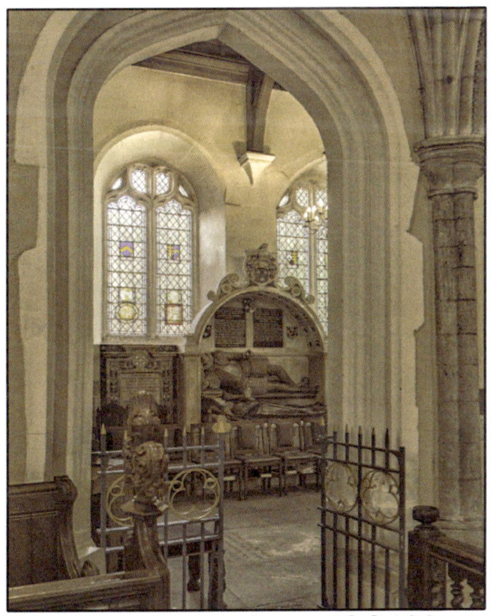

1/60sec f3.5 18 mm ISO400

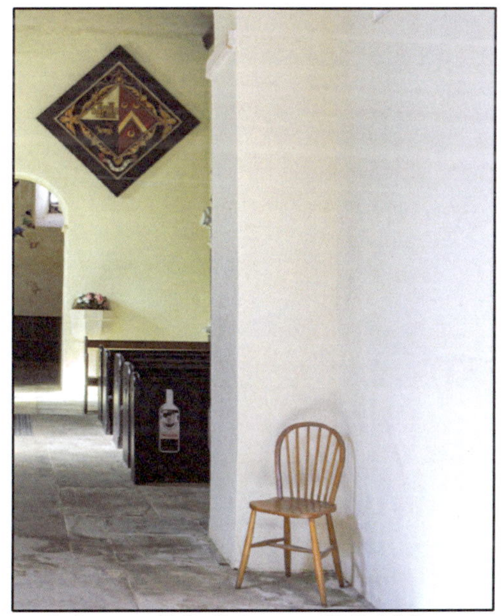

3.0sec f19 24 mm ISO100

SOME OF MY FAVOURITE CHURCH IMAGES

I hope some of these images will inspire you to look at our beautiful country churches in a new light and with a *creative eye*.

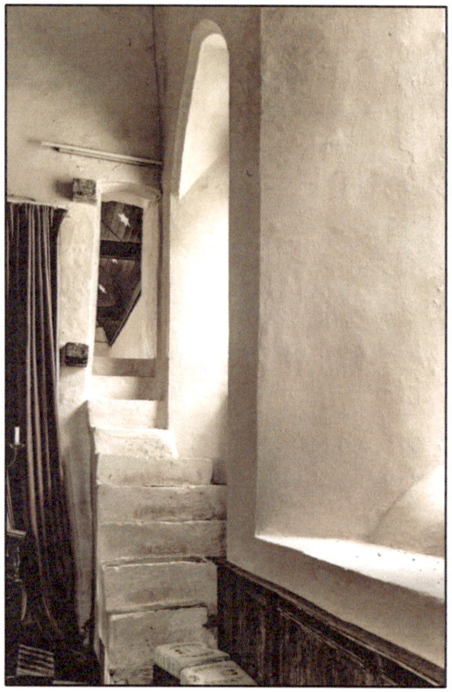

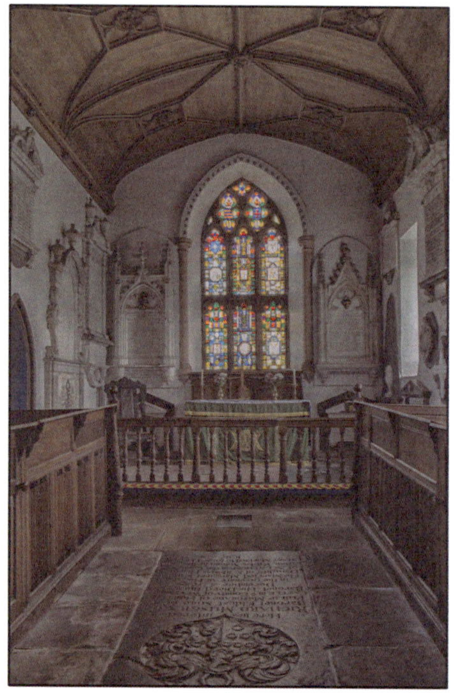

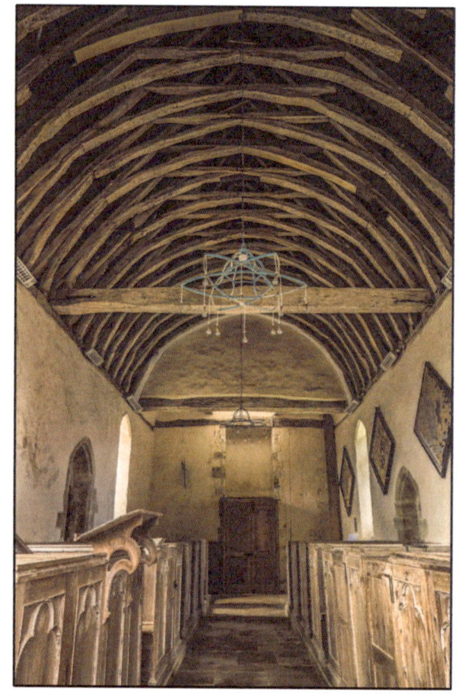

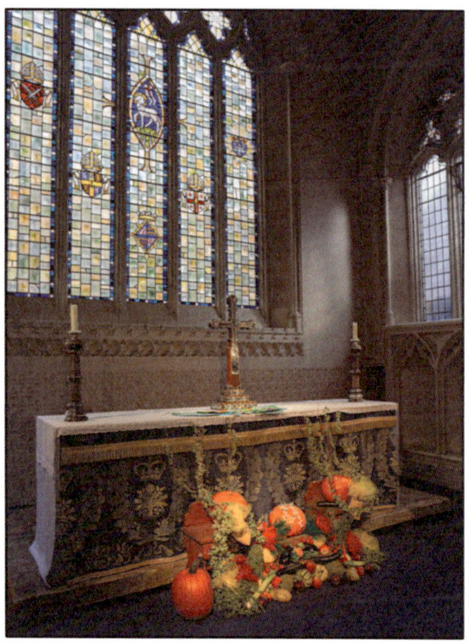

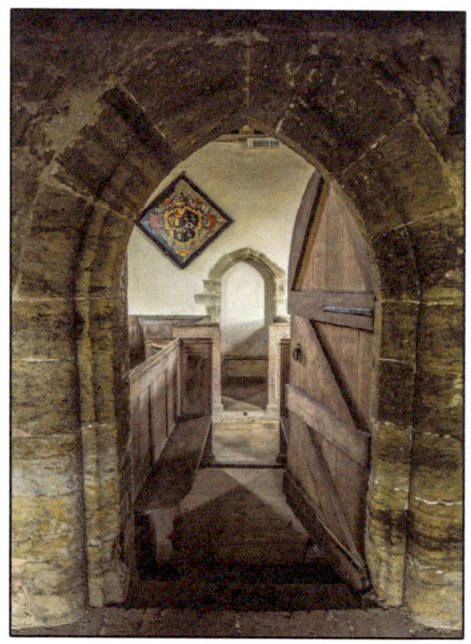

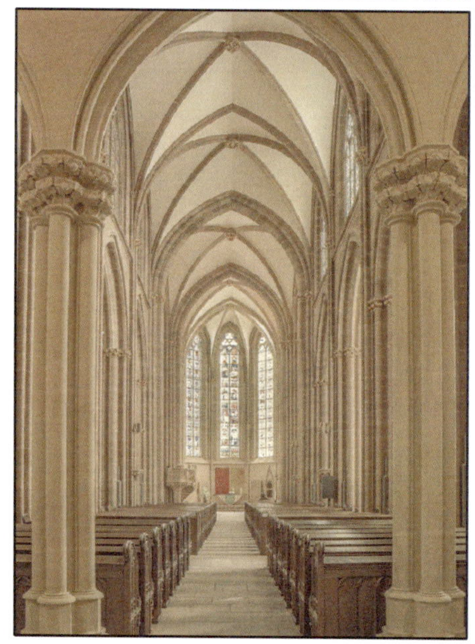

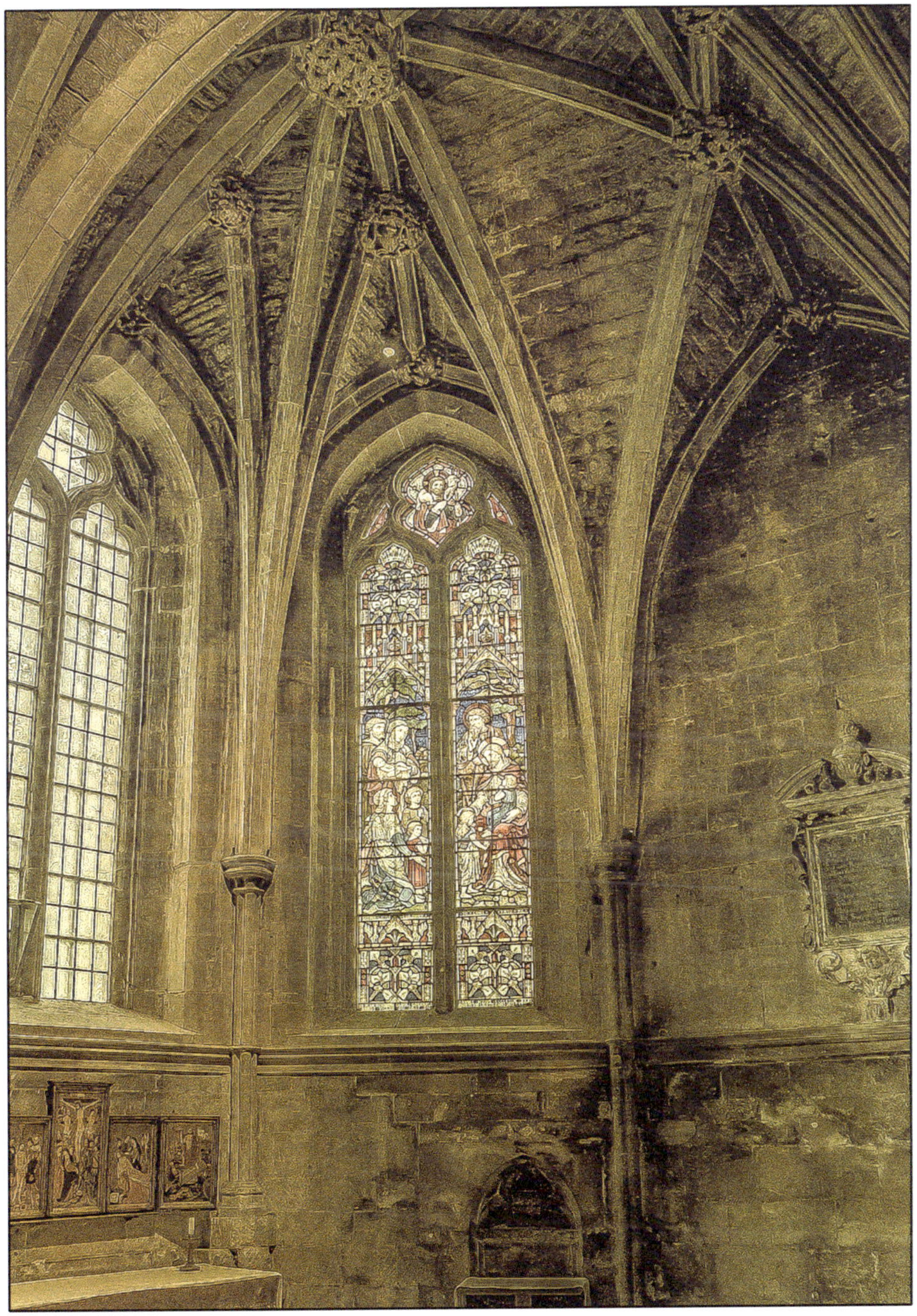

Tewkesbury Abbey, Gloucester

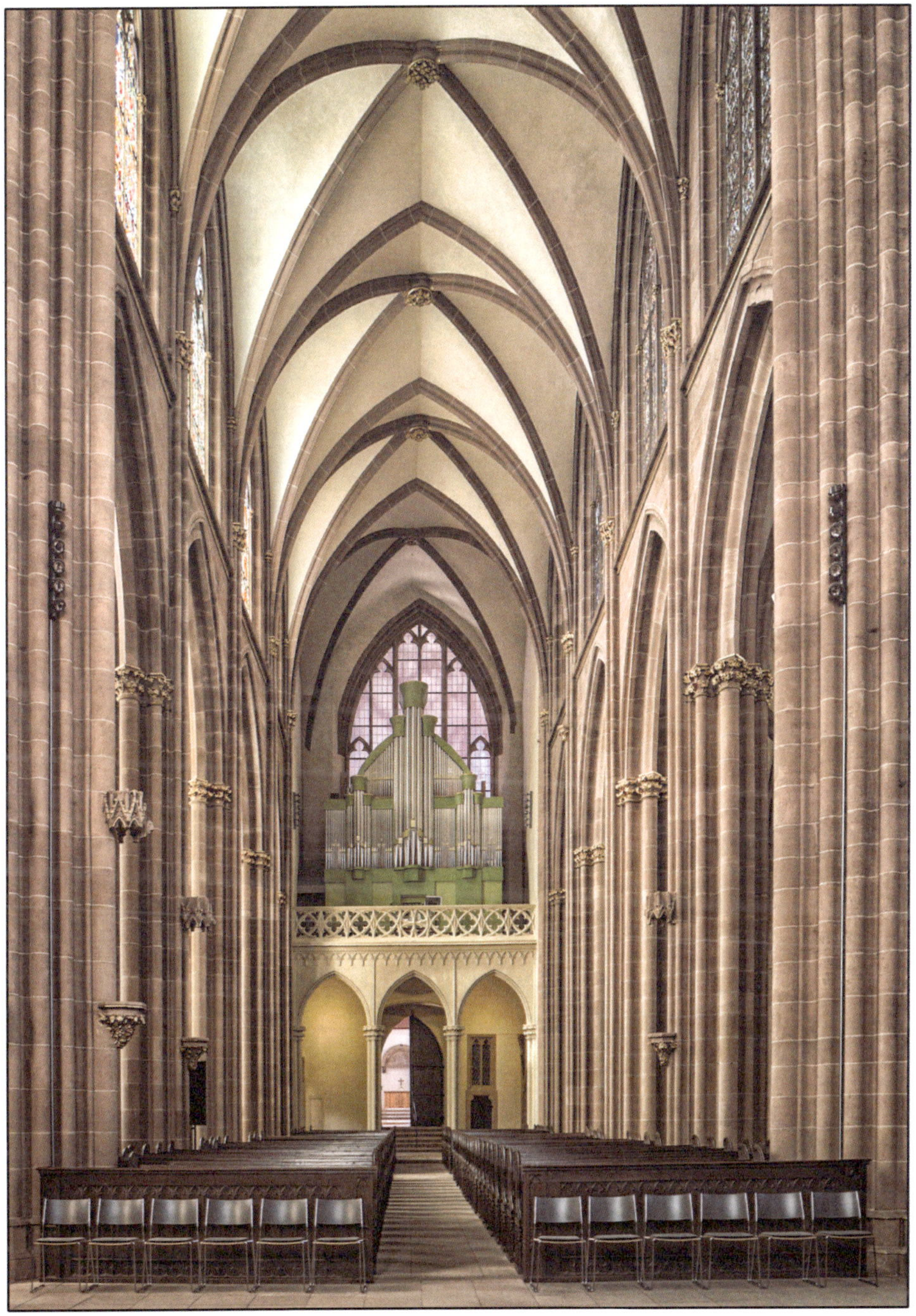

St Katherine’s Kirk,Oppernheim, Germany

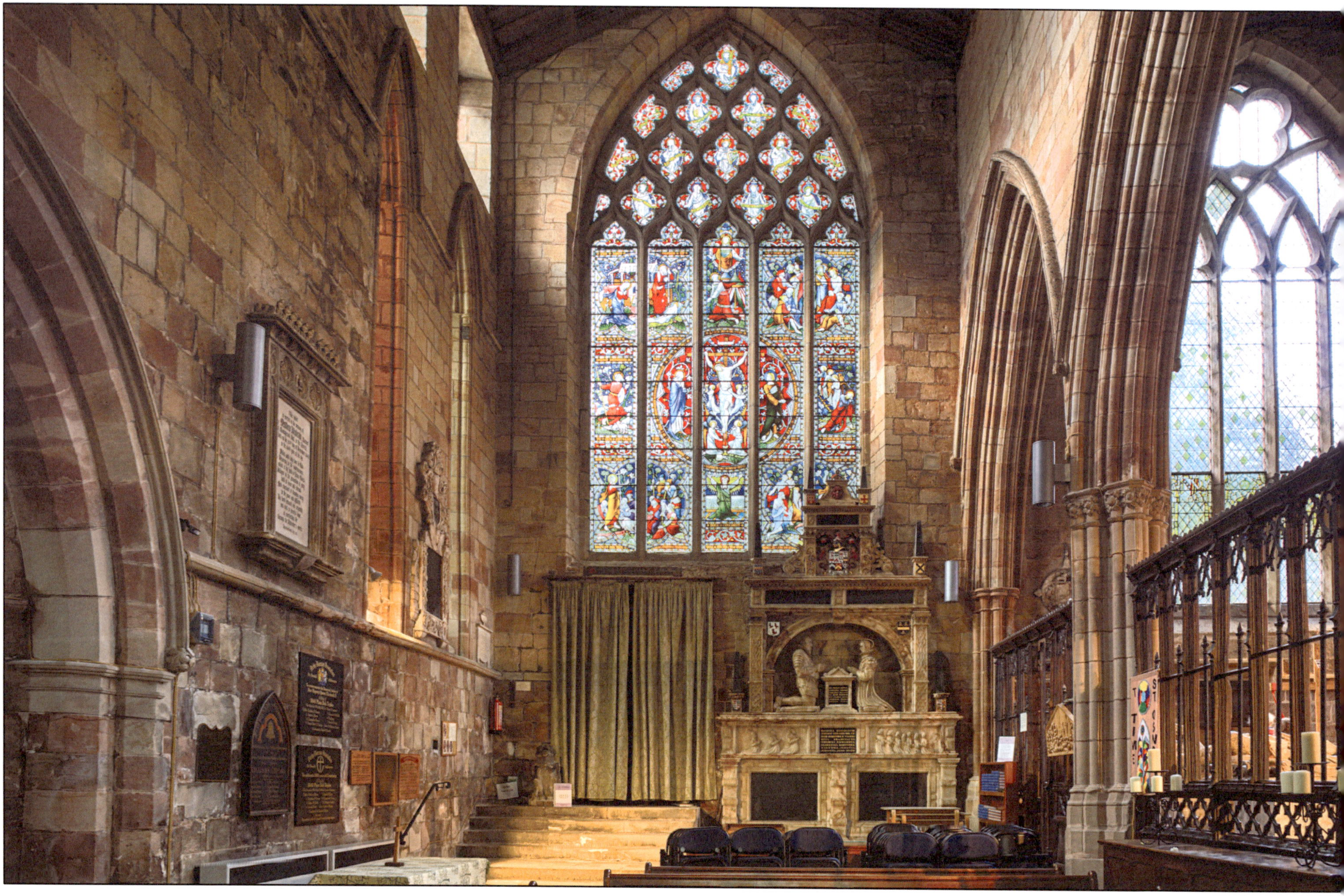

St Oswald's, Ashbourne, Derby

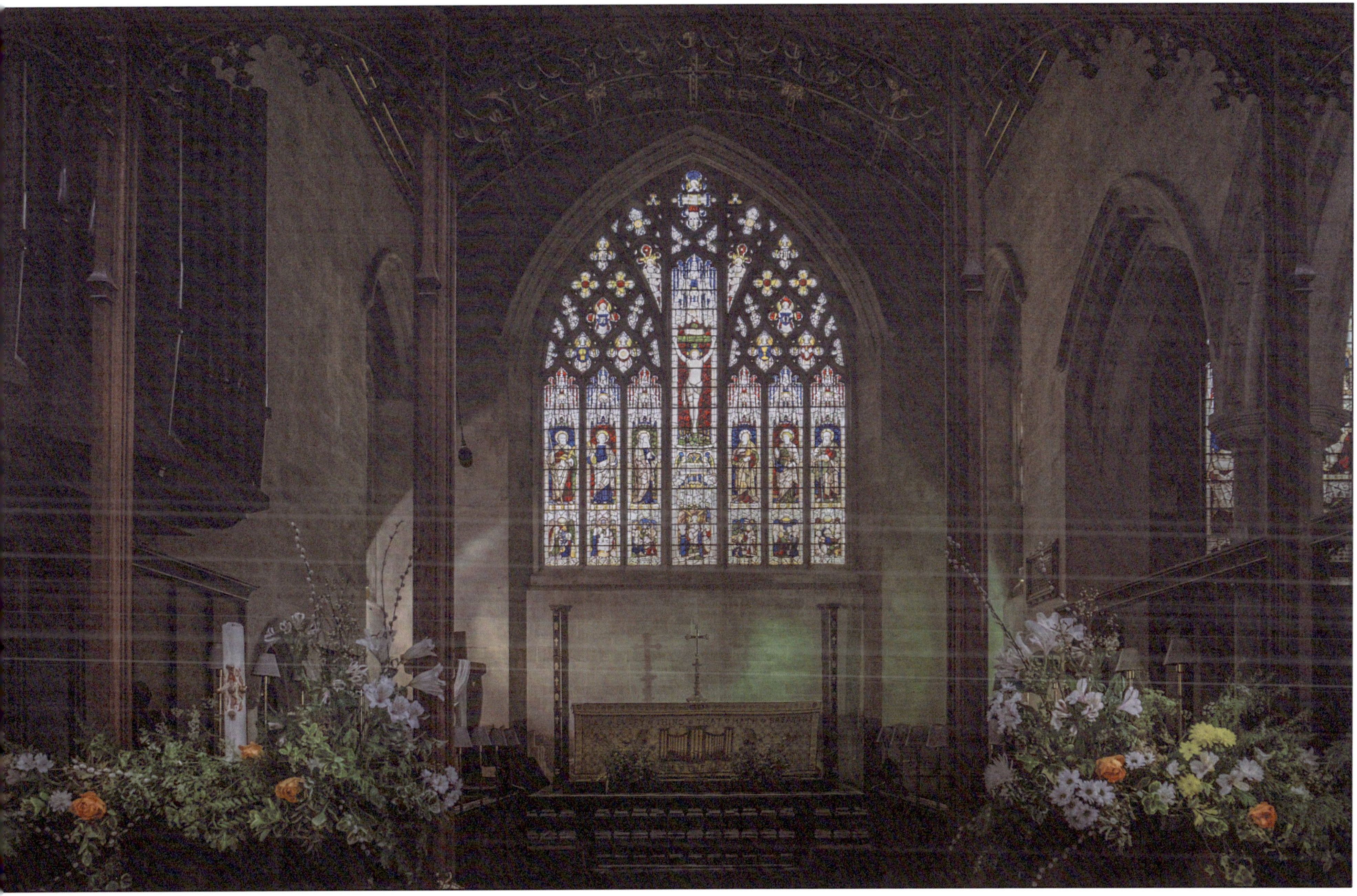

St Mary Magdalene, Richmond, Surrey

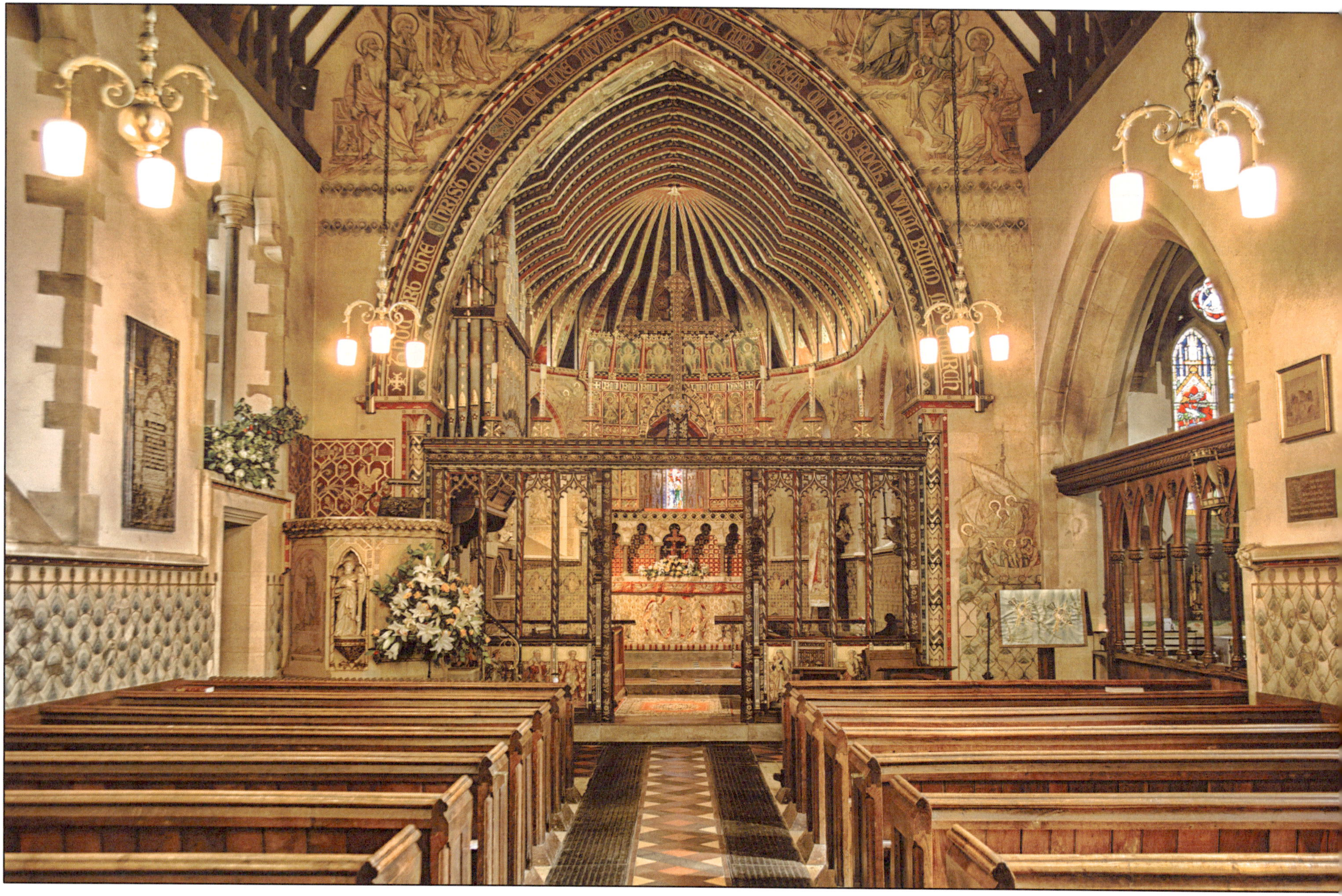

St Peter's, Hascombe, Surrey

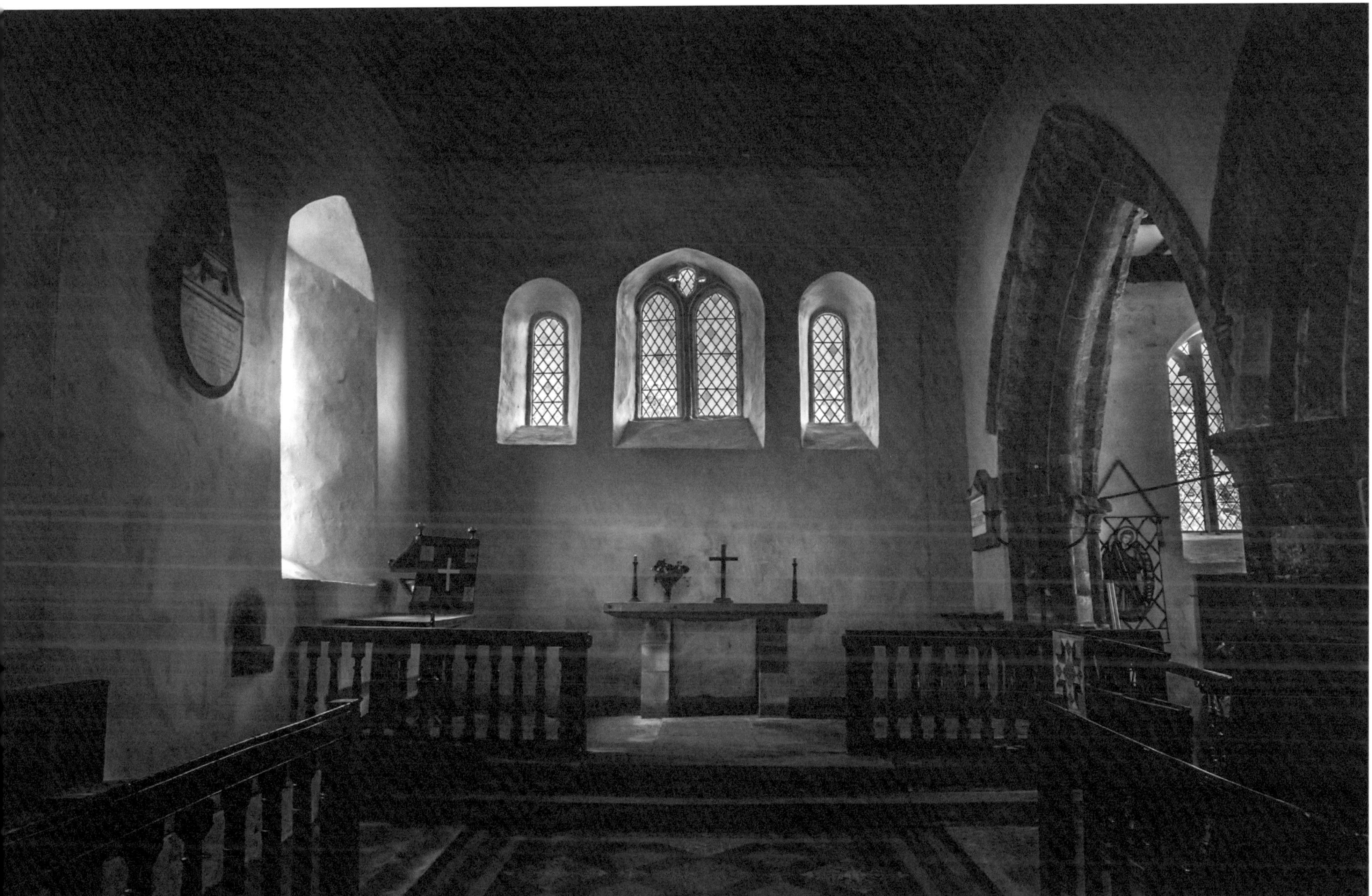

St Michael's, Garway, Hereford

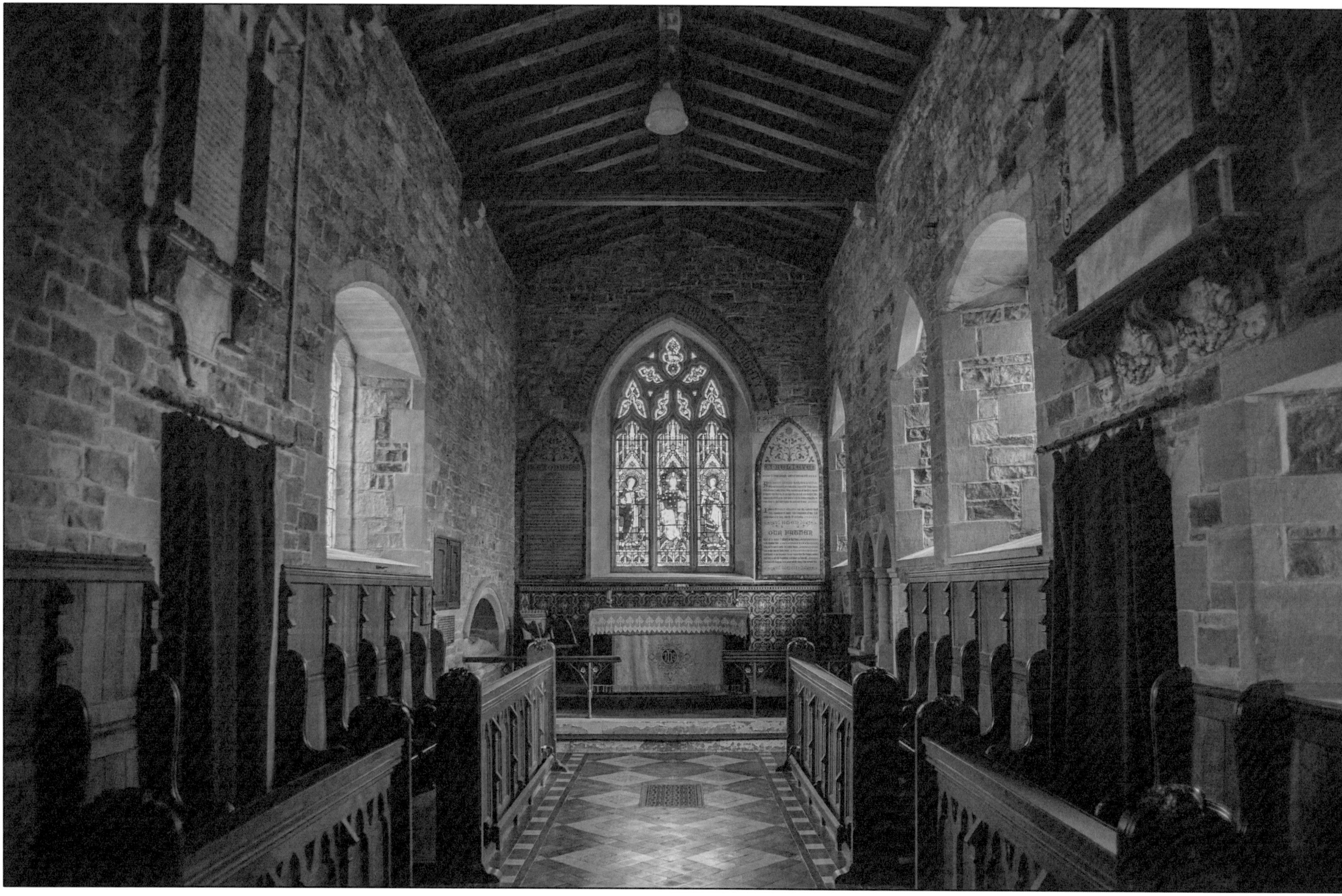

St John the Baptist, Stanwick, Yorkshire

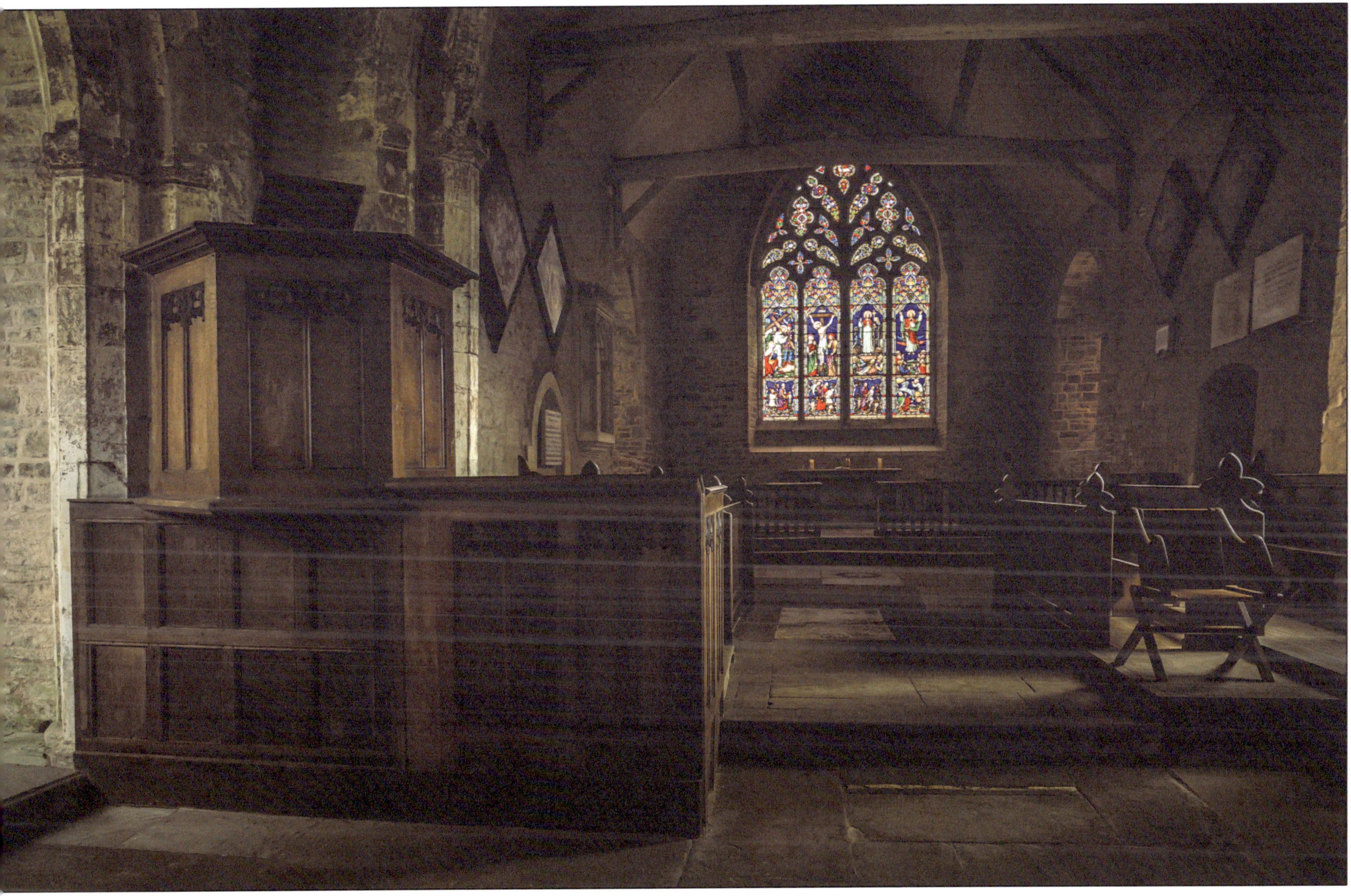

St Bartholomew's, Richards Castle, Hereford

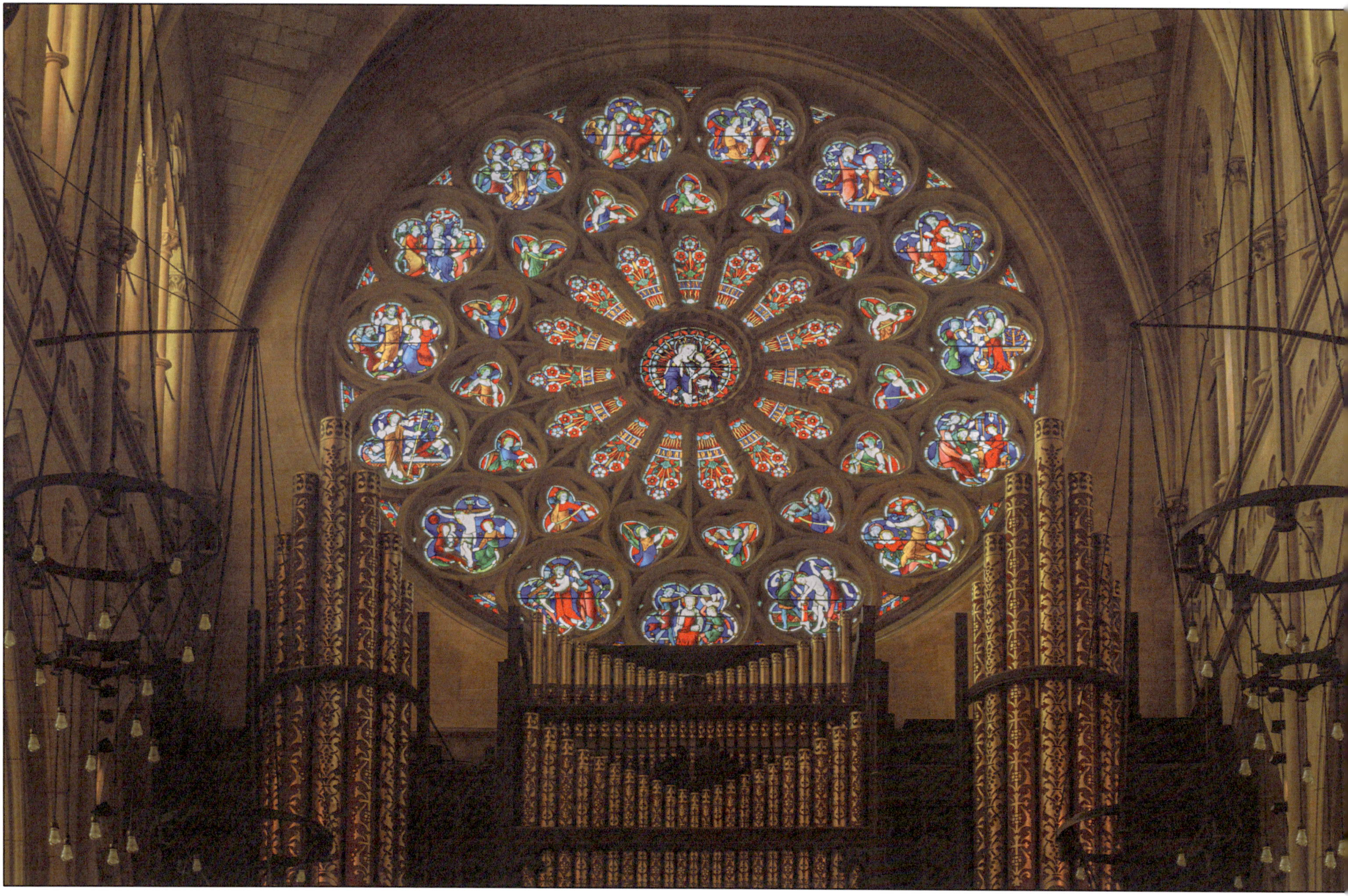

Arundel Cathedral, Sussex

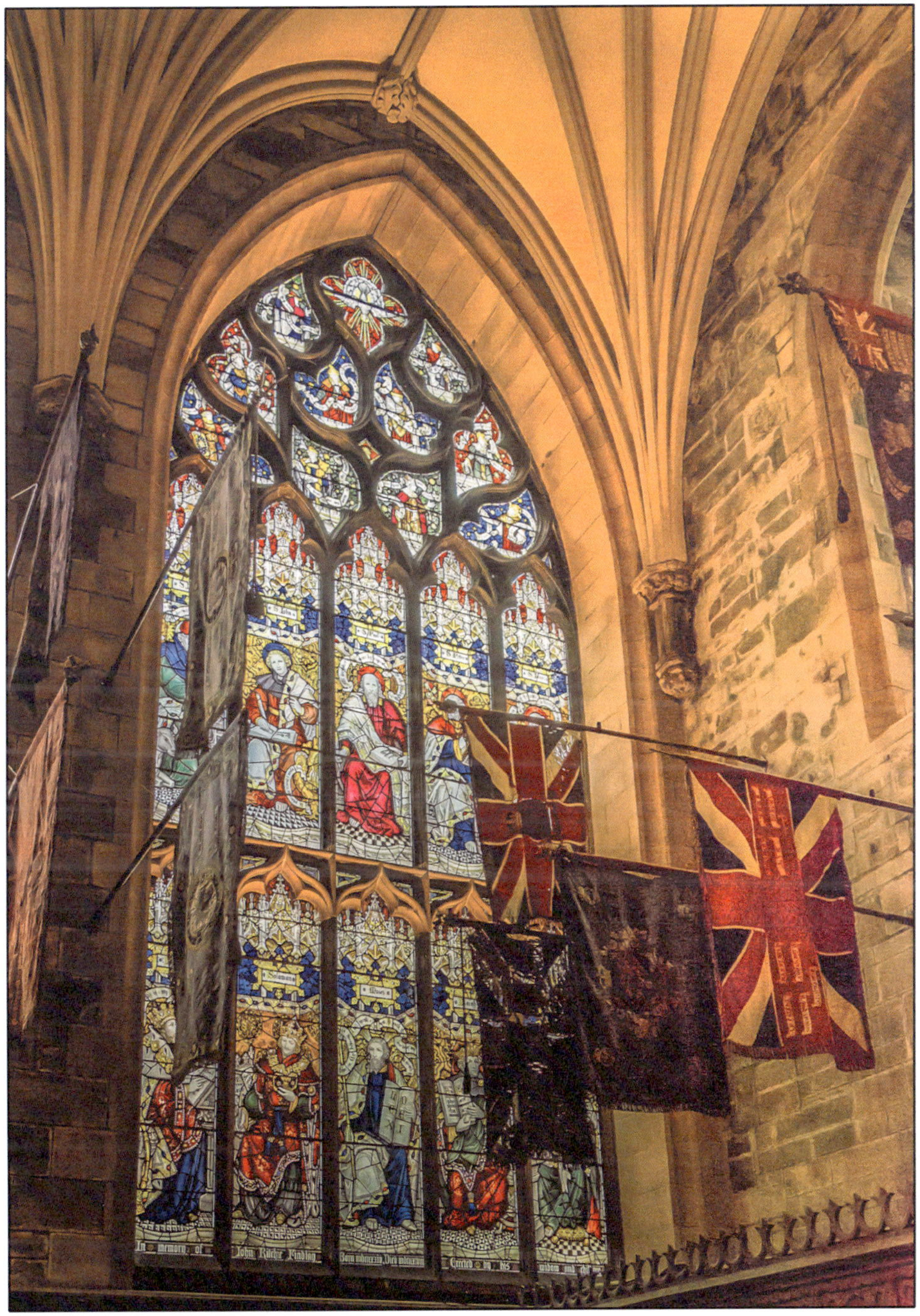

St Giles Cathedral, Edinburgh

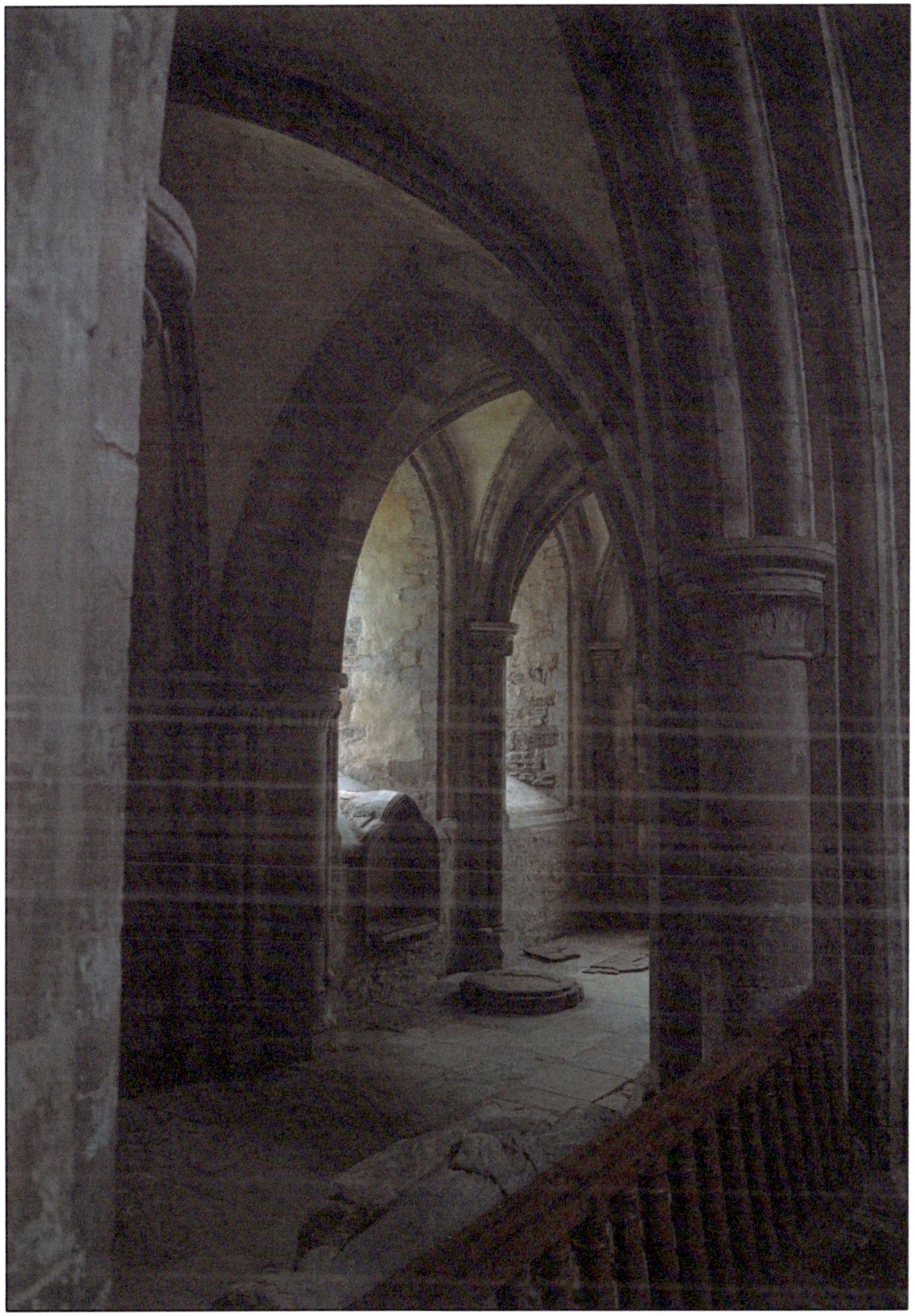

Dore Abbey, Hereford

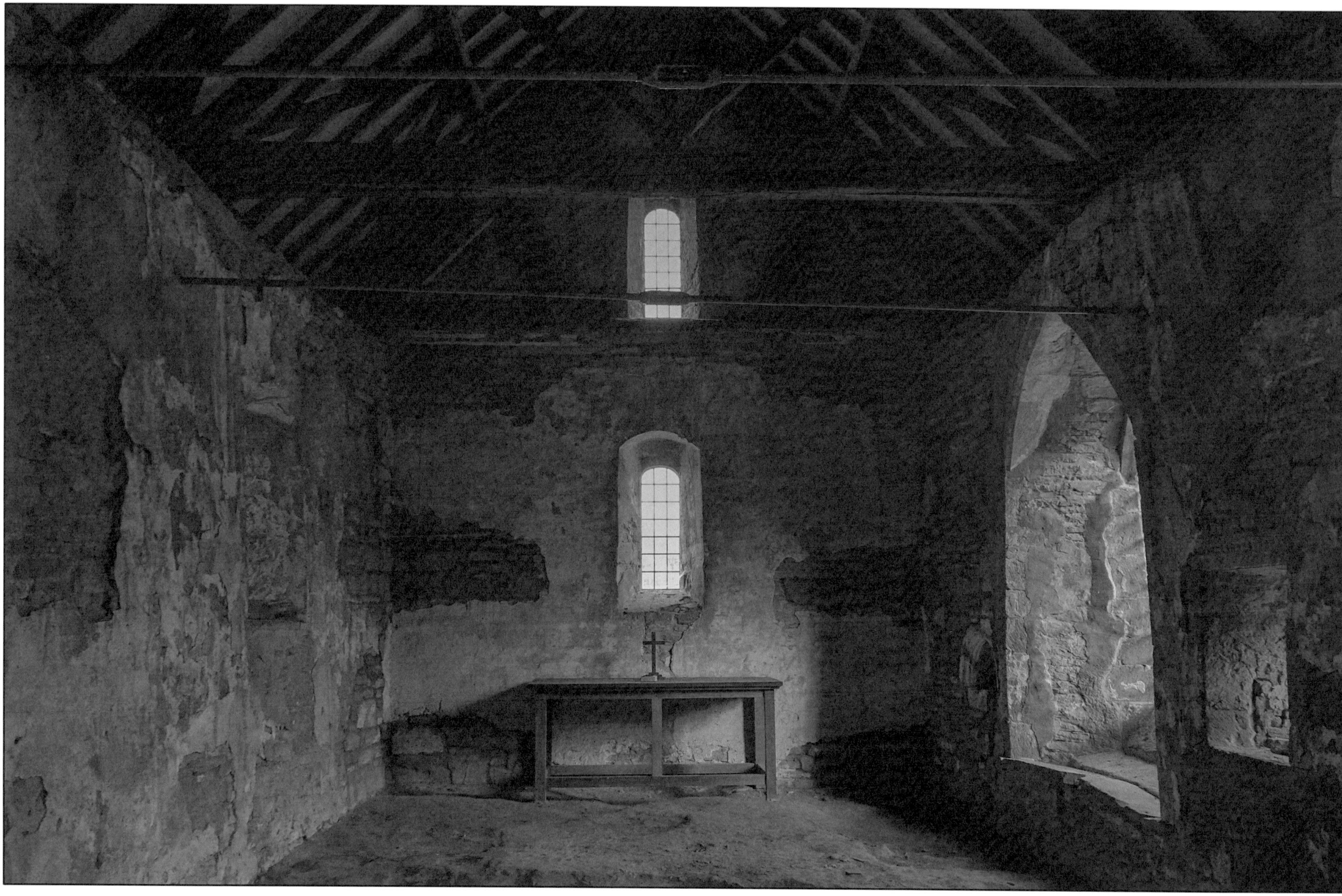

Yatton Chapel, Hereford

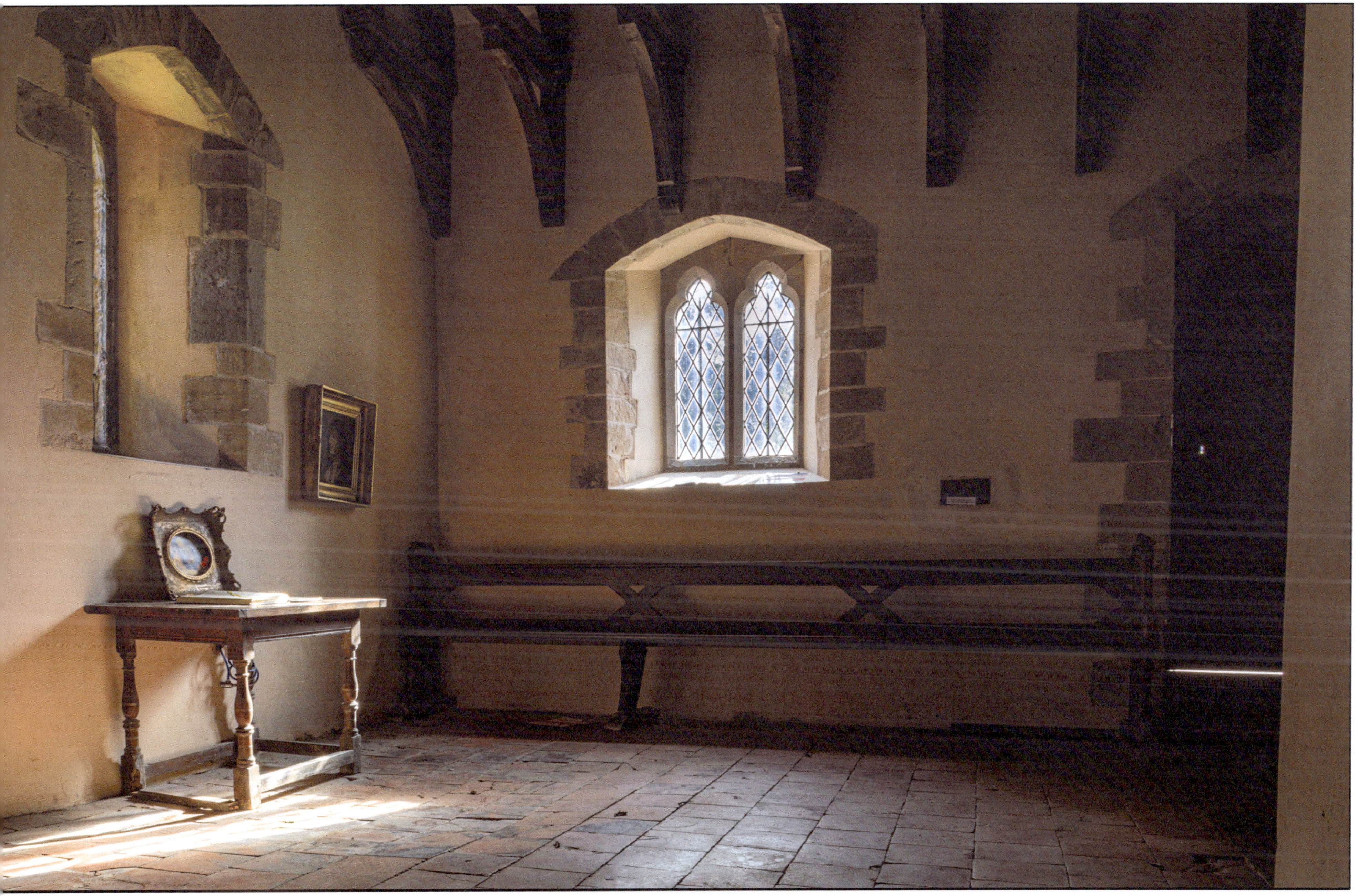

St Michael’s, Upton Cressett, Shropshire

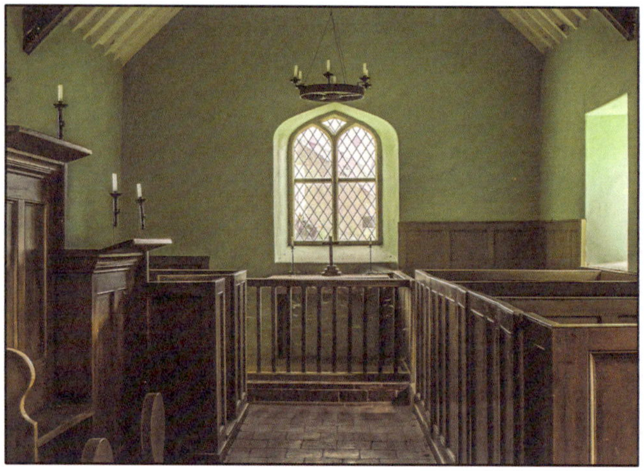
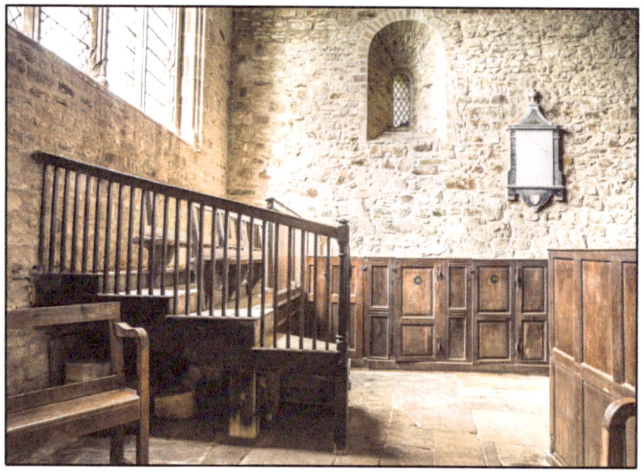
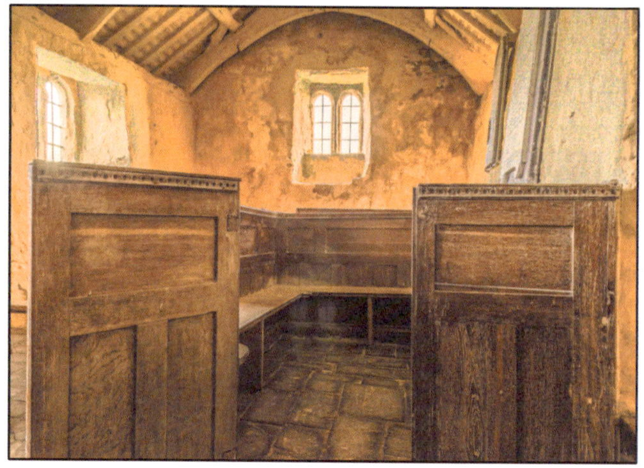
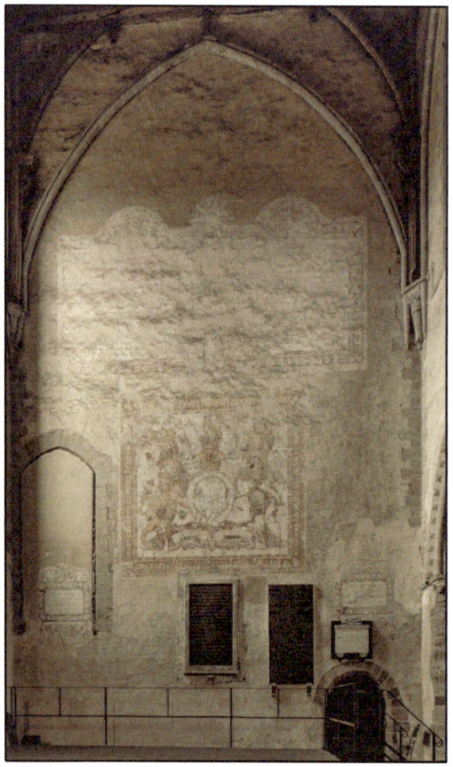
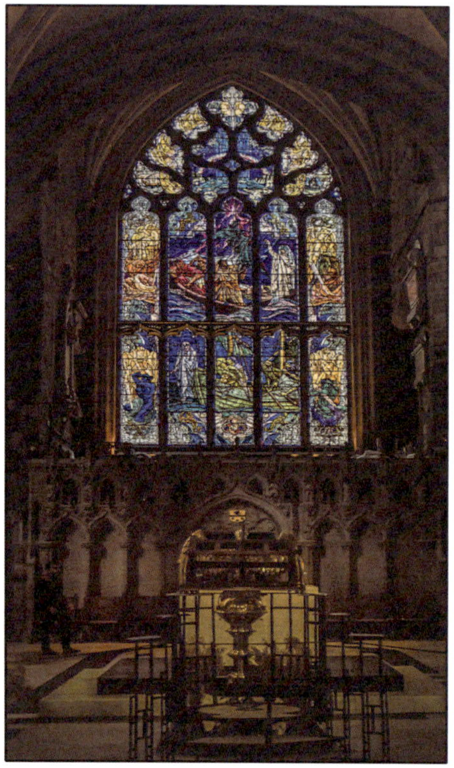
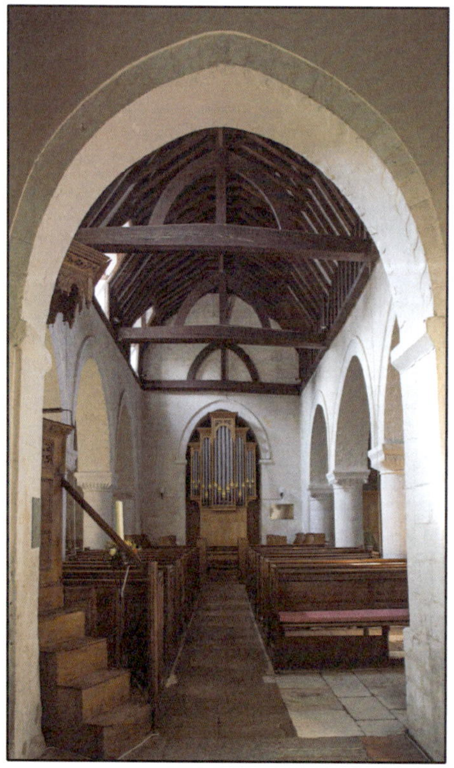
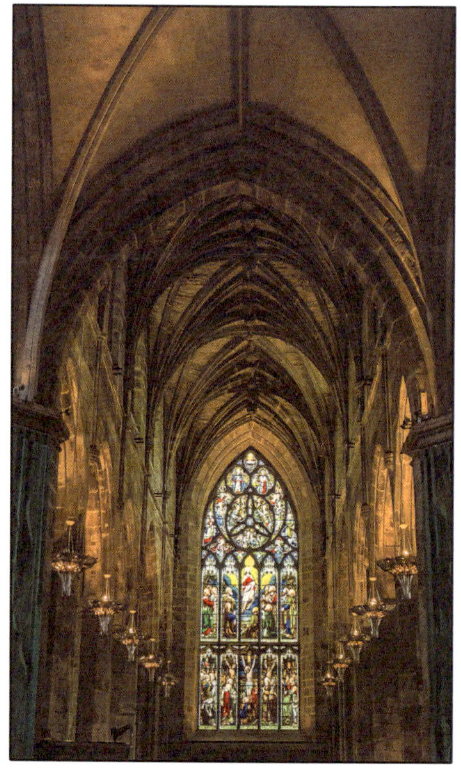

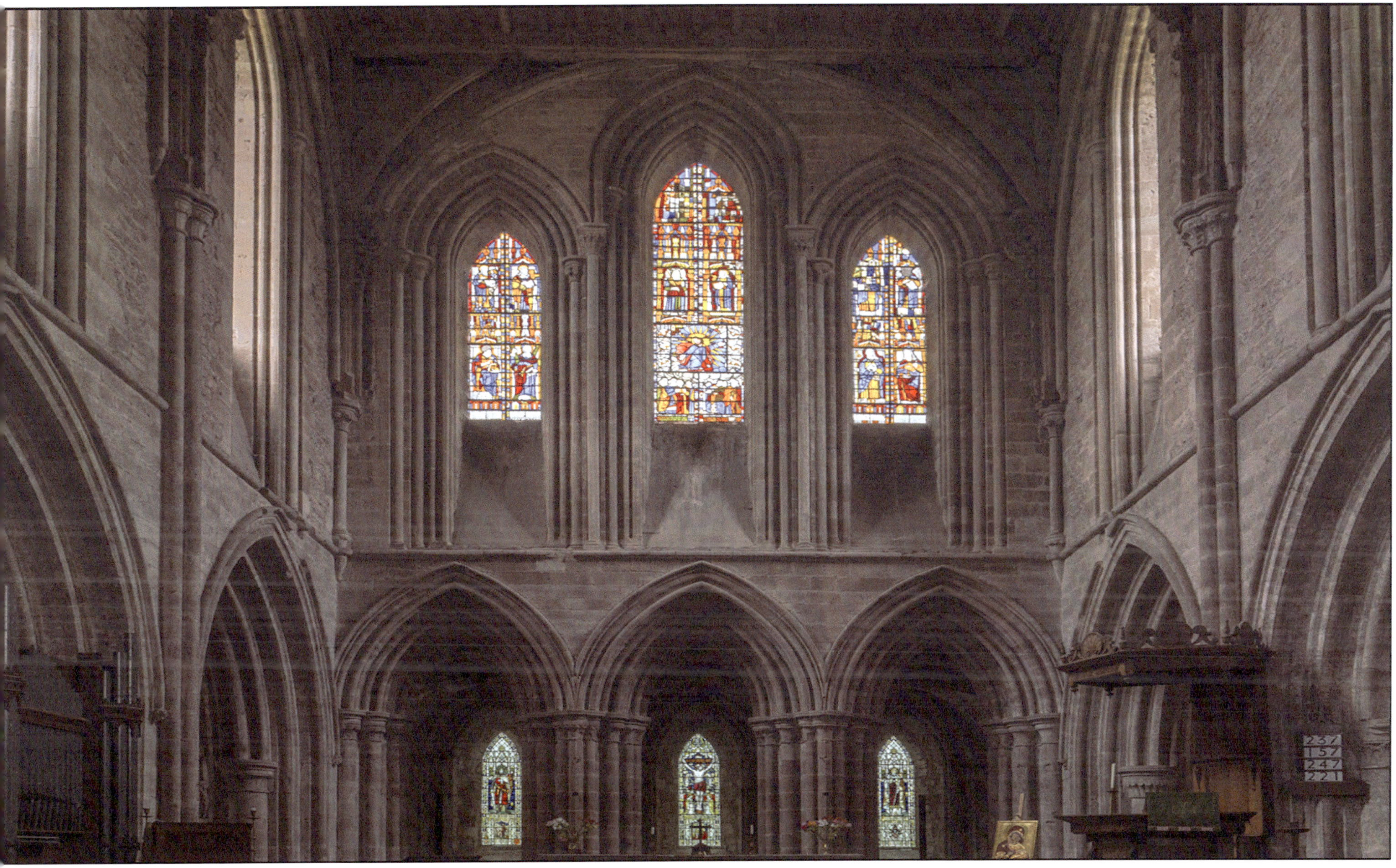

Dore Abbey, Dore, Hereford

REMEMBER WHERE YOU ARE

Take a look outside

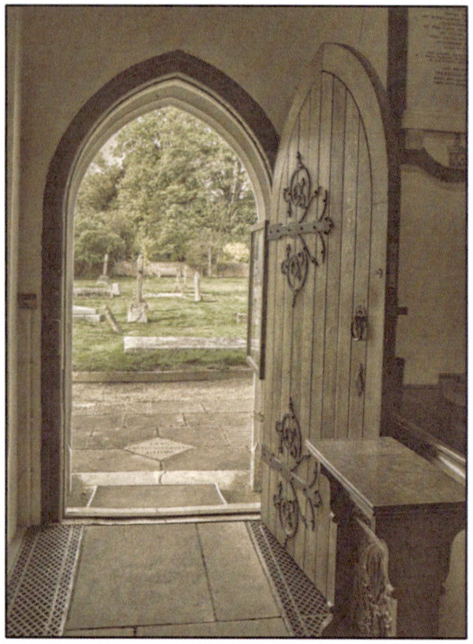
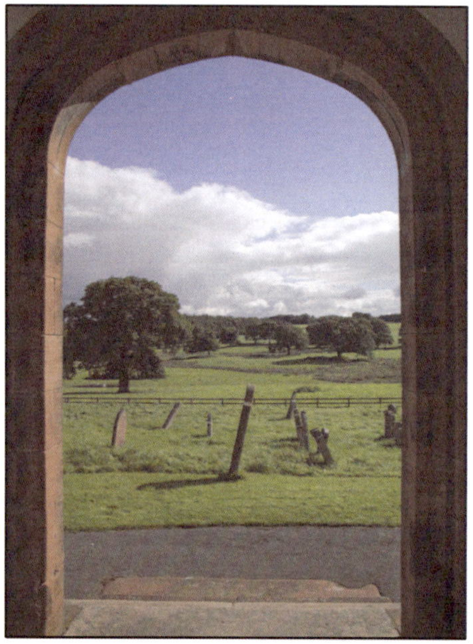
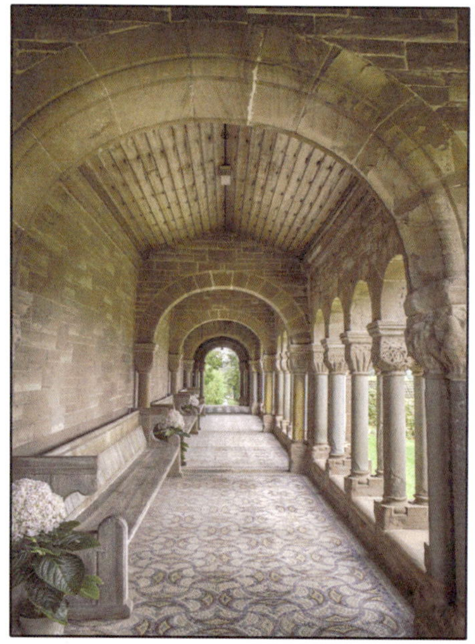
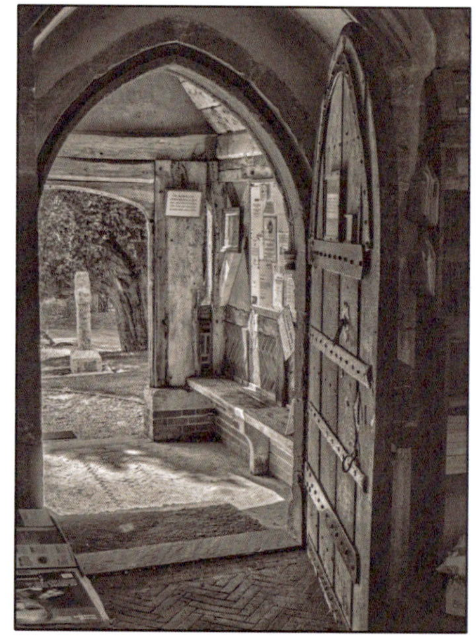
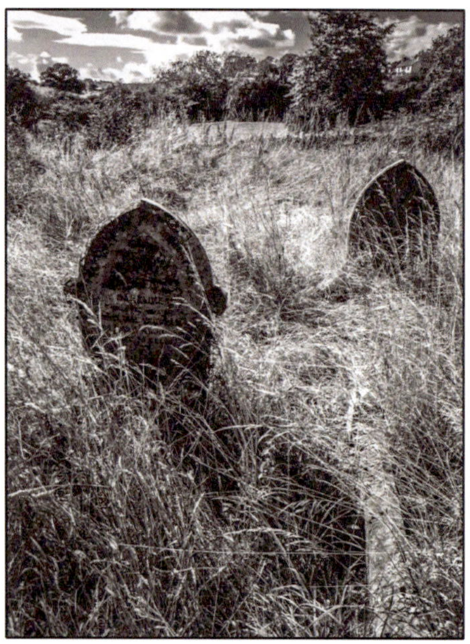
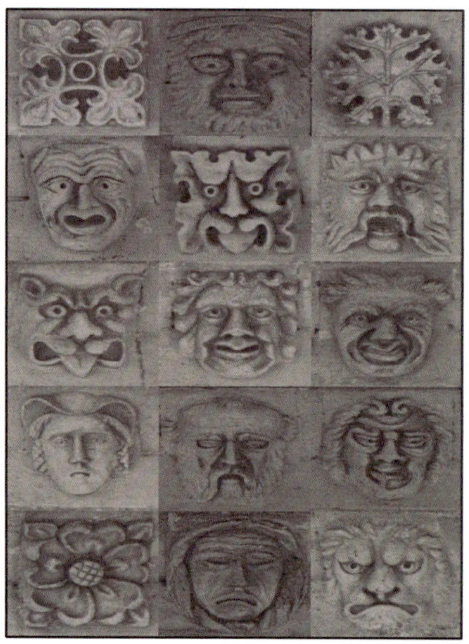
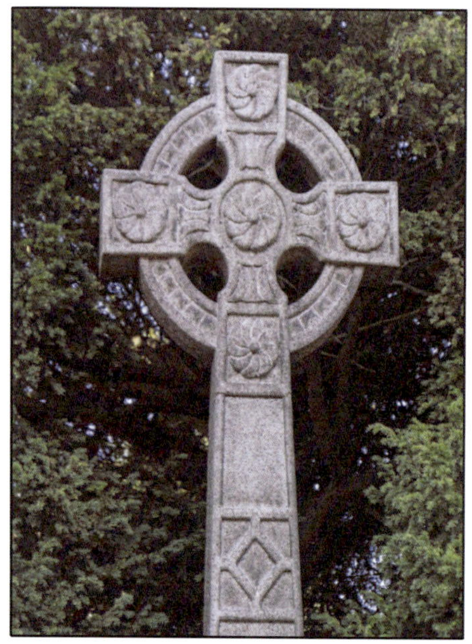
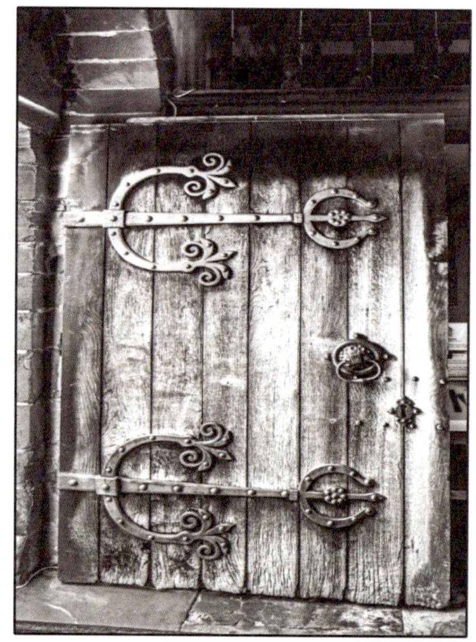

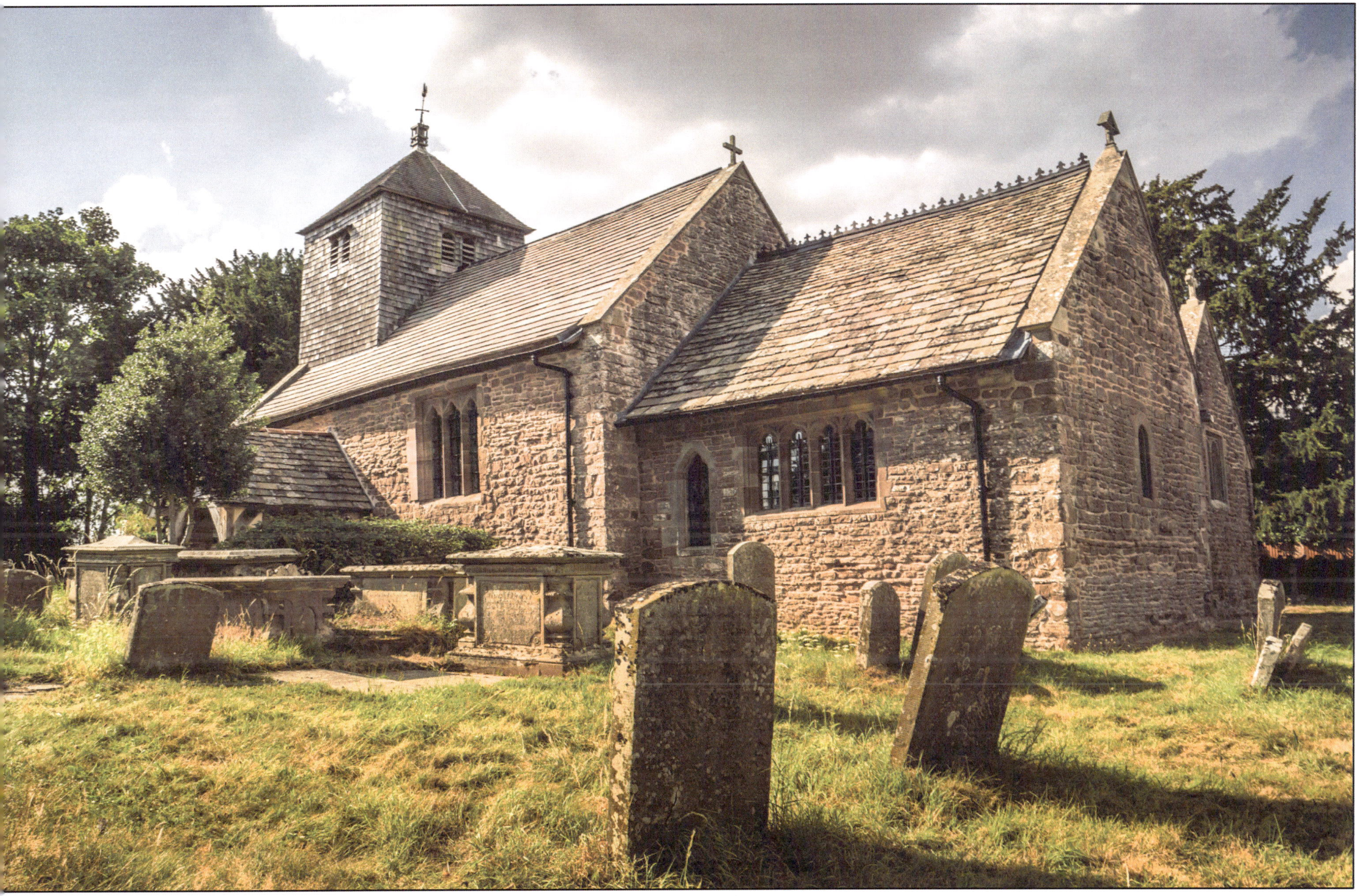

St Michael's, Brampton Abbotts, Hereford

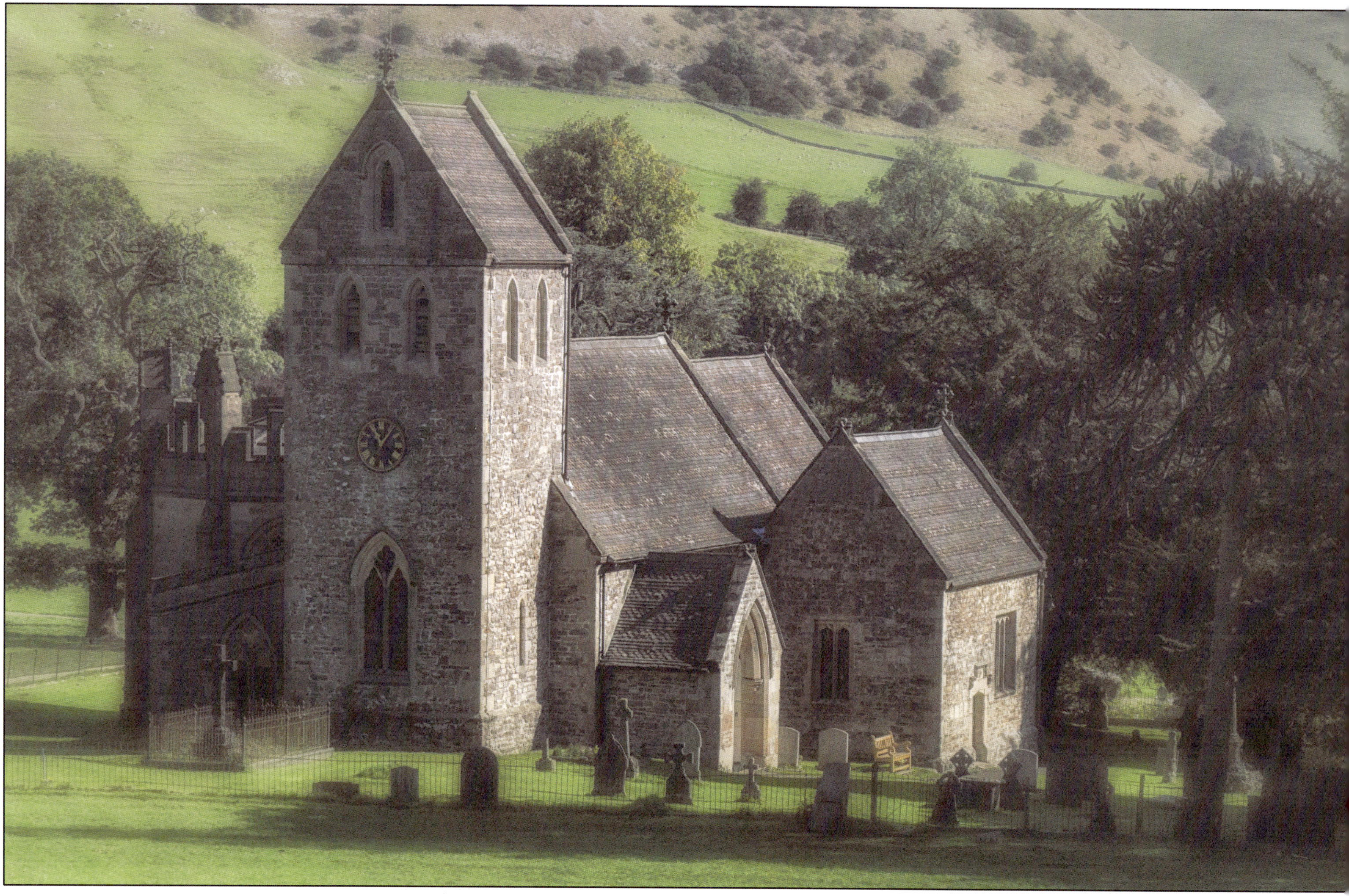

Church of the Holy Cross, Ilam, Derby

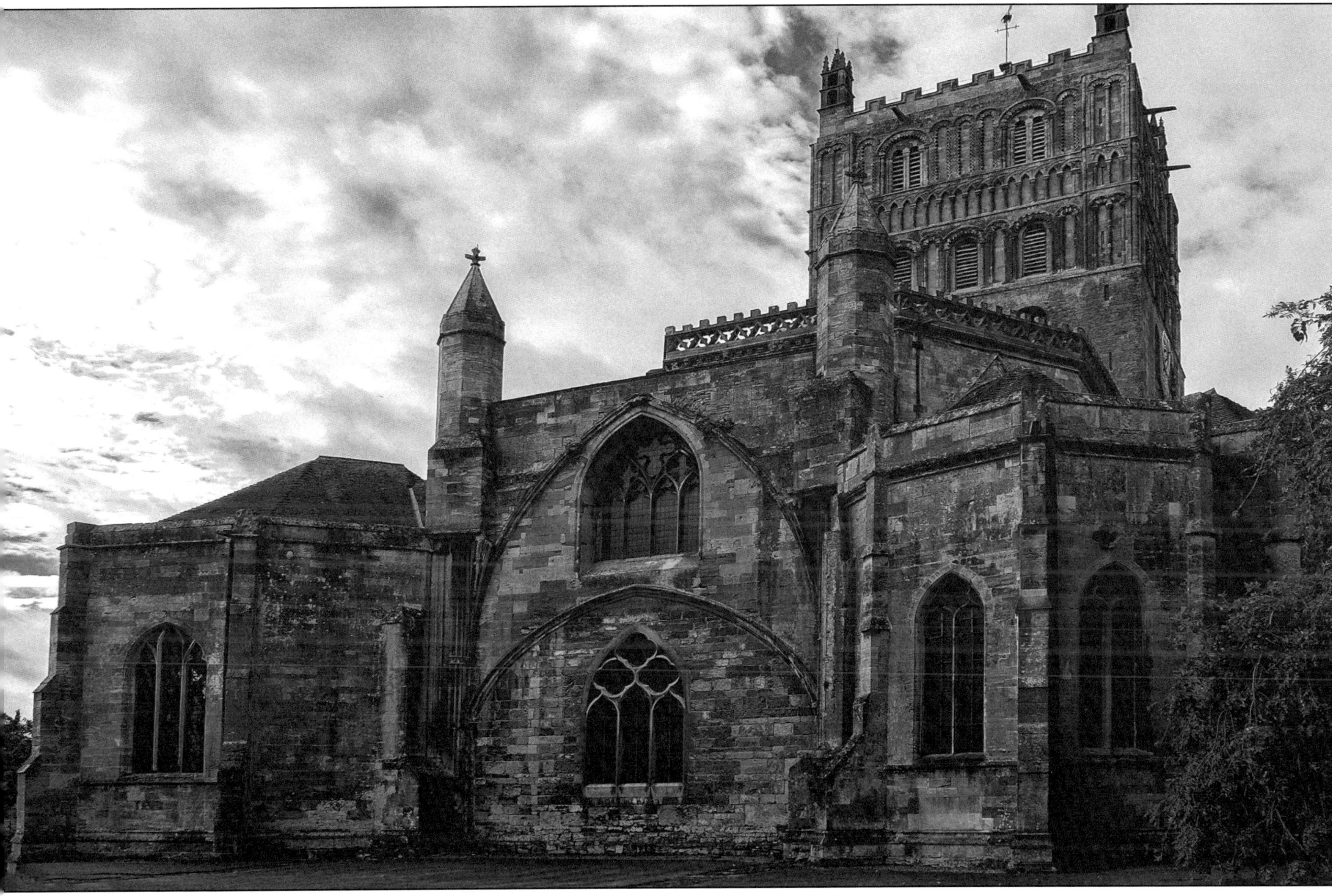

Tewkesbury Abbey, Gloucester

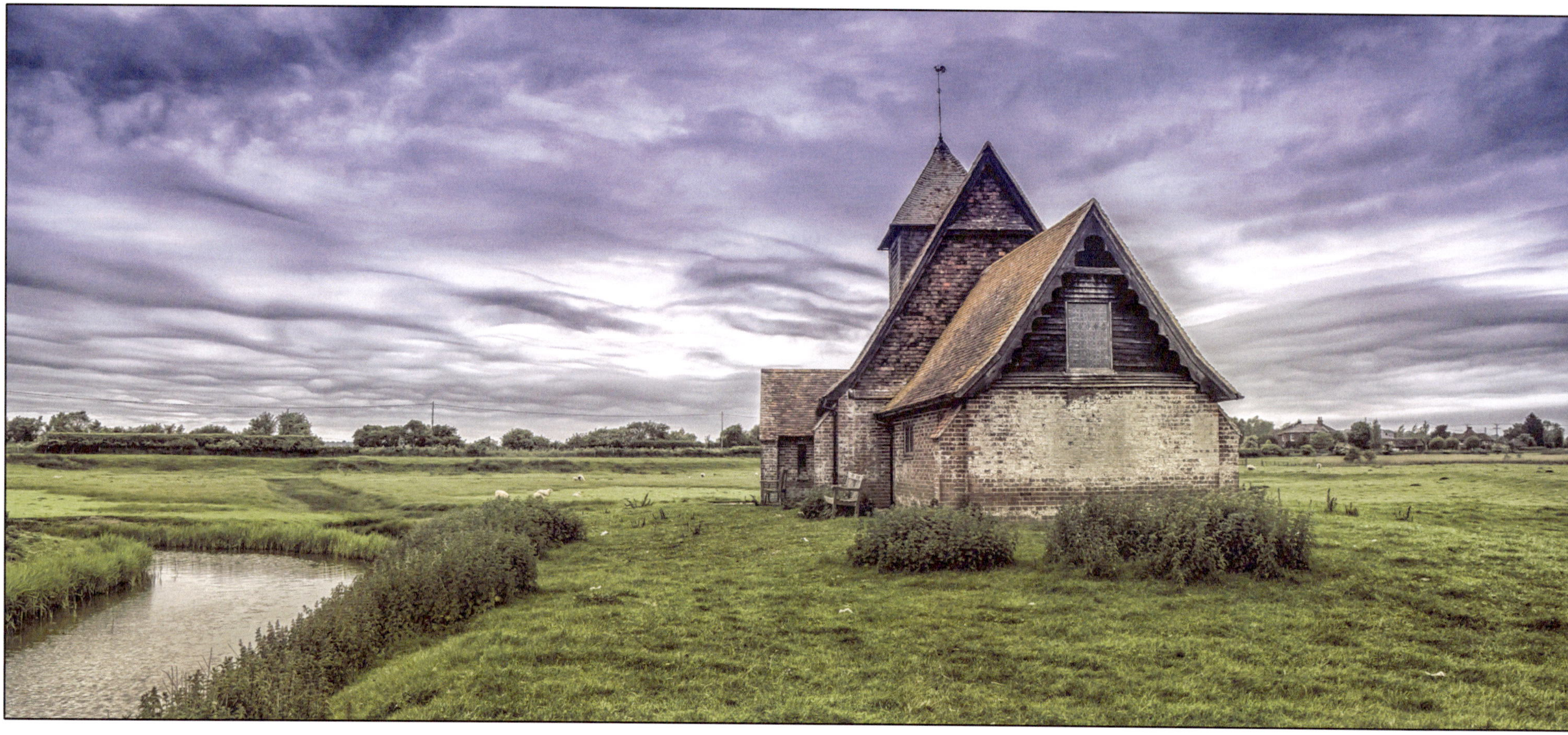

St Thomas à Becket, Fairfield, Kent

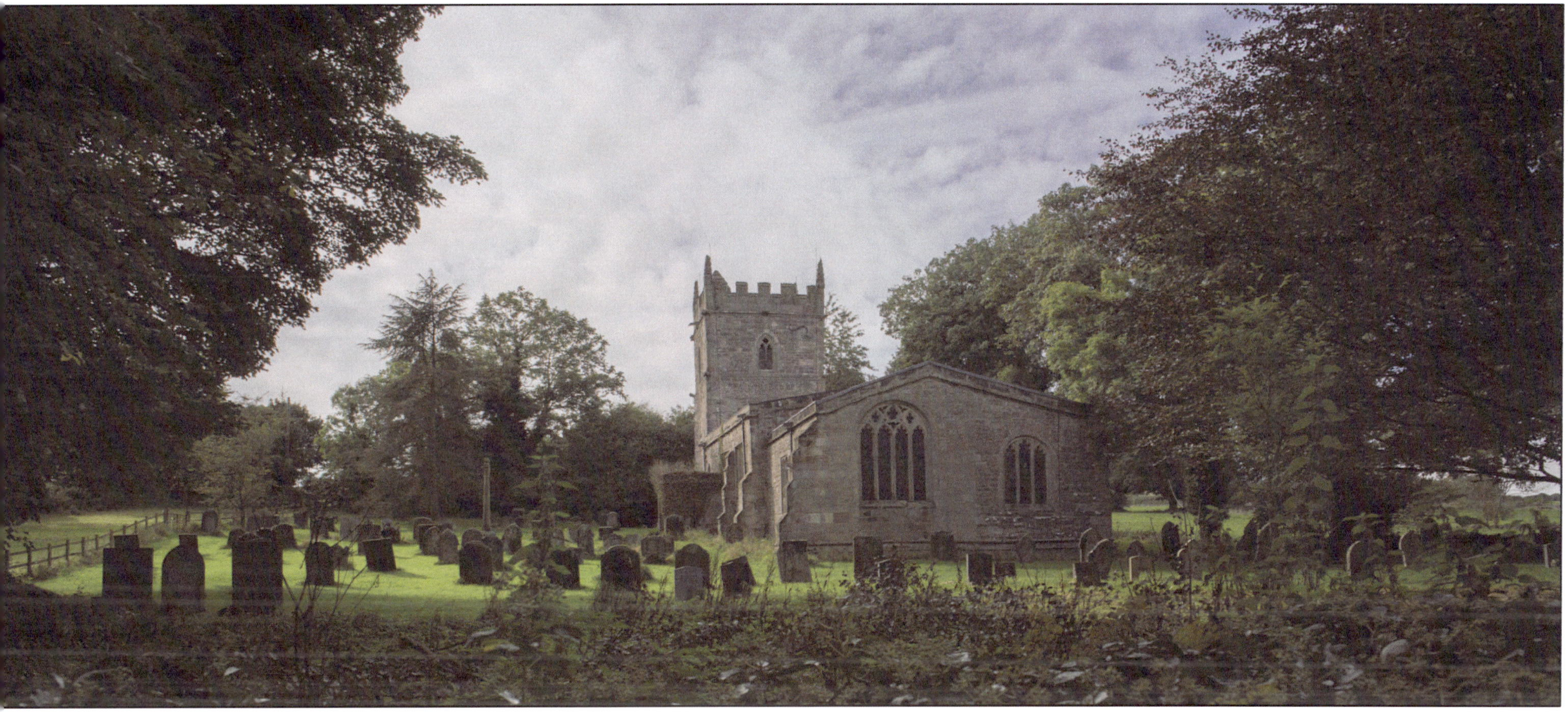

St Bartholomew's, Blore, Staffordshire

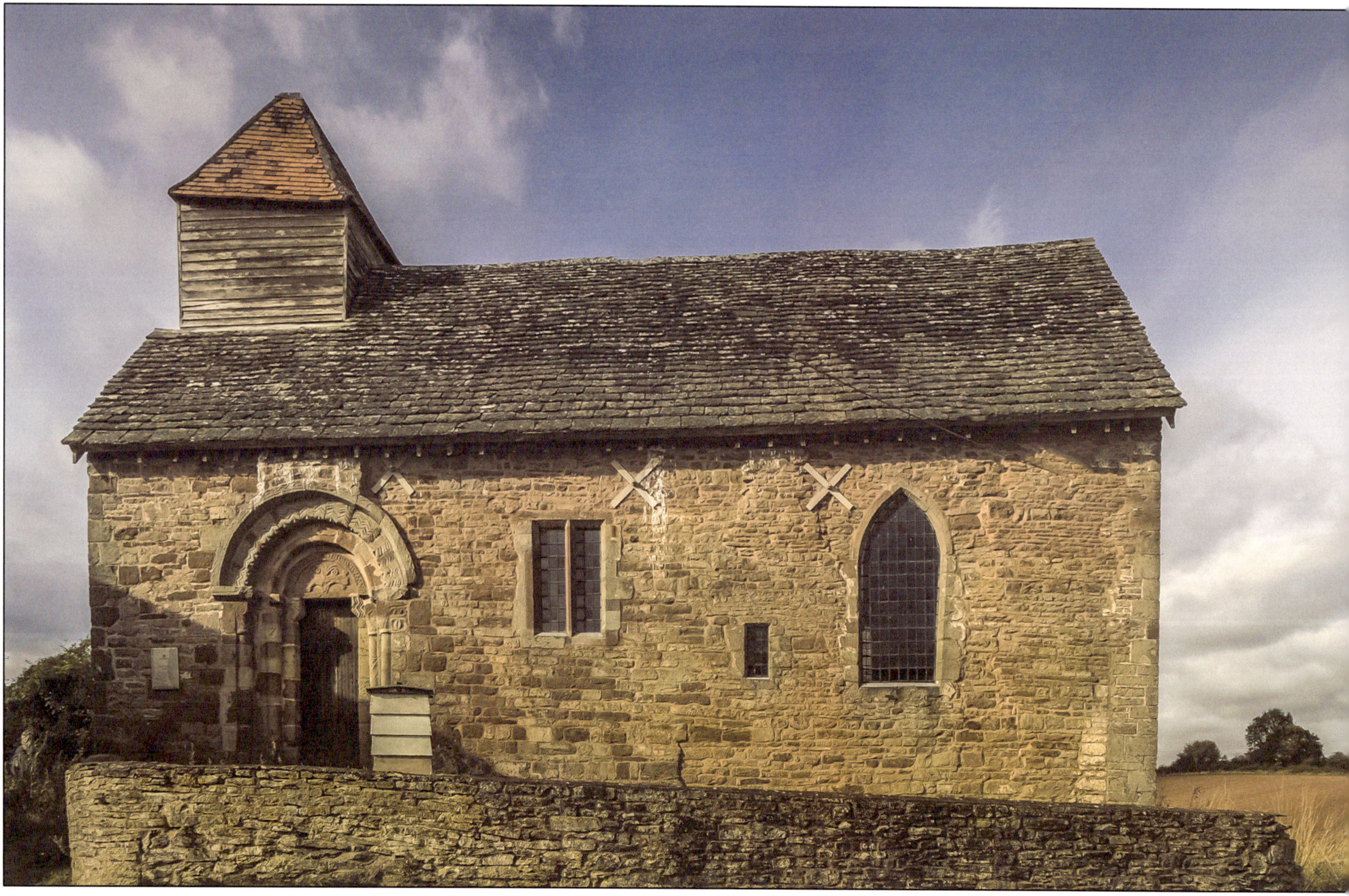

Yatton Chapel, Hereford

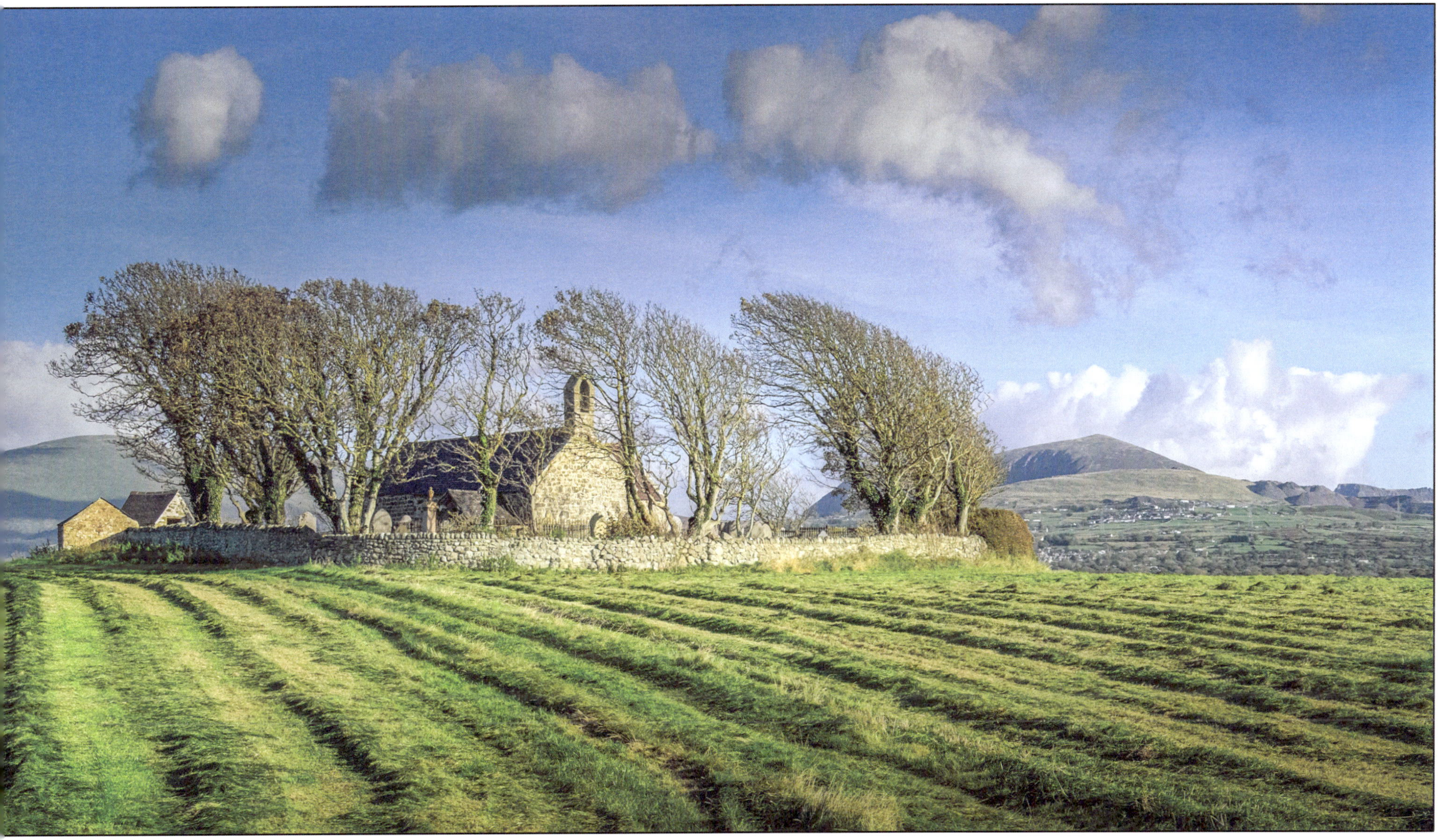

St Baglan’s, Lianfagien, Geynedd

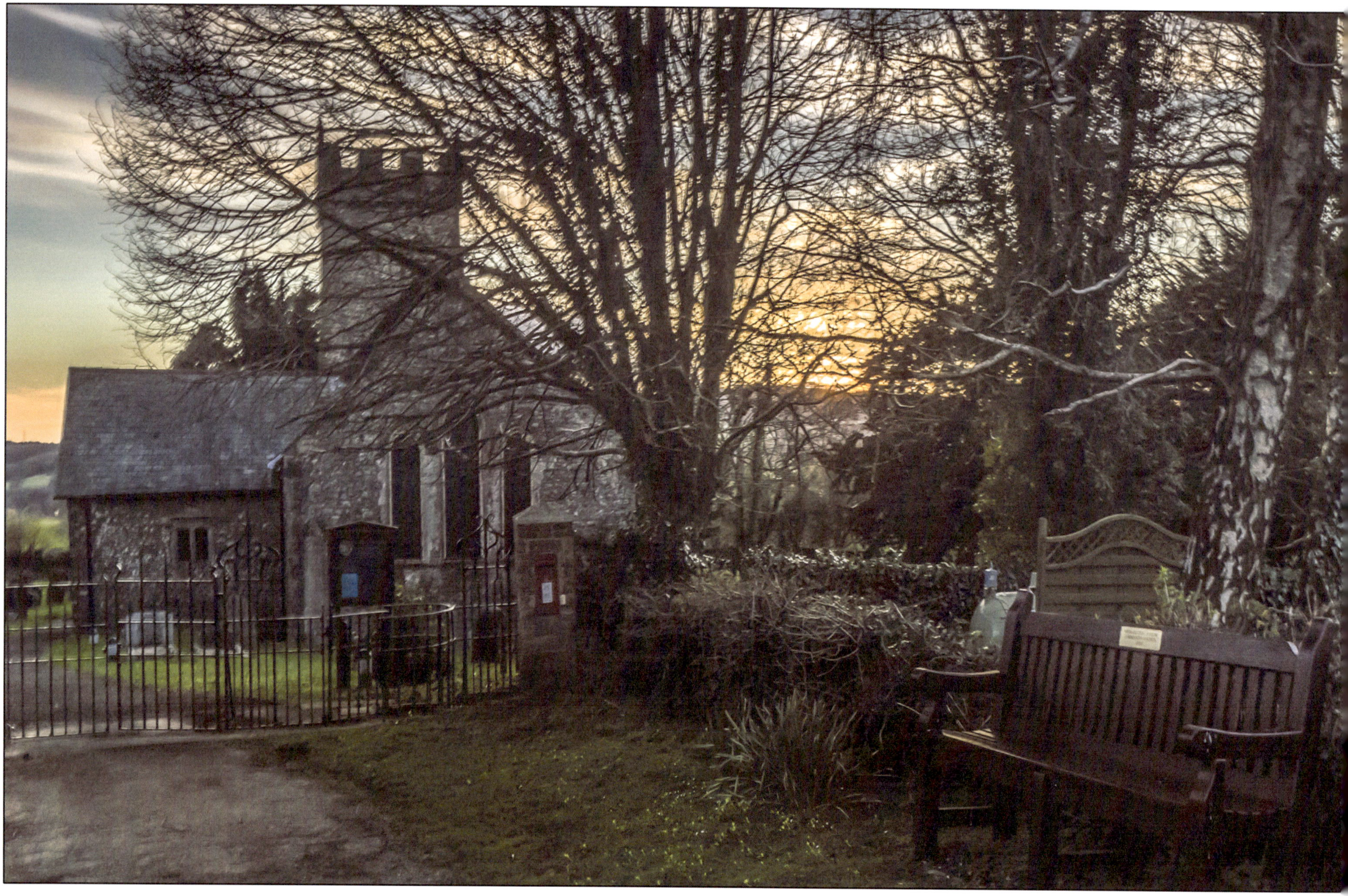

St Michael's Church, Michaelston-y-Fedw, Cardiff, Wales

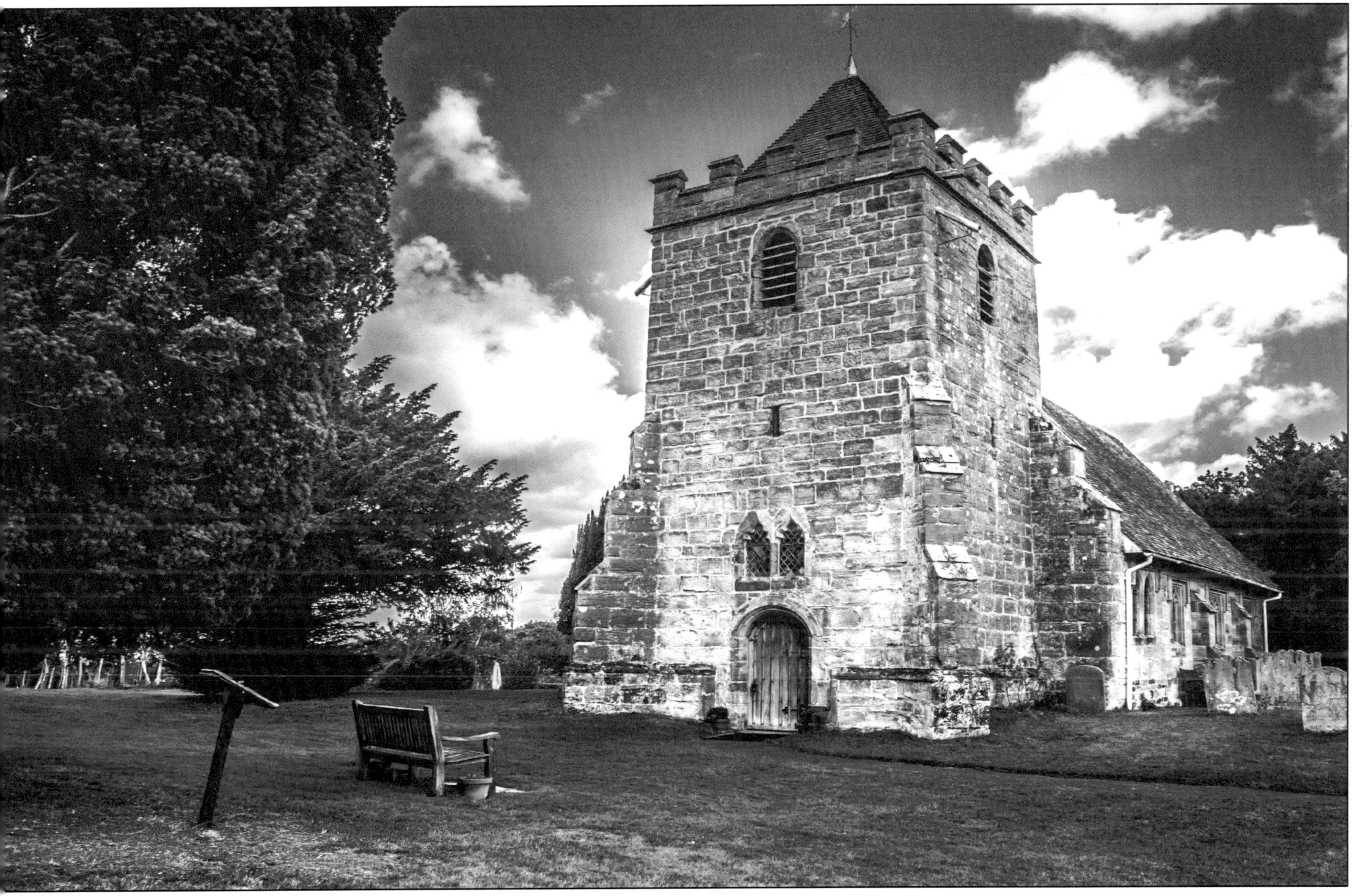

St Thomas, Capel, Kent

If you have found even the smallest part of this book of interest I consider that a success. Enjoy taking photographs. Join a Club (if not already). Get out there and experiment – it's the only way to learn.

If you would like to see more of my church images I have a website: *www.debphotosonline.com*

Thank you

David Balaam

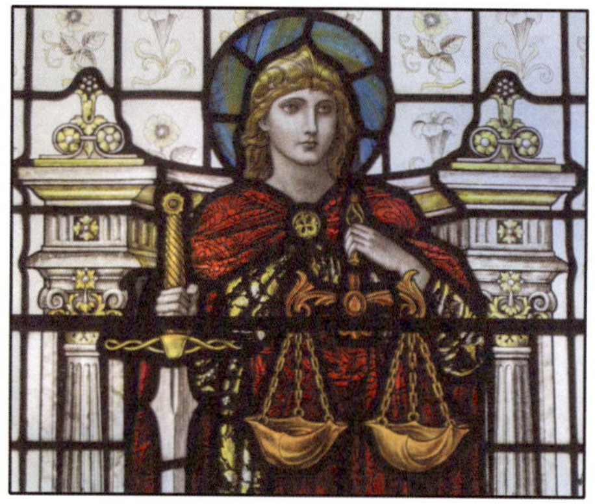

Acknowledgements

My sincere gratitude to Ron Smith ARPS DPAGB, and Vic Piper for their help and guidance on all matters technical and architectural.

References

History of British Organs by Dominic Gwynn can be found on-line; www.buildingconservation.com/articles/survivors/early-british-organs.htm

Book: Architectural Photography by Eric de Mare

Book: Guided by a Stone-Mason by Thomas Maude

www.ingramcontent.com/pod-product-compliance
Ingram Content Group UK Ltd.
Pitfield, Milton Keynes, MK11 3LW, UK
UKRC032309290726
14090UKWH00004B/408

9780993586477

9 780993 586477